GENERATION DECKS

THE UNOFFICIAL HISTORY OF GAMING PHENOMENON

MAGIC: THE GATHERING

TITUS CHALK

SOLARIS

First published 2017 by Solaris
an imprint of Rebellion Publishing Ltd,
Riverside House, Osney Mead,
Oxford, OX2 0ES, UK

www.solarisbooks.com

ISBN 978 1 78108 490 8

10 9 8 7 6 5 4 3 2 1

A CIP catalogue record for this book is available from the
British Library.

Designed & typeset by Rebellion Publishing

Printed in Denmark by Nørhaven

Contents

A note on pictures: I highly recommend using Wizards of the Coast's official *Magic* Card Database, Gatherer, to look up the names of any cards mentioned in this book. There you will find the latest artwork, text and rulings all in one place. Go to gatherer.wizards.com, check the "Name" tick-box, enter the name of the card in question and instantly discover cards from the game's entire history.

CHAPTER ONE
It's a Kind of Magic

"So do you wear, you know, a cape or something?" Poppy asks me. "Because I could definitely imagine you doing *actual* magic. Like tricks and stuff."

Poppy is trying. A great friend, she always forgives me my eccentricities, but this particular pearl is passing her by. Talking to her, I can't help but feel stranded in some humiliating time warp; inside its whirl, I live out the same faintly ridiculous conversation again and again. Yes, I admit, I play a mysterious card game. No, I say, it is not like snap. Yes, I suppose you could call it a cross between stamp collecting and *Dungeons & Dragons*. No. You're right. Not many girls play it.

The cape question is at least wonderfully leftfield. On a drab winter morning in yet another new and unfamiliar hometown, I'll settle for that. This time it is Berlin. It has been numerous cities and countries before. Various social settings. Different friends. But somehow, always the same unease grips me as the conversation plays out – a sense of never quite knowing if I am happy enough with whom I am to reveal every component of my identity. Never quite knowing how much I want to be defined by belonging to a community. Never wanting to be defined by the judgements others cast on tribes which are not their own.

If you have tried as best as you can to walk your own path, however much of an illusion that may be, it is not trivial to hand the power of sweeping generalisation to someone who may wield it indiscriminately.

Nonetheless, like a recalcitrant alcoholic at an AA meeting, let me begin that conversation all over again. Hello. I'm Titus. And the card game I play is called *Magic: The Gathering*. Thankfully, I am not alone in this world. Since the game exploded into being in 1993, 20 million fans in 70 different countries have fallen under its spell. We meet in sweaty, poorly lit backrooms to play a fantasy game with special, sometimes valuable, collectible cards. Some of us even make a living out of it, raking in prize money at professional tournaments, writing about the game for its legion of fans, or speculating and trading on the fluctuating value of the cards used to play. Most of us though, just have cupboards full of expensive cardboard to which we feel a puzzling emotional connection. To which we compulsively add via mouse clicks and credit cards when no one is looking. To which our thoughts drift during mundane conversations. And whose infinite possibilities keep us awake at night, making our minds spin and driving us online to play against distant opponents, in far-flung time zones, in an Esperanto of gaming jargon.

Whether I am always comfortable with the notion or not, I belong to a vast and motley crew of *Magic* players. I have, since picking up the game as a teenager, become part of an 'us' and not simply an observer of 'them'. This has troubled me at times, challenging my perception of myself and picking at my insecurities. I have been forced to wonder what room for friendship and fun my own heaving ego ever leaves me. And yet at the same time, the murk of my own identity has inspired me to write about a hobby that has remained a part of me, even when I have occasionally cast it aside. When I began work on telling this story in late 2012, I did so with the kind of hand-wringing the well-adjusted might scoff at. Was I deranged for caring so much about something I felt an unease at caring about? Could I overcome my own aloofness to tell the story of a game which, I would learn, has affected more than just me down its decades hiding in tatty backpacks on the shoulders of an entire generation? How much did I have in common with that generation? Could I throw my arms around their shoulders with affection, without patronising them? Learn whether I belonged in their ranks? These were the questions I realised I needed to answer for myself as I began to tell the story of a card game, whose resonance goes beyond one conflicted writer and far wider into the outside world than most muggles could ever believe. Not just a game. Not just a business. Not just a community – *Magic: The Gathering* is an epic story worth sharing. And, like the best of stories, *Magic*'s started a long time ago, in a galaxy far, far away.

CHAPTER TWO
Great Minds

USENET.

Two simple syllables.

Once, they represented a glittering new way of communicating. But as the digital age's advances have clocked up (and in some cases, cocked up) at an astonishing rate, they have long since receded into the past. Usenet was the text-based precursor to the World Wide Web and in many ways, cyberspace's Old West. It was a wild frontier. Sparsely populated. A far-off and unfamiliar idea to all but the most pioneering of souls. In 1991, it boasted around 12 million users worldwide. They were almost exclusively techies, academics and pornographers. It handled two, sometimes three gigabytes of traffic per day. By contrast, today, over two billion of the world's population are online and gigabytes have long given way to petabytes. Still, there are Usenet archives out there, where former devotees can pour over the traces of their rambling, un-moderated discussions like historians poring over sepia-tinted photographs.

Archaeologists mining the Usenet archives might have more interesting posts to uncover, but for *Magic* players, discussions on the forum rec. games.board.design are of particular importance. It was here that in June 1991 an ambitious role-playing fan named Peter Adkison began posting about breaking into the gaming industry. Adkison was an employee at aerospace giant Boeing by day and the boss of a fledgling games company called Wizards of the Coast by night. At the time, Wizards operated out of Adkison's basement at 23815, 43rd Avenue South in Kent, Washington. Or, more usually, from Adkison's desk at Boeing, long after the lights had gone out and the cleaners were making their rounds.

Despite the late nights required to get his new venture off the ground, Adkison was undeterred. The enthusiastic entrepreneur was driven by a passion for gaming he had acquired as a child growing up in Idaho (a state counting only 20 inhabitants per square mile) where he cut his teeth on family *Monopoly* sessions. Later, he took up *Risk* and war games by the American manufacturer Avalon Hill with his father. Then, in 1978, he discovered the love of his life: *Dungeons & Dragons*. Adkison stumbled on it in a local games store where he was drawn to the unfamiliar product by a nascent fascination with J.R.R. Tolkien's fantasy works. Despite not knowing what a role-playing game was, Adkison snapped up a copy. He was, and remains, a firm believer in embracing new ideas.

Adkison's Usenet posts caught the attention of a maths student in Philadelphia named Mike Davis. Davis was keen to plug a game he had co-designed with a fellow mathematician at the University of Pennsylvania. It was a frantic board game called *RoboRally*, in which players guided out-of-control factory robots through a gauntlet of obstacles. Davis hoped Adkison's new company might be interested in publishing it, underestimating how expensive and tricky board games can be to produce. Today, Germany is their spiritual home – a land renowned for its manufacturing prowess. A start-up in the Pacific Northwest, with little capital, could not realistically take a punt on such a complex product. Nonetheless, Adkison enjoyed a sample of the game and agreed to meet its creators in Portland, Oregon a few weeks later.

What followed was a seminal moment in geek history: something akin, at least in gaming terms, to John Lennon and Paul McCartney meeting at St Peter's Church fete in Woolton, Liverpool in 1957. It was serendipity. It was alchemy. It was rock and roll. On 17 August 1991, Adkison met *RoboRally*'s co-creator for the first time, an unassuming and taciturn maths expert by the name of Richard Garfield. It was an encounter that would transform both of their lives.

Writing later in *The Duelist*, Wizards of the Coast's in-house magazine that existed between 1993 and 1999, Adkison described the meeting as an epiphany. Garfield was an almost monastic observer for much of that first encounter, clearly disinterested in talking business. But, what got to Adkison, was his love of not only role-playing games but of all games. *His vision was clear and went to the heart of gaming*, wrote Adkison. *He was looking for entertainment, social interaction, mental exercise, creativity and challenge. I suddenly felt stupid, remembering the time I had refused to play* Pictionary, *even though I knew I would probably enjoy it.*

Like Gary Gygax (co-creator of *Dungeons & Dragons*), Klaus Teuber (inventor of *Settlers of Catan*) or Will Wright (designer of *SimCity*), Richard Garfield is now a name that inspires awe among gaming cognoscenti. Just over 20 years ago though, he was a disorganised post-grad student scrabbling around for a suitable pair of shoes. His important visitor waited patiently, whilst his friend steered the conversation towards *RoboRally*. Garfield had not had a single game published and was as much concerned with "The distribution of the binomial coefficients modulo p" (his thesis) as he was with fantasy worlds and gaming mechanics. He was, remembered Adkison, a scruffy sod to boot: "Then, as now, he wore mismatched socks, had strange bits of thread and fabric hanging from parts of his clothing and generally looked like someone who had just walked into the Salvation Army and grabbed whatever seemed colourful." Then, as now, it would have been foolishness of the highest order to judge him on appearances.

Garfield was in no way disheartened when Adkison explained to the *RoboRally* creators that he was unable to publish their board game. Instead, at once pragmatic and keen to demonstrate his game-designing chops, Garfield piped up, "If you don't want *RoboRally*," he asked, "what do you want? Describe a game concept – any concept – and I'll design a game around it for you," he told Adkison.

What Adkison was looking for was a game for the convention circuit: something portable, something quick, something that jaded role-players could distract themselves with during their down-time or while waiting for a tardy dungeon master. As a fan of the fantasy art he also saw at the numerous conventions he visited, Adkison wanted a vehicle for great illustration, too. The solution, he felt, was some kind of card game. Garfield nodded, took in Adkison's off-the-cuff brief and the conversation moved on.

Garfield stayed on at his nearby parents' house for a week and met up with Adkison the following weekend for a Seattle gaming convention called

Dragonflight. There, at Adkison's behest, he demonstrated *RoboRally* to convention-goers and got to know Adkison's few associates at Wizards of the Coast. After the show, he hitched a ride with Adkison and Wizards co-founder Ken McGlothlen. The trio stopped off at the Seattle Center, near the city's iconic Space Needle, and as McGlothlen popped out to collect something, Garfield and Adkison stretched their legs. Garfield turned to his new mentor: "Remember that game concept you described?" he said. "Well, I have an idea that might work."

By the time Garfield had finished describing his idea, Adkison was bowled over in a way he had not been since first discovering *Dungeons & Dragons*. In some grungy corner of a Seattle car park, he started, he says, "dancing around, whooping and hollering". When McGlothlen returned to the scene and heard the idea, he was blown away, too. It was good. It was really good.

Having dropped Garfield off at his parents' house, McGlothlen did his best to rein in his excitement. But it was too much for him. Turning to Adkison, he let it all out: "You know," he said. "This game could make a million dollars. Maybe even *two*."

CHAPTER THREE
Meet Kird Ape

IN LATE 1994, I had just uprooted to New Zealand from rural England after a traumatic time in my family's life. My dad, a fantasy illustrator and suitably corrupting influence, had started a business designing and selling war games, along with a partner from his days working at fantasy powerhouse Games Workshop. Sadly, the partnership failed, the Conservative government shepherded the UK economy down the toilet with a series of violent flushes and the Chalks, like numerous other families the country over, lost everything.

In practical terms, that meant our house, almost everything my parents had in the bank and a cosy middle-class existence in a neat Northamptonshire village. I left my posh fee-paying school mid-way through the year, ashamed, confused and unable to describe to friends, who never wanted for anything, what was happening. Why my parents could no longer afford the fees, let alone pocket money for music, tuck, clothes or whatever my peer group thought the measure of a man-cub back then. We were in dire straits and, of the few possible escape routes open to us, my parents hit upon the idea of emigrating to New Zealand (English-speaking and home to a few friends at least) as the best of a bad bunch. As a 13-year-old boy finding my feet in school, it was not a move I relished. All I wanted was to cement my first lasting friendships and to listen to Pearl Jam, Juliana Hatfield and the Wonder Stuff, occasionally with girls. New Zealand was, so I heard, all sheep.

If only it had been. Instead, it was also a terrifying new school, distinctly agricultural in appearance, all tin roofs, huts on stilts and concrete walkways.

A fine educational institution Mahurangi College may have been, but compared to my private all-boys school in Warwick, founded by Edward the Confessor, it felt like the back-end of beyond. Helpfully, regular racist taunts (ethnically, I am half-Chinese) from white co-pupils made me feel especially welcome. "They told us we were getting a new kid from England," they informed me on my first day. "Imagine our surprise when a nip walked in!" As if that was not bad enough, I was also one of the sinful few in my new environment not to revel in participatory team sport. A passing interest in football was derided as "gay" and quite clearly I had never done PE outside in my bare feet before. All in all, I was ill-equipped to embrace the pillars of New Zealand culture.

In such circumstances, I couldn't help but hover from group to group at break-time, trying to find one with whom I felt I belonged. Slowly but surely, I gravitated away from the idiots to whom I was first assigned and had a crack at a more popular bunch. There I failed miserably. A lack of self-confidence and overriding cultural incompatibility (I wore trousers instead of shorts) scuppered me. That left me chatting to some kids from maths, who seemed to gravitate towards the library on cold days.

Already au fait with fantasy gaming through my dad, I had more luck infiltrating this last clique. Perhaps that is too grand a word for three or four awkward teenagers with bad skin and bookish tendencies. But from them, I discovered that painting metal figurines for kitchen-table skirmishes was in fact a gateway drug to far harder substances. The new stuff on the street was called *Magic: The Gathering* and, as 1994 rolled into 1995, I would duly take my first hit.

Into the library I went with the Mahuranghi *Magic* gang, comprising Simon, Jamie, Brad and James and a few kids younger than ourselves. The latter would flit around, join in occasionally, trade us the odd card, but were never part of the *Magic* inner sanctum. We didn't have much – no cars, girlfriends, the right trainers or parties to go to – but we did have standards. A requisite disdain for anyone younger than ourselves. Turf even. Reeking of wet wool and adolescent odour, the library was that turf – our preferred table, a couple of chairs, the same cheap carpet that finds its way into educational institutions everywhere. It wasn't much. But despite regular set-tos with the fussy old librarian Mrs Hughes, it was ours.

I had tried to grasp the concept of this unknown game from fragments of back-of-the-class chatter. But until someone pressed a slightly battered wad of cards into my hands, I didn't really get it. Was *Magic* tactical like a war game, the cards replacing toy soldiers on a mocked-up battlefield? Was it as banal and random as *Top Trumps*? Where did this game even come from? "No", "No", and "America" came the rapid-fire answers as the *Magic* players huddled around me and tried to explain the game's rules.

Clumsily, I shuffled the deck I had been lent and prepared for my first-ever game. Brown, book-like card backs tumbled through my hands as I mixed them. Then I drew a starting hand of seven, as instructed, and stared blankly at my opponent. I was, to put it mildly, lost. But then I fanned open my first grip of cards and came face-to-face with a startling fellow called Kird Ape. The card's illustration, a hulking silverback gorilla lurking in the undergrowth, stared out at me with piercing red eyes. Instantly, I knew that for all my confusion, for all the meaningless jabbering in my ear, for all my questions about what I was doing in a library 11,600 miles from home, *I got it. Magic* was special. And it was something for me.

Magic is perhaps best described as a singularly rich gaming environment. Its genius lies in the premise outlined by Richard Garfield to Peter Adkison in that Seattle car park, back in 1991: where other games had one set of rules, Garfield told Adkison, his game would have almost endless rules. Where other games came neatly sorted in one communal box or deck, his would be sold in incomplete chunks and every player would be free to assemble their own set. Whereas other games were finite in scope, his would be endlessly expandable. The math whiz's 'two-million-dollar' idea was not simply for a card game, but for what he dubbed a "collectible card game", something that had hitherto never existed. 'Collectible', like sports stickers or cards. And playable, like a strategy game. It would be, just as *Dungeons & Dragons* had been to tabletop wargaming, a paradigm shift. A new gaming form entirely. One set of rules would govern the game as a whole. But each card printed would also have its own rules written on it, too. Interacting with the universal rules in a unique way, a card could then be collected by a player, sized up for its strengths and weaknesses and slotted into his or her personalised deck. Both the design of the game and the decks of cards used to play it would be completely modular. It was a deceptively simple idea but absolutely revolutionary at the same time. Adkison, who knew a good game when he found one, was right to jump up and down with glee.

Still, as I fumbled *Magic* cards for the first time, it took me a while to understand what any of this meant. The backs of the cards provided the first clue to understanding the game. Each was textured to look like a leather-bound tome and featured a ring of five coloured dots in its middle; red, black, green, blue and white. These were, said my friends, the game's different colours of 'mana'. Mana is the main resource each player must marshal in the game, using it to deploy the other cards in his or her hand. In the game's parlance, players use mana, to 'cast' a mixture of 'spells'. Those spells are broken down into different types, cost different amounts of mana to use and have different effects on the game. Sorceries, instants, creatures, artifacts, enchantments, planeswalkers and tribal spells – all of them can be used in one way or another to reduce the opponent's life total from 20 to zero points, the main path to victory in the game.

Kird Ape represented one of those card types, a creature as its name suggests, and a red creature at that, as I could tell from the card's coloured frame. Each appropriately coloured card has a slot for a picture, a main text box detailing what the card does, plus other textual tit-bits dotted around the card's surface. In the top left is the card's name – 'Kird Ape'. I read it several times, as I tried to beat my puzzlement and make my first-ever play. To do that, I then had to look in the opposite, top right-hand corner. There, symbols would show me what I needed to do if I wanted to play the card – to take it from my hand, introduce it to the game and have it do what it says it does in its text box. In Kird Ape's case, there was a single symbol in the corner, a little red swirling flame, showing me that to cast him, I had to spend one red mana. Mana functions like a currency – once generated by a 'land', it can be spent to pay the casting cost of the spells in a player's hand. Each colour of mana has its strengths and weaknesses, each is represented by its own symbol and each colour of mana is produced by a corresponding basic land that produces one specific type of mana. Each turn, players alternate and can put one more land into play, giving them progressively more mana to play the cards in their hand. Each player gets to draw a card each turn and as their resources grow, each can play a wider range of the new options being drawn from their 'library' (the more flavourful name for their deck used during the game). With each turn, come new decisions about how to overcome one's opponent or to stop them from charging to victory first.

With that goal in mind, I scratched my head and tried to figure out how best to smash the grinning and impatient rival sat across the library table from me. Reducing your opponent's life total from 20 to zero is the key and here, Kird Ape and his fellow creatures are vitally important. Each creature has two numbers down in the bottom right-hand corner, separated by a '/'. In the case of Kird Ape those numbers read '1/1' – the mighty beast's 'power' (before the '/') and 'toughness' (after the '/'). These stats dictate how much damage a creature can deal (to an opponent or to another creature, should your opponent throw one of their own into its path to block its attack) and how much they can soak up before dying themselves. Kird Ape can deal one damage (its power) and survive being dealt one damage, too (its toughness). Unlike a toy soldier in a war game though, once Kird Ape is in play, he is not manoeuvred with a tape measure or advanced following a die role. *Magic*'s battlefield is metaphorical and pieces are laid out according to convention rather than tactically arranged or physically moved into contact with one another for combat.

Instead, cards in play have an effect on the game specified by the individual rules text printed on the card. Kird Ape, for example, is no ordinary monkey. The words in his text box read, *While controller has Forests in play, Kird Ape gains +1/+2.* What does that mean? Simply, that if you build your deck to include red-mana-making Mountains with which to cast him and Forests with which to fuel him, you can make Kird Ape a bigger threat to your opponent – a 2/3 creature instead of a 1/1 creature, something not to be sniffed at. Lastly, Kird Ape, like every other card in the game, includes an artist credit. Ken Meyer Jr was responsible for Kird Ape's look and feel: a brooding beast waiting to leap out from his verdant habitat, all the while fixing his prey with fiery red eyes. Those single dots of crimson paint lit up a grey New Zealand day and compelled me to become a *Magic* player. So thank you Ken. The bill is in the post.

More importantly though, Kird Ape's gaze sparked joy in me, which I realised I hadn't felt since departing Heathrow airport in tears. That card was more than a playing piece. It was a handhold for my teenage self, flailing above a gaping void of my own ill-defined identity. Slapping down Kird

Ape on a chipped Formica tabletop in the library at Mahurangi College was liberating. The newness of the experience hinted at a world that had not yet been defined, as grand in scope perhaps as Garfield had intended. To me, that signalled hope. That, having lost the world I thought I knew, I could find another place for myself within this game. These cards then, these simple cards, would be the key to a new community. A home away from home. Solace during a miserable exile. I smiled as I held them. They have proved almost impossible to put down since.

CHAPTER FOUR
Testing, testing: 1, 2, 3...

"There's something you should know," Richard Garfield told Peter Adkison almost immediately after explaining his concept for *Magic* to him. "I'm not sure it's possible to design this game." It was a rare admission from the designer confident he could rise to any challenge. His concept was so radical and so vast – a game whose modular design could be endlessly expanded with collectible cards – that even he was having trouble getting his head around how to execute it. To think he would be deterred, though, would be to misunderstand Garfield's way of looking at things. Designing such a complex system was a game itself: a quest to be undertaken, a pushing at established boundaries and a tinkering with the rules defining what a game should be. Despite having lowered Adkison's expectations, Garfield returned to Philadelphia to do what he did best: roll the proverbial dice and begin playing.

Anyone looking for Garfield in those days would have found him camped out in the David Rittenhouse Labs, on the southeast corner of 33rd and Walnut. There, west of Philadelphia's Center City, over the slithering Schuylkill River and past the ornate, art-deco 30th Street Station, was the University of Pennsylvania's maths department. Like many PhD students, Garfield could be found in his office there at all hours of day and night. Ostensibly, he was hard at work on his thesis. But, more often than not, he could also be found playing card and board games with his colleagues. He was a good student – a great student even – but one whose love of combinatorics (the science of counting) was very much in the service of his true passion: games.

Garfield was loath to waste his brainpower on anything else. He wore permanently mismatched socks, for example, having given up sorting them early in life. And indeed, sometimes even his teaching of undergraduate students was a game to him. In one infamous incident in the Penn maths department he and a colleague swapped roles to dupe a first-year maths class: Garfield stood in front of the lecture hall, prattling on – only to be interrupted incessantly by someone sat in the crowd, telling him he was wrong. As the interjections increased and the 'teacher's' mistakes were brazenly exposed, Garfield feigned exasperation and stormed out of the room shouting, "Well if you're so clever, why don't you teach the class?" As jaws dropped amongst the assembled students, the know-it-all did just that – finally revealing that he was in fact the real teacher all along. Garfield was just playing a role for laughs. For a challenge. To see how far a game could be pushed.

Barry Reich, who became friends with Garfield at the university bridge club, says his gaming buddy was fascinated by fun. By strategy. By the different shapes a game could take. "If you sat down with Richard in a restaurant he would have the salt shakers and sugar packets arranged into a game before you knew it – condiment chess or something like that. It wasn't just silly, it was fun. Because Richard really understands what people want." It was the same all-encompassing understanding of gaming that had so impressed Peter Adkison. It was also what destined Garfield to create a game like *Magic*, which, it would turn out, extends far beyond sitting down and playing cards with an opponent.

Perhaps it was Garfield's well-developed strategic instincts which had led him to downplay the possibility of making *Magic* work to Adkison. In fact, the avid game designer had had related ideas crystallising for some time. His variations for the traditional card game hearts, played competitively in the maths department, often included a number of special cards. He was also a huge fan of the cult game *Cosmic Encounter*, in which each player takes on the role of a different alien species. Each one is capable of breaking one of the game's rules. This mechanic fascinated Garfield and would find its own expression in *Magic*'s interactions between card text and game rules. It is remarkable, though, just how quickly the 'un-designable game' began to fall into place. Garfield's revelation was that both players need not have the same cards – and as he sought to build a framework for that idea, he was reminded of a card game he had been working on since the early 1980s called *Five Magics*. It, too, contained land cards and five different colours of magic, each with their own flavour, and provided the backbone of the prototype that Garfield would develop for his new game. Just a month or two after telling Adkison that creating the game could be beyond even his powers, he created a deck of 120 cards that demonstrated its premise. This was known as the Alpha playtest set: a single deck made up of small, business-card-sized cards, sometimes of confusingly different colours, covered in Magic Marker scrawls explaining their names and functions. While the finer points of the execution were perhaps too prosaic to bother Garfield, he was quietly confident his concept would work. Now all he needed was an opponent.

"HEY BIT," SAID Garfield to Barry Reich, using the nickname he had bestowed on his diminutive, computer science-studying friend. "I've created this game and I want you to try it with me." It was now the late summer of 1991. The invitation in itself was not surprising. Garfield constantly had a new game on the go. But Reich was more than happy to indulge his close friend, who he credited with introducing him to so many other great games. The pair grabbed some food, and then headed off to one of their preferred hangouts, the lounge in the university's astronomy department. Located in the heart of the building, what it lacked in windows, it made up for with comfy seating and large coffee tables ideal for gaming on. Garfield produced his deck of cards, split it roughly in half and explained the rules to his first *Magic* guinea pig. The pair shuffled up their cards, then set aside one at random from each of their piles as ante for the winner (an unpopular rule that would be dropped officially in 1995, but unofficially much quicker by players who treasured their cards). Then they began to play.

Things started slowly, but as the rules Garfield had invented held up, the pair began to play with more confidence. The game's rapid pace grabbed Reich – a single game might last five minutes or 10 or sometimes 15. Compared to board-gaming, role-playing or tabletop wargaming, it was an instantly gratifying all-you-can-eat gaming buffet. The pair gorged on it, throwing down the unfamiliar cards in their rudimentary decks featuring spells of all colours, as well as colourless artifacts, with no regard for the time.

Eventually, they battled each other to exhaustion. "I love this game!" Reich told his friend. "But it's five in the morning, I've got to stop." Giddy with excitement, the two collaborators stumbled out of the astronomy lounge and into the daylight. It was, in fact, 8.30am. They had played through the entire night. Both knew then that *Magic*, as it was almost instantly christened, was a special game indeed.

The days that followed were a blur as Garfield, aided by Reich, figured out how to transform the single Alpha deck into a game that could be playtested more widely. Central to Garfield's thinking was that cards would be unevenly distributed. Three levels of card rarity would exist – common, uncommon and rare – which would make the game a process of discovery and accentuate the collecting aspect. Each player would have to seek out the less frequent cards to score for their decks. Reich helped him devise the ratios for the distribution of the different cards, so they knew how many test versions of each rarity to mock up. Once the maths had been done, they could head to the David Rittenhouse Labs, which were well-stocked with everything a would-be game designer needed: not only computers, printers and assorted stationary supplies, but an army of fiendish gamers ready to try their hand at anything new. "You have to understand," says Skaff Elias, whose office was across the hallway from Garfield's, "Richard would grab people for games all the time. If you said 'yes' once, you were in the loop."

As he had done with Reich, Garfield introduced Elias to the game with the rudimentary Alpha deck. And like Reich, Elias was instantly impressed. The Pennsylvania native and fellow maths student helped to up Garfield's production values for the full-blown playtest set. Sacrificing the stack of comics in his room in a flurry of scissor blades, he plundered artwork to help illustrate some of the experimental cards. Then, following the plans drawn up by Reich, the group of friends made up a sheet containing all the rare cards and printed it off in the computer room. They then photocopied it and stuck both sheets to cardboard backing, before slicing them up into individual cards. Then they made the uncommon sheet, following the same method, but producing more copies. Finally, they devised the common sheet (which also featured lands), photocopying it still more times to produce the desired number of playing pieces. This produced a mix of cards, notably featuring only two of each rare card (usually the most powerful cards in the game). Garfield felt this was analogous to the kind of mixture groups of friends would have access to when the game was finished. Elias then stirred up the resulting card pool in a big black bin bag and dished out its contents to willing gamers in and around the maths department. What was known as the Beta playtest set was ready to go, and the game that Garfield had feared might be un-designable began to take shape.

Although an attempt to draft a rulebook was not attempted until much later, the game would already have been graspable by modern *Magic* players. One of the key mechanical notions of the game, 'tapping,' was in place from the word go: Tapping – or turning a card through 90° until it is horizontal – is an elegant solution devised to show when cards are being activated or used. Tapped cards can then be untapped again at the start of the player's next turn during the untap step. Basic lands are, for example, tapped to produce one mana each, which can be used to cast spells. The next turn they are untapped and can be used again to cast further spells. Creatures tap when they attack or use certain specially activated abilities. Artifacts, too, can in some cases be tapped to generate a powerful effect.

The most striking difference with finished *Magic* cards was the way the casting cost of each spell was notated. Serra Angel, for example, is an iconic creature card that costs a total of five mana to cast, two of which must be white and three of which can be any colour. Today, that is notated with a "3", then two instances of the white mana symbol. The playtest version of the card cost the same total amount to cast but was notated "5", then "WW" – meaning five total, of which two must be white. While that notation would be simplified on the finished product, Garfield had otherwise got the game's grand lines in place from the off. Although many new cards would be devised during playtesting, with many of the students contributing ideas that would make it into print, very few were taken out. As Reich said, Garfield's strength was knowing what people wanted. He instinctively delivered a version of *Magic* that captivated its first audience. Even he would be surprised (and delighted) though, by some of the twists his game took during testing.

*   *   *

ALTHOUGH THE SINGLE Alpha playtest deck had been adequate for demonstrating the actual playing of the game, when everyone had their own deck, *Magic* took on a new dimension. Some of the game's individual elements may have existed before – but Garfield had brought them together in a new and brilliant synthesis. Most importantly, the game's social aspect quickly revealed itself. For Elias, that was when *Magic* went from being "good" to being "a great, great, great game." He says, "It was just amazing! And it was instantly like that for everyone who laid their hands on it." The importance of trading cards to improve decks (often depleted by losing cards to the ante) shot to the fore.

"It was fascinating," says Reich. "It was like a little stock market. Like an economic simulation that was occurring as we were playtesting. Some cards were clearly very powerful, like Time Walk [which for just one colourless and one blue mana reads 'Take an extra turn after this one'], while others would rise and fall in value depending how people played them." To tempt others into trades, the playtesters realised they could showcase specific cards in their decks while playing against their opponents and inflate the value of a card they no longer wanted before trading it away. Scruples went out the window as the playtesters got more and more hooked on the game and tried to master the rapidly developing environment. "The game took on a life of its own and did things Richard never expected," says Reich.

Over the winter, Garfield tweaked *Magic*'s rules and cards. Then he pressed the maths department's computers, photocopiers and guillotines into service once again. Elias sacrificed more of his comics and together they printed a new, fully illustrated set of playtest cards named Gamma in the spring of 1992. The Rittenhouse Labs became a hothouse of *Magic* development. And as the academic year rolled on and Garfield hit the home straight of his thesis, the game's first focused deck-building strategies began to emerge.

Chris Page, a maths student and tester, remembers some of the ideas being concocted. Garfield, he says, had a Snow White and the Seven Dwarves theme deck built around a card called Super Hero and seven copies of War Mammoth. Others had picked up on how to abuse the set's most powerful cards. "At that point Time Walk and Ancestral Recall were both common cards and someone was able to break those by using all small creatures with them," says Page. After petitioning from the playtesters, Time Walk and Ancestral Recall were moved to rare in the final printed set. Today, the two cards are part of a long-out-of-print group of the game's most powerful cards dubbed the 'Power Nine' by players for their game-breaking effect.

Reich, meanwhile, was also innovating and highlighting the strength of *Magic*'s other power cards. A capricious player who had plunged headlong into the game since his introduction by Garfield, he had become particularly attached to the card Sea Serpent. Whenever he cast it, he would launch a toy plastic snake on to the table hissing like the monster in question. It was this same sense of fun that led him to pursue various thought experiments in building his decks, which would elucidate some of the game's subtle interactions. "I bet I could make an all-artifact deck," he told Garfield, who was sceptical about the idea of making a functioning deck with only one class of cards, albeit one that can be cast with any colour or colourless mana. Reich leapt to the challenge and began trading in earnest to build his theoretical deck. Key to his strategy was a sub-set of the game's artifact cards dubbed the 'Moxes' or 'Moxen'. There are five original Moxen – one for each colour. Each is a zero-to-cast artifact, which can be tapped to add one mana of a specific colour to its controller's mana pool. At first glance, that is the same function as a basic land. But as only one land can be played each turn, the fact that a Mox is an artifact becomes relevant – it can be played *as well as* a land in a single turn, and with a casting cost of zero nets its controller mana. Each Mox highlights the brilliant complexity of Garfield's design – because each *Magic* card has its own unique functionality, the game can constantly break its own rules. If you play a Land *and* a Mox on your turn, you have essentially taken two turns in a row, advancing the development of your resources while your opponent twiddles his or her thumbs.

Reich managed to amass seven of the 10 Moxes available to the group (one of each of the five colours, each being rare and thus printed twice), a handful of Sol Rings (which can be tapped for two colourless mana) and a variety of other artifact mana sources. "It was hard because people were beginning to be clued in about the strength of these cards," says Reich. "But because I wasn't limited by the rule that says you can only play one land per turn, I could dump stuff down really quickly. I had a Hive to make Bee tokens and a Hill that generated Ants and I just swarmed and overwhelmed people. The fact that it worked at all blew Richard away."

Reich then used the Moxes he had amassed to make the group's first fully functional five-colour deck, again using the artifact mana sources to break the one-land-a-turn rule. This allowed him to cast the biggest threats available in each of *Magic*'s colours. Reich's strategy presaged some of the decks the wider public would build when *Magic* was released, as well as the value the game's most powerful cards would accrue: "When I built these decks and used the Moxes to dump out mana sources so fast, everybody said, 'Oh my god, these things are super-powerful!'" he says. "The price skyrocketed and people tried to get them back from me. I might have traded one or two of them back, but only for exorbitant prices."

While Reich's tinkering illustrated the inordinate strength of certain card combinations, the playtesters remained relaxed. As Chris Page remembers, the risk that anyone would amass as many power cards as Reich was considered tiny. "We were working off a different model before it came to market," he says. "We thought that somebody might buy one deck [the game would initially be marketed in 60-card Starter Decks, alongside 15-card Booster Packs – the primary way cards are sold today]. Perhaps there might be a few extravagant people who might buy two Decks and a Booster Pack or two a year." That meant the chances of any one player or group even discovering all the rare cards, let alone collecting them, would be slim. That was just the way Garfield wanted it: he hoped players would be blown away each time an opponent threw down a mysterious card they had never seen before. In fact, by the time Garfield had completed his thesis and taken up a teaching post in Walla Walla, Washington in the summer of 1992, he decided to play a similar trick on the playtesters. As he drew up the final list of all the cards that would see print (the Delta file which was never itself playtested), he kept the exact list of rare cards secret from all the testers. It would be as much a surprise for them as it would be for the *Magic*'s first real players. Garfield never could resist a little game.

CHAPTER FIVE

The Basement Blues

As Magic-fever gripped the David Rittenhouse Labs in Philadelphia, life 2,371 miles away in Peter Adkison's basement was somewhat different. In the weeks following Adkison's meeting with Garfield, the Wizards chief had moved his initial enthusiasm to the backburner. He and his small staff were focused on getting the company's first-ever product out of the door. This was to be a role-playing book called *The Primal Order*, designed to complement other publishers' rules-systems.

Editor Beverly Marshall-Saling was steering the challenging project. She was helped in particular by Wizards' new vice president Lisa Stevens. Stevens had joined from role-playing company White Wolf and brought with her one thing the company sorely lacked: gaming industry experience. Adkison was so keen to get her on board, he had driven her from Atlanta to Seattle, with all her worldly possessions in a U-Haul rental truck directly after his meeting with Garfield. It was Stevens who had now devised a strategy to get Wizards into the market place. First would come *The Primal Order*. Then a series of products for the role-playing game *Talislanta*. Wizards had bought the rights to the existing game by designer Stephan Sechi as a way to boost their slender product roster and attract an established fan base.

As autumn 1991 began to set in and the final push on *The Primal Order* got under way, a parcel from Philadelphia arrived at the Wizards office. Adkison unwrapped the package to discover a box stuffed with Beta *Magic* playtest decks and a rough set of rules drafted by Garfield. It was Wizards' first glimpse of the game so tantalisingly dangled before Adkison in Seattle a month or so previously. The reaction was immediate. "It was incredible," says Adkison. "The office shut down for like three weeks because all we did was play *Magic*. That seemed like a pretty good sign."

Adkison could see that this was not simply another game – rather a paradigm shift in gaming, the creation of a whole new gaming form, as radical as role-playing (and his beloved *Dungeons & Dragons*) had been in its day. Immediately, it became the game he wanted to produce more than anything else. As Marshall-Saling and co-editor David Howell put the finishing touches to *The Primal Order*, *Magic* consumed all his time. He and his few Wizards employees were playing it relentlessly, trading with each other to tune their decks and mercilessly winning ante from each other. It was a sudden febrile outbreak – but one not without its dangers.

"We were very excited," says Stevens. "But we were also scared, because we were such a small company, and we didn't have much money at all. Here we had this great card game that we were all addicted to right off the bat. But we didn't have the money to publish it and, if we showed it to anyone else, it might get stolen from underneath us." From a base of almost nothing, the tiny role-playing company with not a single product on the market, had in its a lap a golden ticket. They just had no idea if they could cash it in. It was a daunting situation and one Adkison felt was best pushed aside, while Garfield developed the game further and tried, simultaneously, to rustle up a finished thesis. "You pretend it's not there and charge forward," says Adkison. But things got far, far worse before they got any better.

ON APRIL FOOLS Day 1992, Wizards of the Coast took delivery of *The Primal Order*, the culmination of over four years' work. When the product hit the shelves, it should have been the realisation of a long-held dream and the first step in a well-defined strategy, designed by Stevens. Unfortunately, it quickly turned into a nightmare. With their ambitious book, Wizards had hoped to allow role-players using different rules systems to play together more easily. But by referencing other manufacturer's products, they were treading dangerous ground. A rival publisher took offence and decided to defend its trademarks. In June 1992, Palladium Books and its owner Kevin

Siembieda instigated legal proceedings against Wizards for copyright and trademark infringement. It was an exhausting, expensive mess that dragged the young company into the mire. By December, Adkison was at breaking point – and writing the last pay-roll cheques he could afford for his skeleton staff. Wizards was on its knees.

That meant *Magic* was in danger of finding itself homeless – or worse, of being snatched up by a rival publisher. Under extreme pressure, Adkison wracked his brain for a solution that would protect the new game from the wolves and preserve the great hope everyone at the company (and indeed anyone who had played the game) had for Garfield's creation. His solution, when it came, saved the card game from a stillbirth: Adkison set up a new company called Garfield Games in which both Wizards and Garfield held stock. Garfield Games would own *Magic*, guaranteeing its creator an appropriate share of any profits if it really did turn out to be the hit it had the potential to be. The new company would also protect prospective investors from the fall-out of the Palladium case. "If we hadn't created Garfield Games," says Adkison, "I don't think we would have been able to raise the money to make *Magic*."

Still, Wizards was fighting for its life, haemorrhaging money on legal fees that it needed to release its *Talislanta* products and fund *Magic*'s development. Morale was low and life for everyone at the company had become a spirit-sapping grind; a masochistic labour of love. Stevens remembers shareholders coming to the office to make the dejected staff – who by the end of 1992 were working for stock rather than cash – a hot meal now and again. Paying the rent became impossible. And everyone was forced to take on part-time work while the Palladium case rumbled on. It was a bleak time, far removed from the fun outsiders might suppose a games company is all about. It was also a scene that was playing out simultaneously on the other side of the Atlantic, as my parents' own games company went under. Days ended in tears, shed behind closed doors and wiped away when my sisters or I entered the room. Hair went grey overnight. Tempers and bonds and futures frayed.

I am glad someone survived.

*   *   *

ALTHOUGH PALLADIUM'S CASE was thin and their pursuit of legal action primarily about being seen to protect their trademarks (an important aspect of intellectual property law), a preliminary court hearing failed to throw it out. As 1992 became 1993, it was time for Wizards to try a different avenue. Lisa Stevens' gaming-industry connections would prove vital in finding it. She was friends with Mike Pondsmith, the designer of seminal future-noir role-playing game *Cyberpunk*. At the time, Pondsmith was also president of the Game Manufacturer's Association (GAMA), an America-wide gaming-industry body. Stevens was able to convince him to mediate between Wizards and Palladium. Pondsmith was an honest broker with the diplomatic skills and peer respect to arrange a deal between the two companies. After his intervention, Wizards agreed to remove all references to Palladium's games in future editions of *The Primal Order* and to pay a small amount of compensation over a number of years. It was a common-sense solution, but coming early in 1993, it was the breakthrough the company needed. Spring hit Kent, Washington, early, and Wizards put up green shoots, which strained for air, light and life.

Thanks to the creation of Garfield Games, progress on *Magic* had not stalled completely. A few pieces of artwork had been commissioned and with these, Wizards had put on a number of local events aimed at generating investor interest in the game. Every cent brought in was a boon to the game's development, but progress was slow and laborious. Convincing investors to back a completely new gaming form, designed by a maths student, and published by a largely unproven company was a tough sell. Thankfully though, some could identify with Wizards' vision.

Adkison was still working full-time at Boeing and using the superior computers in his office for Wizards business, after his colleagues had gone home. He had been pulling 80-hour weeks for two years straight, the charismatic captain at the wheel ready to go down with the ship, should it – as it almost had – go under. His dedication and belief were unflappable. And would result in one very special investment in *Magic* from an unlikely source.

"It was a very specific amount, I remember that," says Adkison. "Something like $1,293." It was written on a cheque and pressed into Adkison's hands by Marilyn, his janitor at Boeing. She had seen Adkison working late every night and would stop by and ask him what he was doing as she made her nocturnal vacuuming rounds. Now – much to her family's fury – she had decided to invest her life savings in *Magic*, buying stock from Adkison at 50 cents a share. "I don't know anything about these games," she told Adkison. "But I see how hard you're working every night and that you're so excited about what you're doing. I think you're going to make it."

It was a heartfelt vote of confidence, but a reminder to Adkison of the seriousness of his undertaking. He knew the risks of start-up companies and yet knew how desperately *Magic* needed investment if it were to see the light of day. Reluctantly, he pocketed Marilyn's cheque and redoubled his resolve to make *Magic* the success it deserved to be.

Raising money wasn't the game's only teething problem, though. Just as Garfield had struggled to figure out how a trading card game might work, Wizards were struggling to figure out how it might be produced. Up until that point there were two broadly analogous products to *Magic* on the market. These, though, were diametrically opposed to each other. On the one hand, trading cards existed as a pure collectible – they were printed on a glossy thick stock, suited to full illustration or photographs of the sports stars they usually represented. On the other hand, playing cards existed on springy, flexible card stock designed to be durable and easy to shuffle rather than carry lavish artwork. How to produce a card that was somewhere between the two was a huge barrier for Wizards of the Coast, a company that had been founded to publish rules books. Their enquiries with playing card printers received blank looks. Adkison meanwhile was reluctant to approach trading card producers who would be best-placed to snaffle the collectible card game idea and rush it to market before Wizards. Again, Stevens' industry connections – plus a dash of serendipity – helped solve a problem that was giving everyone at Wizards headaches: Stevens' former boss at White Wolf, Mark Rein-Hagen, was the key. When Adkison got really desperate in his search to raise the $100,000 he needed to bring *Magic* to market, he turned to other games companies. Everyone – including the famous Steve Jackson Games – turned him down. Only White Wolf could see *Magic*'s brilliance and agreed to back one of their peers.

At America's biggest gaming convention, Gencon, in 1992, Rein-Hagen happened upon a representative from a Belgian printers called Carta Mundi.

Knowing that Wizards were desperately trying to find a printing solution, he dashed off to find them and did his bit in bringing the two parties together. Carta Mundi, whose card-printing expertise stretched back to the 18th century, assured Wizards they could print the cards they wanted. Figuring out how to collate them though, into the semi-randomised decks and packs that Wizards wanted... well, that would take a maths genius. Luckily though, Wizards knew one of those.

Although most players who picked up the game in the earliest days may scoff at the notion that *Magic* was playable right out of the box, Wizards got their finest brain working on the problem – another first – of how to get 60 semi-randomised cards into a Starter Deck that could be shuffled up and played by a new customer. It was intended that each deck would contain two cards from the rare sheet (printed least), 13 cards from the uncommon sheet, plus a mixture of 45 common cards and lands (which in the earliest days were printed on the same sheet). Before the encounter with Carta Mundi, Wizards had been trying to devise a way to get a playable mix into the decks with some back-of-the-envelope blue-sky thinking, including such off-the-wall schemes as using a giant blower to mix up the cards. Once Carta Mundi were on board though, Garfield was able to work directly with them (even flying to Belgium to see how their plants worked) and devise an algorithm to collate the cards as they were cut from their respective sheets. It was important that if people got a number of blue cards in their Starter Deck, for example, that they also got a number of Islands (the land which taps for blue mana to cast those blue spells), too. For Garfield, it was just another puzzle – and a chance to instil some method in the *Magic* madness.

ALMOST TWO YEARS to the day after Mike Davies had contacted Peter Adkison on Usenet, the first finished *Magic* cards began rolling off Carta Mundi's printing presses. In mid-July 1993, as Adkison prepared to travel to the Origins gaming convention run by GAMA, he took a phone call from the Belgian company. They informed him they already had a small sample of cards they could send to him. The call took the still inexperienced Wizards CEO by surprise. He had been expecting to get his hands on the finished product a month later. With an excited "Whoop!" he asked Carta Mundi to courier the cards to his hotel in Dallas (Origins was to be held in nearby Fort Worth), so he could show *Magic* to the gaming public for the very first time.

Asked how well *Magic*'s debut went, Lisa Stevens gives a rueful laugh. Having only had the finished cards in hand for a matter of hours before demonstrating them at the Wizards booth, the publishers themselves were as baffled as anyone by the new product. As Stevens concedes, they simply did not know how to build playable decks from the samples Carta Mundi had sent them. It had been Garfield, remember, who had sent Wizards playtest decks to get started with. That meant that at Origins, Wizards were jamming all manner of cards into big unplayable piles, which did little to entice punters. "The decks we were playing with were horrible," says Stevens. "I'm surprised more people didn't just say: 'This game is stupid!'"

One Origins attendee, John Scott Tynes – who would eventually work for Wizards – wrote about the experience in a later article for Salon.com. Tynes had been at Origins with his own small gaming company Pagan Publishing and after a few drinks with Adkison was talked into trying out the new game. "It was a disaster," wrote Tynes later. "The game creaked past an hour and was an interminable bore. Peter assured us that this first batch mostly consisted of specialised rare cards, which in practice should only be used sparingly. Whatever. We left the convention thinking that Wizards had an expensive failure on its hands." All in all, it was not the reception Wizards was hoping for, having bet the house on the game (literally in Adkison's case – he had re-mortgaged his home to print the cards). If *Magic* was going to fly, particularly at the all-important Gencon convention a month later, it would need all the help it could get.

With that in mind, an increasingly frazzled Adkison decided to take drastic measures. A batch of *Magic* proper would be delivered to Wizards' booth at Gencon in Milwaukee a day before the convention opened on 19 August. Adkison resolved to race it there, driving to the site with his then wife Cathleen. On the way, he would stop at every game store he could on the West Coast, before swinging up through Arizona, New Mexico and the centre of the United States, on towards Milwaukee. The most direct route from Renton, Washington to the convention centre was 1,990 miles. Adkison's route took in twice that distance. But, he hoped, it might just convince gamers that *Magic* was a game worth backing – rather than snake oil being peddled by a travelling charlatan. With two weeks to go until the gaming convention which could make or break Wizards, Adkison slung a small amount of product into the back of a rental van. Then he waved his colleagues goodbye, braced himself for a long ride and put the pedal to the metal. Like every good story, *Magic* was a journey. Like every good American story, it was also, in part, an epic road trip.

"The first store I got to," says Adkison, "they had received a small order of *Magic*. But it was still unopened in the storeroom. They were kind of embarrassed, so they opened it up and I taught like three people who were hanging around how to play." It was not the most auspicious of starts. And at the next store Adkison visited, the reception was much the same. "Oh well, this is a waste of time," he thought and climbed dejectedly back into the driving seat.

But at the third store, things started to pick up a little. There, they had opened the small amount of the product they had ordered – and loved it: "One guy had put his *Magic* cards in a binder," says Adkison. "That was the first time I ever saw someone do that, sorting them like sports cards and putting them away in plastic sleeves in a binder. We take that for granted today but I just thought, 'Wow! That's cool!'"

Little by little, Adkison began to make progress. For every uninterested store or tough crowd he fell upon, he found one which had opened its cards and was keen for more. Some players would even trail Adkison to his next stop, just to have a second crack at purchasing cards from the back of his van. As he wound his way south, the gaming public's interest in *Magic* was beginning to stir. The Wizards founder, fretting about bankruptcy, could start to see light at the end of the tunnel. The game was coming to life before his very eyes. As he pulled up in Albuquerque, word of his trip and the game itself had spread. The first signs of a genuine phenomenon were appearing. "In Albuquerque," says Adkison, "I was treated like a celebrity."

Around 70 people had turned up at local store Wargames West to greet the weary and saddle-sore traveller as he pulled into town. Staff at the gaming hangout had literally laid out a red carpet for him. And excited gamers had even brought video cameras to the event and captured Adkison on camera answering questions – "mostly incorrectly," he says – about how to play their new favourite game. It was a reception to warm the Wizards CEO's cockles.

After an epic odyssey across the rolling asphalt between Washington and New Mexico, his spirits were up. With days to go until Gencon, he allowed himself some cautious optimism. Maybe, just maybe, Wizards would have a good show.

On Wednesday 18 August 1993, Milwaukee's MECCA arena was a frantic anthill of geek activity. Exhibitors at Gencon busied themselves preparing their booths for the four-day onslaught of frenzied gaming fans which would be unleashed the next day as legions of punters descended on the fair to explore, test out and purchase the latest gaming products. Having started in 1967 as a small gathering at *Dungeons & Dragons* co-creator Gary Gygax's house in Lake Geneva, Wisconsin (hence 'Gen'), the convention had been growing year on year. Some 20,000 gamers would make their way to Milwaukee for the 1993 edition. The crowd who filled the venue only weeks later to watch Wizards' fellow Seattleites Nirvana on their *In Utero* tour could not have been more rabid. This was the gaming convention that mattered – and Wizards were primed to make a splash.

Except that they weren't. As other companies put the finishing touches to their booths and stacked them high with product, Wizards were anxiously awaiting a shipment of *Magic* to adorn their Spartan stand. The cards, on their way from Belgium, had been held up in port at Los Angeles. Lisa Stevens was desperately trying to get them flown out to Milwaukee to prevent impending disaster. Her fixing powers had proved invaluable so far, but now she was helpless, hammering the phone and imploring Wizards' customs company to get the shipment unloaded, out of LA and on to a plane as fast as possible. Adkison was tearing out what little short-cropped hair he had: "We were calling the guys and they were like: 'Yeah, yeah. It'll be there... probably tomorrow,'" he says. "I'm like, '*Probably* tomorrow? What the fuck?!'"

Thursday arrived. Gencon opened. The hordes swarmed in. Already, gamers who had encountered Adkison on his cross-country drive could be seen crouched in corridors with *Magic* cards in front of them, playing the game in the lulls between other events, just as Adkison had envisaged. Curious onlookers were asking what this strange new game was and were being helpfully told to speak to Wizards of the Coast. They would surely have cards for sale. Lines at the booth started building up – and were being turned away by the powerless Wizards staff. Adkison meanwhile was pacing the loading bay at the back of the convention centre, his normally bouncy and hyperactive demeanour giving way to nervous agitation. Still, his product did not arrive.

It was not until late on Friday afternoon, with almost half the convention gone, that a truck finally swung into the loading area bearing precious *Magic* cards. (If you can find a sealed Starter Deck from *Magic's* first printing for sale today, expect to pay around $9,000 for it.) With the exhibition halls scheduled to close at 6.00pm, the Wizards team swarmed to the loading bay and summoned a Herculean effort to get the long-awaited stock back to the booth in time to finally start selling their new game.

As fast as they could open the shipping crates (and scrawl hand-written receipts), Wizards started selling *Magic* cards. The crowd of gamers who had been hovering near the booth for a day and a half pounced – and finally got their hands on the curious game that was proliferating amongst the Gencon crowd. It was a rush for Wizards, a flurry of activity that confirmed – albeit briefly – that they had a saleable product on their hands. As the first wave of buyers subsided, though, the unglamorous business of selling the game to the unconverted began in earnest. "What? Each player needs his own deck?" they would ask incredulously, before buying a Starter Deck and trundling off into the crowd, muttering under their breath. But as the lights went off in the main exhibition hall and Gencon activity moved to nearby bars, those same reluctant customers, refreshed with a cold beer, broke open their new game. After thumbing the Lilliputian 32-page rulebook that came in each Starter Deck, rifling through the full-colour cards which were like nothing they had seen before, and shuffling up their decks for the first time, they began, with a shrug of the shoulders, to play Richard Garfield's brainchild. As the sun came up on the Saturday morning, they were still playing. Red-eyed, hung-over and wearing the maniac grin of zealous converts, they had just one thought on their minds: this game was pretty damn cool!

On Saturday, as soon as the exhibition halls re-opened, they returned to Wizards to buy their first Booster Packs.

On Sunday, they came back to buy whole boxes of Booster Packs.

And on Monday, an exhausted, euphoric Peter Adkison returned to work at Boeing having sold $25,000 of *Magic* in little over 48 hours. As soon as he reached the office, he handed in his notice. His boss Vince was only too glad to accept. Peter had been a hopelessly distracted employee of late. And besides, Vince had invested in *Magic,* too.

CHAPTER SIX

The Sub Pop of Gaming

IF GENCON '93 confirmed one thing, it was that Wizards' modest hopes for the game were going to need drastic revision. Quite what caused the instant public reaction to the game is open to interpretation – the gameplay was undeniably brilliant, but the playtesters had enjoyed the same experience and still only counted on punters buying a deck or two. Chris Page, one of the East Coasters who was at Gencon and witnessed the scramble for *Magic* firsthand, thinks the playtesters may have underestimated how much people would buy, simply because they themselves had not been able to buy cards: the quantity of cards in their environment was fixed and only via trading could they accumulate new tools for their decks. He also points to another factor that hooked the game's early adopters: "I think the art added a big part to the game," he says. "There was certainly a huge difference in seeing the finished cards compared to the playtest cards, which might have had like a black and white picture of an aeroplane or something stuck on them. I wound up buying two boxes worth at Gencon myself." That would be music to the ears of Jesper Myrfors, who along with Lisa Stevens, had another complex production problem to solve during the game's development: how does a new company, with very little cash, commission 302 pieces of full-colour artwork for a brand-new type of game?

MYRFORS IS A towering presence. Part artistic eccentric, with his long mane and black, paint-smudged leather jacket; part Viking, too. The gentle giant with a famously boisterous streak was born in Stockholm, Sweden, before his father was recruited out of the navy by Boeing to work in Seattle on the 747. He now lives surrounded by Lake Washington's lapping waves on Mercer Island, a landmass reachable by road bridge from East Seattle, where inhabitants sip strong coffee and live for the glorious moments the sun breaks through the low-hanging cloud. Quite how one small island contains Myrfors' boundless creative energy, brimming passion and bonhomie is a mystery. But, by common consensus, without those qualities, *Magic* would have been a far poorer product. Ask Richard Garfield if Myrfors helped raise the game's production values and you get an emphatic, "Absolutely!" in response.

In the early 1990s, Seattle was the world centre of misfit culture. Grunge music was taking over the airwaves in a raucous whirlwind of screeching guitars and flannel shirts, and reluctant artists were being thrust upon the world as standard-bearers of a new avant-garde. While Nirvana and their Sub Pop stable-mates floored fans with their heavyweight riffs, a new generation of local visual artists was flourishing, too, not least at Cornish College of the Arts. Housed in the handsome 1928 William Volker building on Leanora Street, just over the road from the *Seattle Times* headquarters, you cannot miss the school: painted in contrasting grey and maroon livery, today its name is stencilled on to the side of the building in huge letters. Contrary to some of their teachers' expectations, the graduating class of 1993 were instrumental in making that name by deploying their brightly burning creative skills in the service of *Magic*. "There was just something in the air," says Myrfors. A student at the college himself, it was he who bridged the gap between the misfits in the city's creative scene and those striving away in Peter Adkison's basement.

The young Myrfors was an avid gamer and a huge fan of the fantasy artwork he discovered in role-playing books and board game boxes. His hero was the British illustrator Ian Miller, whose haunting, gothic artwork had helped define the look and feel of wargaming juggernaut Games Workshop. He was also a big fan of the role-playing game bought up by Wizards of the Coast to seal their push into the market, *Talislanta*. Having heard rumblings about the game being discontinued, a concerned Myrfors headed to his local game shop, Games and Gizmos in Bellevue, to find out what was going on.

There, the staff informed him that a local company had bought the game and would be bringing out a fresh version. Myrfors scribbled down Wizards' details, popped them into his wallet and promptly forgot about them.

More than anything else, Myrfors wanted to be a fantasy artist. His work at Cornish was dedicated to his favourite genre. But despite the technical skills he was learning from his most inspirational teacher Preston Wadley, he was getting little practical help on how to break into his chosen industry. Instead, staff at the college pointed him in two directions: Album covers or book jackets. And, they told him, he would have to move to New York or Los Angeles to crack either of those markets. Frustrated but undeterred, Myrfors promised in the summer of 1992 that he would not return for his final year at Cornish without a piece of published fantasy artwork to his name.

It was then that he remembered the scrap of paper lodged in his wallet and phoned up Wizards. Lisa Stevens, art directing between her many other roles at the start-up, agreed to look at Myrfors' portfolio. Although she felt his artwork wasn't the right look for Wizards, she put him in touch with her old employers White Wolf and John Tyne's Pagan Publishing. Very soon Myrfors had his first published fantasy artwork under his belt. Mission accomplished. But Myrfors couldn't stop there – the *Talislanta* fan in him wouldn't let him.

"How about I do a piece on spec for you?" he asked Stevens. He would do a piece of artwork to her brief and she could decide whether she wanted to buy it or not. Stevens acquiesced and asked Myrfors to do a piece for *Talislanta* within a week. Eager to impress, Myrfors produced two paintings in one weekend. Stevens showed them to *Talislanta* creator Stephen Sechi for his approval and suddenly Myrfors was on board, working on his favourite game, on his own doorstep.

The larger-than-life Myrfors quickly made a name for himself at the Wizards office with his infectious enthusiasm, sense of fun and determination to make great games. Soon, he was attending Wizards' weekly Thursday meetings and helping out with any odd job he could to cement his role at the company. But popular as he was, he noticed that he was not invited to a series of secret meetings that the key employees kept slipping off to. 'The Project', as they dubbed it, was off limits to him. It took tenacity and plenty of grunt work before he could ingratiate himself with the inner circle. Finally though, he managed to infiltrate one of the shadowy pow-wows. Someone thrust a *Magic* playtest deck into his eager hands. And Myrfors had his first crack at a game that would instantly supplant *Talislanta* in his affections. The seasoned gamer's reaction was instant: "I don't want any money for the work I've done," he told Peter Adkison. "Just pay me in stock." These little cards were going to change everything; Myrfors could sense it in his bones. But something would have to be done about the photocopied *Calvin and Hobbes* artwork.

Although Cornish College's staff knew little about the fantasy industry, they were correct that book covers and album sleeves were the main outlet for full-colour fantasy artwork. Although boxed games, role-playing rules books and fantasy magazines were packed full of illustrations, much of it was by necessity black and white. Printing in full colour was still an expensive undertaking, particularly for a start-up, and full-colour artwork was reserved for high-impact covers, because it cost so much to commission. Part of Peter Adkison's thinking when he gave Richard Garfield the brief to create *Magic,* was that there was a stockpile of existing artwork to be mined. Much of it was produced by artists who, outside of the convention circuit where their work for small gaming companies was on show for hardcore fans, got little exposure. By buying up second- and third-use rights to existing artwork, Wizards figured they could quickly and affordably assemble enough artwork to populate Garfield's game. But the idea of pasting existing artwork on to such a radical new game, necessarily giving it a generic look and feel, horrified Myrfors. At once artist and gamer, he sensed that the game's customisable nature meant that it was crying out for each card to be an individual treasure; to be discovered, collected and curated in its owner's deck. At once, Myrfors petitioned Adkison to do everything he could to use original artwork.

In his gut, Adkison knew Myrfors was right. But the budget for the game would only stretch so far: the best deal Adkison could come up with for each piece of artwork was $50 cash, $50 in stock and 50 artist proofs (one-sided versions of the finished card which artists could hand out to promote their work). But the key incentive would be a slice of a royalty pool established for the artists – a certain percentage of sales would go into it and the money would be divvied up according to how many *Magic* images the artists had done. For established artists, it was not a hugely enticing offer. But Myrfors knew where to turn for help: "Peter," he said. "I can get you the artists."

JULIE BAROH IS Seattle born and bred. Today, she works out of an ex-industrial unit in Georgetown in the south of the city with fellow artist Mark Tedin. The young Baroh, though, was a sports-loving tomboy with energy to burn, who preferred cutting class to planning her academic future. When it did become time to figure out what to do after high school, she opted for the local art college. Even with a low grade-point average, she figured, she had a chance of scraping in. Besides, she had been drawing since she could hold a pencil and Cornish College seemed like a cool, creative place in tune with her mindset and Seattle's prevailing vibes at the time.

Her first two years were hell. The illustration course she had enrolled on demanded that students take two years of graphic design, before any actual illustration began. That felt like a waste of time to the rebellious young Baroh, who was soon dodging class again and plotting an escape route out of the lessons that were dragging her down. Her art student friends, including Jesper Myrfors with whom she had grown up on Mercer Island, Amy Weber and Sandra Everingham, made life tolerable – but when she was unceremoniously booted off the course, she was only too glad to go. Instead, she found a place for her talents on Cornish's fine art programme, where she decided to major in print-making and sculpture. Still, she talked regularly with her friends from across the curriculum. And, it was not long before Myrfors put the Wizards deal to her – and indeed all his peers at Cornish.

Baroh, along with Weber, Everingham, Andi Rusu, Cornelius Brudi and recent Cornish drop-outs Anson Maddocks and Drew Tucker, all jumped at Myrfors' offer. Tedin, meanwhile, was a friend of Maddocks' looking for work after finishing a masters' degree in St Louis. There, his tutors had despaired at the doodles of Klingon battle cruisers littering his sketchbook. "To us, it just sounded a lot of fun," says Baroh. "And Jesper really loved the concept. He emphasised to us what a completely new type of game it was and pretty soon, we were all caught up in his enthusiasm for it." For most of the artists involved, including Baroh and Tedin, it was their first paid gig. They took to it with gusto, even if fantasy illustration was not something they had done before, even without fully understanding the game, or indeed, without being fully formed artists. Wizards was their Sub Pop Records: the DIY, punk rock upstarts of the gaming world and the outlet for a new wave of alternative art.

To Myrfors, this was exactly what such a radical new game needed – up-and-coming artists with equally new ideas. "None of them were particularly fantasy artists," he says. "But I liked that." For Myrfors, now the de facto art director for *Magic*'s first print run, variety would be key to the game's appeal. He would rather include bold art that risked polarising players than re-tread the same old fantasy tropes for the nth time. His other guiding principle was that the art should be recognisable from a few feet away, so that anyone walking past a table of *Magic* players could spot that they were playing the startling new game. "I didn't want book covers reduced down to a muddy mess," he says. "It had to be clean, iconic images."

The artists Myrfors had contacted (plus some recruited by Stevens from her White Wolf days) went into overdrive. Soon, they were comparing notes, enthused by the collective buzz of working on a new project together, their first as professionals. Myrfors remembers doing much of his work while hanging out with other painters watching John Woo movies. Friends such as Mark Tedin and Anson Maddocks would egg each other on. And Julie Baroh found herself locked in alien debates with Myrfors about what exactly a blue spell called Clone, her first piece, should like look. It was a creative explosion that turned up fantastic results – and came as no surprise to Myrfors' mentor at Cornish, Preston Wadley. He remembers the class of 1993 with great fondness and an avuncular chuckle: "I remember the first day we had a homework assignment due and everybody pinned their work to the wall for a critique," he says. "The gauntlet was laid down. It was going to be the homework wars, I could see that. There was a supportive, nurturing competition within that group and no-one wanted to be the one that didn't give their best."

Soon the work was rolling in as quickly as Myrfors could process it on his rudimentary set-up at Wizards: a Mac Centris 650 with Version 2 of

Photoshop and a tiny flatbed scanner that restricted everyone's artwork to the maximum size of 5" x 7". Myrfors was teaching himself the software on the fly – and along with fellow artist Chris Rush, working on the graphic design of the cards themselves. Rush designed the *Magic: The Gathering* logo (*The Gathering* having been added because Wizards were unable to trademark the word 'Magic' alone) and the mana symbols for the five distinct colours in the game. Myrfors designed the borders that would frame each illustration and present the card's title, casting cost, rules text, and power and toughness if it was a creature. One feature he included was a different texture to each colour of card, so that even colour-blind players could distinguish between them. He also designed the card back, which to this day remains unchanged – just.

Previously, games had used a single illustrator for their components. But the impossibility of asking one artist to produce over 300 pieces of colour art was turned into a virtue by Myrfors and the 25 artists he assembled to produce *Magic*'s artwork. Variety was the key value – and one thoroughly embraced by Richard Garfield. With Myrfors dishing out only the most minimal of briefs, there were few guidelines in place, although it is worth noting that from the word go, female nudity was ruled out. Scantily clad maidens being rescued by beefcake barbarians represented the very worst of generic fantasy art. Unfortunately, it was a misogynistic rut that the largely male *Dungeons & Dragons* player base had at times dragged role-playing into in the late 1970s. Wizards' decision was in tune with more politically correct times and signalled their hope that with a new female-friendly game, women gamers could be reached in more significant numbers.

That rule aside, the artists were to give free rein to their imaginations. Baroh worked quickly in coloured pencil to produce cards with names like Clone and Mindtwist. Tedin tapped into his comic-book influences for images such as Timetwister and Chaos Orb. Myrfors produced desolate landscapes for powerful special lands such as Bayou and Tundra, while the artist Drew Tucker produced distinctive loose watercolours for cards such as Plateau. Uncharitable souls might have called it a hodge-podge but the results were exactly what Myrfors and Garfield wanted – a wild mixture of bold imagery that reinforced the game's modularity. They hoped the art would excite players, as much as it did the Wizards staff who hotly debated the pieces as they flowed in. A new gaming form deserved a new aesthetic, says Mark Tedin, who fondly remembers seeing the game's visual world take shape. "The bonus of having so many different artists from so many different fields and backgrounds, was that there was no pre-conceived notion about what the art should look like," he says. "It was really rewarding seeing everyone's different efforts coming together."

THE IMPACT OF *Magic*'s art was very real on us in our far-flung corner of New Zealand. This was a startling and gripping universe, completely removed from the drudgery of our teenage existence. We had imagined we would recognise the artists' names at the bottom of each card, from other fantasy games or magazines. But instead, we were left startled by the unknowns from Seattle. They had opened our eyes to a new world with their bold brushstrokes, just as bands from the same city had opened our ears.

My best friend at the time, Simon Hope, had even managed to get his hands on a bizarre promotional poster released by Wizards of the Coast. It featured images of dozens of iconic *Magic* cards. But, perhaps as an attempt to foil would-be counterfeiters, the cards were reproduced without any text on them. Even the names were omitted. And yet, every time we met to play, sprawled on Simon's bedroom floor, we would drag the damn thing out and pore over it. We were searching for clues as to what each card might be called or what each might do. But ultimately, that was just a pretext. We were in the sway of these images, more complex and often more abstract than any fantasy art we had ever seen before. They were simply, undeniably, 'cool'; that intangible virtue marketers all seek to inject into their products. And, if these images were cool, it was because they pushed at the boundaries of what was considered fantasy at the time, calling us to artistic realms beyond the confines of genre.

What never occurred to us when we were looking at that poster though, was to ask whether *Magic* needed artwork at all. The illustrations had us in their grip. But after all, many of the world's most enduring games are played out with abstract components (such as go and backgammon), tiles or cards organised by suit and number (such as poker or mah-jong) or imagery simplified to the symbolic (chess). Their popularity is due not only to the quality of their gameplay, but because such components are instantly understandable. That helps makes classic games graspable by players from across continents and cultures – and indeed by those who may harbour prejudices against a specific genre, in this case what in the broadest brushstrokes gets called 'fantasy'.

Indeed, ask most top players today which images adorn the cards in their *Magic* decks and they probably won't be able to tell you. While that may say something about the more homogenous direction the game's art has evolved in since Jesper Myrfors last worked at Wizards in 2000, it is also due to modern players' focus on the mechanics of each card, rather than their aesthetic impact. For them, the game could be about cops and robbers, cars or robots. Indeed, some of those themes may have introduced the game to a different audience. But it is worth noting, that however hard it can be for a 30-something man to explain his excitement about a new goblin card to sceptical norms, *Magic*'s genre is intrinsic to its quality as a game. Unlike any of the classic games mentioned above, which are played with a fixed number of pieces, Richard Garfield's modular concept meant an identity of some kind had to be mapped on to the cards. *Magic* would never have been able to grow as per the implications of its design if the cards, instead of being divided into five colours with individual names, were divided into five suits with a number like traditional playing cards. It would have been nigh-on impossible to conceive new designs and create the richness of the game (now with around 13,000 unique cards) if each card was only an abstract value. This is particularly true of recent 'top-down' *Magic* sets where cards have been designed to represent a certain theme, like gothic horror in the popular *Innistrad* expansion. More broadly, too, though: creating a game with an infinite variety of pieces requires giving each of those pieces an identity. And fantasy was the perfect fit.

"It's easy to say fantasy is an element of so-called 'geek culture,'" says Skaff Elias. "But it's not. It's an element of culture generally. You can walk up to a person in the street who has never played a game of any kind before and ask them what they a think a shield should do versus a sword. They will automatically know that. If you try and think about what kind of intellectual property you can map over a game like *Magic*, you will be hard pressed to find anything remotely close to fantasy in terms of its ability to convey comprehension." Fantasy tropes are largely drawn from myth and whatever technological advances we may trumpet in the 21st century, that remains a deeply engrained part of who we, as humans, are.

While *Magic* may never be as popular as *Uno*, there is little point in its fans banging their head against the incompatibility of their pastime with friends who claim simply not to 'get' fantasy. Like it or not, *Magic* would not be the game it is without its genre. Without the artwork that enraptured its players in the early 1990s, sprawled on bedroom floors everywhere.

SOME TWENTY YEARS on, Preston Wadley is still teaching at Cornish College. A 61-year-old whose mixed media work juxtaposes found objects and photographs, he is the one teacher the Cornish *Magic* artists immediately mention as their most influential. Without him, many would never have learned the skills or indeed the self-confidence to produce the work for the game that they did. He is, in short, the spiritual grandfather of *Magic* art. And like any grandfather, he is immensely proud of how his charges turned out. Batting away any notion that he should take credit for the success of his former pupils, he says that, on the contrary, it was easy teaching the students who trained their brushes and pens *Magic*-wards. "They had desire," he says. "And you can't teach that." While Wadley says that Myrfors was the leader in that sense, none of the artists who learned their trade at Cornish and graduated on to *Magic* would have done so without that same gnawing need to achieve excellence. They were hungry. They were ambitious. And they weren't afraid of hard work. "Assessing your weaknesses, realising what you have to do to overcome them and making your goals manifest," says Wadley. "That's where real talent lies."

CHAPTER SEVEN
Unleashing a Monster

HELLO ALL, BEGAN a cordial Michael Smith, posting on the Usenet discussion group rec.games.board on 5 August 1993. *I have decided to post my opinion of the game* Magic: The Gathering. *Most of the previous opinions I have read on these groups are from people who insist on flaming a game before they actually play it. Not an informed way to make your opinions known...*

I have purchased two packs of the 'Starter Deck' to duel with a friend of mine who also has two of the Starter Decks. We love the game! We have played about a dozen games and have found it to be a very thought-provoking game. From what I have seen, there is no monster that is too powerful or no spell that is too useless. There are, of course, some combinations of things that give you a distinct advantage. There is no obvious limit to the number of these powerful combinations so I feel that they give no great advantage to either player.

The marketing method, I admit, seems a bit unorthodox, but, it does add to the mystery of 'I wonder what my opponent has in his hand?' I believe that I have enough cards with two decks (of 60 cards for $7.95 each) to enjoy the game for quite a long time. If I wish a little variety, I can always plop down an additional $2.45 for a pack of fifteen more cards. Overall, I enjoy the game...

While such a measured online post might itself seem archaic, the responses, too, reveal a different gaming age. One poster named Patrick Rannou sniped back regarding the cost of buying four decks for a total of $32. *That's a bit much for a card game don't you think?* he wrote. *Personally, I'd even say it's WAY TOO MUCH!!!* (Emphasis his own).

Thankfully for Wizards, Gencon '93 proved that whatever the Rannou camp's grumblings, the gaming crowd's appetite for *Magic* – when stimulated by that lip-smacking first taste – was voracious. The curious marketing method that foxed sceptical customers foreshadowed the 'freemium' business model that has gone on to become popular in the digital realm. Players felt enticed to upgrade their decks and, from the get-go, pounced on any Booster Packs they could find. No wonder then, that after a mind-blowing four days at Gencon '93, Wizards returned to the northwest dazed, giddy and $25,000 the richer.

Peter Adkison and co had an unprecedented hit on their hands and the nascent internet would soon be swamped with talk about their astounding new game. Indeed, before the week was out, an official Wizards' FAQ, written by production manager Dave Howell, was doing the rounds on rec.games. board and alt.games.misc. Another week or two later and playtester Chris Page was fielding rules questions online. By mid-September desperate players were trying to track down stores where they could buy the game; the game's first degenerate combination of cards (or 'combo') Channel and Fireball, was being discussed; disgruntled rec.games.board users were calling for the creation of a separate newsgroup just for *Magic* and, by 17 September, Michael Smith had posted a full list of all the game's cards for the frenzied first wave of buyers to check their collection against. Wizards' first release of the game, dubbed *Alpha* like the first playtest set, weighed in at 2.6 million cards – enough, they thought, to last the first year. Instead, *Alpha* sold out within a week and a scramble ensued to get the second part of the first print-run back from Belgium and out to the growing number of gamers eager to get their hands on the hotly tipped product. *Beta*, as the next 7.3 million cards released would be dubbed, fixed some of the small mistakes in the *Alpha* release: dies at printers Carta Mundi were sharpened to produce less-rounded card corners, seven cards which had been accidentally left out of *Alpha* were included (Circle of Protection: Black, Volcanic Island and an extra version of each of the five basic lands) and some typographical errors were fixed, including the casting cost of the card Orcish Oriflamme, for example. As fans clamoured for the new cards, the phones in Peter Adkison's basement struck up a ring that would, as it turned out, never pipe down. Wizards did anything they could to get the cards out to punters. But still, they could not keep up with demand.

Lisa Stevens remembers a typical scenario in the Wizards office in the period of *Magic*'s stunning early success. Demand on the West Coast was particularly high, spurred by Adkison's epic drive to demo the game before Gencon, and retailers there were haranguing Stevens for cards. As she sat fielding calls, as exasperated as the retailers themselves at not having any cards left to sell, a distributor in Atlanta, Georgia called Southern Hobbies came through on her phone. "How's it going?" asked Stevens, expecting her caller to tell her *Magic* was selling like hot cakes. "I haven't sold a single thing and want to return my order," said a miffed voice instead. Without missing a beat, Stevens told him she had a call from Europe coming through on the line and would have to call him back in five minutes to arrange a refund. What she actually did was call all the stores on the West Coast who had been nagging her for cards and gave them Southern Hobbies' number. Ten or so minutes later, she called the distributor back. "OK, here's how the returns are going to work," she deadpanned. "Returns?" came the shrill, excited response. "We just sold out! I need more!" Never mind *Alpha* selling out within a week of its release, *Beta*, three times bigger, was sold out before it arrived on US soil. Conspiracy theorists cried foul and accused Wizards of trying to short the market to drive up demand. But that was nonsense: in reality, the mortgage on Peter Adkison's house would only stretch so far. "The fans credit us with far more intelligence than we had," says Jesper Myrfors. "There was no Machiavellian conspiracy. We printed all that we could afford to and tried desperately to get it out there."

THE GRAND PLAN for *Magic*, which required an immediate tearing to shreds, was to gradually sell the first print run and then to replace it with something completely different a year later. The limited-edition first print run of *Magic: The Gathering* would be available during the first 12 months, then would give way to a new set of around 300 cards called *Magic: Ice Age*. That way players would not get bored, thought Wizards, and would get to enjoy a completely fresh game environment. Already, groups of playtesters had been given responsibility for the future annual releases: Skaff Elias, Dave Pettey and Jim Lin were working on *Ice Age*. Bill Rose, Joel Mick, Charlie Catino, Don Felice, Howard Kahlenberg and Elliott Segal were working on a set dubbed *Menagerie*, which would later form the backbone of the sets *Mirage* (1996) and *Visions* (1997). Barry Reich meanwhile was back in Philadelphia, beavering away on a set dubbed *Spectral Chaos*. Although his work would be overtaken by events and shelved for many years, it would eventually provide many of the ideas for the block of sets *Invasion, Planechase* and *Apocalypse*, released in 2000 and 2001.

Clearly though, with fans battering down game-store doors for the game (literally in fact: one game store was robbed of its *Magic* stock by ram-raiders), a new business plan had to be conceived to keep up with demand. Wizards and Richard Garfield flew to Philadelphia en masse to meet with the East Coast playtesters and come up with a new strategy. Locked in one big room all weekend, the *Magic* brains trust thrashed out numerous ideas on where to take the game next. Key would be an *Unlimited Edition* of the base set, printed with white borders around the card faces rather than black, to differentiate the cards from the first print run (*Alpha* and *Beta*) which the company had marketed as a *Limited Edition*. Secondly, after much discussion, it was decided that new cards should be produced in small expansion sets that were available concurrently with the original base set. The sets need not be as big as the original game or *Ice Age* as it was then conceived. This would be a quick fix for players, easy to collect and keep *Magic* visible at the stores where it was otherwise permanently sold out. The idea for *Magic*'s first expansion, *Arabian Nights*, was born – and Garfield disappeared to his proverbial woodshed to hammer it out. It was, says Lisa Stevens, seat of the pants stuff. "We had no idea what we were supposed to be doing!"

That much would become clear as *Arabian Nights* neared completion. Garfield had decided that the expansion should have different-coloured card backs (like the originals' but in a pink hue), so that players didn't feel a new product that they had to buy was being foisted on them. If the expansion cards were immediately identifiable, he reasoned, they could be separated from players' other cards and used apart.

When rumours of the proposed change leaked out, players were horrified. They, in fact, were desperate to incorporate new cards into their decks, to experiment with wild new combinations and add variety to their creations. Alas, *Arabian Nights* had been sent to Carta Mundi with pink card backs and would, in a matter of days, begin rolling off the Belgian printer's presses. One Friday in late 1993, with the final files for the first expansion sent, Lisa Stevens took a call in her office. The cards were to begin printing on the following Monday.

"We've heard that you guys are going to do different-coloured card backs on the new cards," said the anxious caller from All-Star Games, a store in California. "I'm calling to tell you it is a huge mistake – and all my customers here want to speak to you about it." One by one, the assembled local *Magic* players took their turn on the phone to bend Stevens' ear about the changes. And with each complaint, the colour drained a little more from Stevens' face. One hour of lobbying later and, she says, "I was freaking out!"

Stevens called an emergency meeting of the whole company on Sunday at Peter Adkison's house and relayed the appeals she had heard from the worried gamers. After much heated debate, Garfield was reluctantly convinced that changing the card backs would be a terrible idea. Instead, he agreed that adding a small symbol on the card face would achieve the same effect. A mad trolley dash around the art department followed until an illustration of a scimitar from *Talislanta* was hit upon as the perfect emergency solution. Hurriedly, it was faxed to Carta Mundi with instructions to shrink it down and slap it on the front of all the cards, while the card backs from the original sets should be substituted for the new pink backs. Thankfully, the printers were caught just in time and able to execute the 11th-hour request from their client in far-off Washington State. The only clue that anything was ever amiss was a slip-up on the *Arabian Nights* packaging itself. There, on the display boxes for the eight-card Booster Packs, were images of the pink card back, a reminder for all eternity of what might have been. It was a close call, says Stevens: "We might have ended up killing the game." As it was, with one almighty blunder avoided, the game could come into its own, as players learned to incorporate exciting new cards (indeed, some of the most powerful ever printed) into their favourite decks. While it was a chastening lesson for Wizards and Garfield in particular, Skaff Elias says it also spoke volumes about *Magic*'s creator. "In order to make the game, Richard had to make dozens of major decisions correctly," says Elias. "If you make 40 decisions right in a row but are willing to be proved wrong and change your mind on the 41st, it says a lot about your character."

*   *   *

THE 78-CARD *Arabian Nights* set hit games store shelves in December 1993 and was an almost instant sell-out. A print run of five million cards was nowhere near enough to satisfy the growing legion of *Magic* card-slingers. The mooted *Unlimited Edition* – the white-border run of the main set – followed in the same month, but its name proved inaccurate: Wizards would end up printing 35 million *Unlimited* cards which were snaffled up in a frenzy of ripped-open Booster Packs. The game's second expansion was rushed out of the door in March 1994. Named *Antiquities*, it too sold like cardboard crack and the 15-million print run was again insufficient to keep up with demand. As the months after *Magic*'s release ticked by and the number of players grew, *Magic* just kept selling out and busting all expectations. A *Revised Edition* of the basic set followed in April 1994 and represented a huge departure for the fledgling game. Certain cards deemed to be game-warping were removed from the core set (notably the 'Power Nine' cards which playtesters incorrectly thought would be too scarce to become overbearing), while some cards from the earliest expansions were reprinted with a white border (dear old Kird Ape, for example). Hot on its heels followed the hugely popular set *Legends* in June 1994, which introduced multi-coloured cards to the game as well as a new type of creature, legends, emblematic characters with powerful abilities. Along with *Revised*, it reached a huge audience, thanks to Wizards now having established a truly national distribution network. Both *Revised* and *Legends* would also break new ground abroad and become the first sets translated into a foreign language, in this case Italian, thanks to the efforts of publishing partner Stratelibri. Thirty-five million *Legends* cards were printed in English – again, nowhere near enough to keep up with demand – and speculation on the hard-to-get-hold-of collectible hit new highs. People were buying up boxes of the latest, hottest expansion and flipping them for instant profit.

Playtester Barry Reich remembers *Legends* as a turning point in the perception of the game's value. "That's when I realised, 'you know what? These cards are worth a lot of money,'" he says. For the first time, he took advantage of a cheap deal the original playtesters had been offered and bought five boxes from Wizards for $35 a box, 40 per cent of the retail price. He then did the rounds of other playtesters and bought any boxes going spare – even returning to pay more to one friend when it was clear the prices were climbing steeply. By the end of his *Legends* shopping spree, Reich had accumulated 20 boxes of one of the most-loved expansions in the game – and he wasn't alone. The scenario was being repeated all over the US, earning a pretty penny for the savvy investors with enough cashflow to snap up the sizzling new product. Although the ringing cash tills were good news for Wizards – who made that $2 million in the six months after the game's release – rampant speculation on *Legends* was the first inkling that not all was well in the best of worlds. If players could not afford to buy product, because the market was being cornered by speculators, the risk of *Magic* being a bubble that burst – like almost every other pure collectible in the past – was very real. Something would have to be done, although quite what, remained to be seen. In the meantime, *The Dark* – a moody, gothic set designed by Jesper Myrfors – followed up *Legends* in August 1994 and sold in its millions (64 million cards to be exact), propelling the game onwards, despite complaints that too many new cards were being printed too quickly. *Magic* had its teething troubles, but no-one could dispute that its first year was one of mind-blowing success.

CHAPTER EIGHT
We Are One

THE LESTRÉE FAMILY were a bright bunch. Younger brother Bertrand was studying business, while his older sibling Laurent taught computer sciences at the Université Pierre et Marie Curie in Paris' fifth arrondissement. Located on the Jussieu Campus, it was at the forefront of scientific and medical research in France. It was also just a stone's throw away from the cornerstone of the capital's gaming scene, a shop called L'Oeuf Cube – 'The Square Egg'. On benches outside the store, traders with bulging suitcases packed with *Magic* cards would haggle with excited players from all corners of the Hexagon. On my only trip there, as a provincial adolescent, I traded for a set of *Unlimited* Sinkholes – a major victory at the time. On my way back to meet my parents, I was mugged by two tracksuited, hash-smoking ne'er-do-wells in the Jardin des Halles. They took my money. They took my dignity. But thankfully not my *Magic* cards...

It was Laurent Lestrée who discovered *Magic* first. The computing teacher duelled daily with his students, before introducing the game to his brother in late 1993. It proved the perfect distraction from the pair's academic concerns. Soon they were honing their skills against each other every evening, with the intensity only sibling rivalry can produce. Bertrand mastered the game and became a fixture at L'Oeuf Cube. There, he discovered the burgeoning French tournament scene. And, as his *Magic* chops improved, he started to win. And win. And win.

By the summer of 1994, Betrand had wrapped up his studies. A sunny stretch of languid Parisian days lay ahead of him before his mandatory civic service began in the autumn. He was playing *Magic* religiously: 10, maybe 12 hours a day. Gradually, he was refining his deck and developing an aggressive strategy, featuring small, cheap-to-cast creatures to overwhelm his opponents before their defences were set. It was a plan that led Lestrée to triumph in his biggest tournament to date – the first-ever French national championship. It came with a spectacular prize: tickets and accommodation for Gencon '94, the pinnacle of which would be the first *Magic* world championship.

On the other side of the Atlantic, meanwhile, Zak Dolan was also perfecting his skills. The towering, goateed mid-westerner had discovered *Magic* at roughly the same time as Lestrée, in December 1993, in Eclipse Books and Comics, in Rolla, Missouri. There, a friend had convinced Dolan to part with much of his slim student budget for cards. After tearing open his first purchase of eight Boosters and pulling a mean-looking Force of Nature, an 8/8 green creature with the trample ability, Dolan was hooked. He began playing large free-for-all games with his fraternity brothers at the University of Missouri-Rolla, while trading feverishly to complete his collection of cards. By the beginning of 1994, he had built a black-green deck that was beating up on local players. By the summer, he cut the black and added blue and white to the deck instead, in preparation for what he hoped would be the highlight of his year: a trip to Milwaukee to play in the first *Magic* world championship at Gencon.

Wizards' presence at that convention blew their previous year's showing out of the water. They had gone, in the space of 12 months, from having the second-smallest booth size available to the very biggest. To boot, they were the show's most popular stand by miles. Fans swamped the stall – to buy packs, to meet the creators and get cards signed by a number of the artists in attendance. It was one hell of a first birthday party. Mark Rosewater, a hopeful young *Magic* player and budding scriptwriter, turned up to pitch articles to the editor of Wizards' in-house magazine *The Duelist*. What he saw blew his mind: Gencon had been overrun by *Magic* players, busting out of their local scenes and congregating en masse for the very first time. Particularly for those without internet access (in 1994, a significant proportion), it was like some thrilling matriculation into a wider, geekier world, where all their pent-up excitement about the game could explode for four heady days of *Magic* action. Although this is only speculation, high-fives were probably traded.

"The joke of the convention was that if there was any horizontal space, *Magic* players were playing on it," says Rosewater, who is today the game's head designer. "As you walked through the convention halls, you could see *Magic* players camped out playing all over the floor. It was a sight to see." For Lestrée and the French players who had made the trip with him, it was an awe-inspiring spectacle. In between rounds of the monolithic inaugural world championship – at 500-plus players, the biggest tournament then held – they seized the chance to trade for the rare and sought-after cards showing up in abundance in people's trade folders. Juzam Djinns, Serendib Efreets, Cities of Brass – the hottest cards from *Arabian Nights* – switched hands, as did a Mox or two. And all the while, Lestrée could scope out what decks other players had brought to battle with. None of them were as focused as his and, as the tournament (featuring multiple direct-elimination flights of 64 players per day) rolled on, his confidence grew.

Dolan, meanwhile, not someone low on confidence, was steamrollering his segment of the tournament. Having overcome an expensive mechanical blow-out on his 500-mile road-trip from Missouri, he was not about to bow out easily. His deck was idiosyncratic to say the least, featuring one- and two-ofs of cards, apparently with little over-arching strategy. It was, though, in the hands of its creator, not to be taken lightly. Ultimately, it would carry the bullish, bandana-wearing Dolan all the way to the finals.

Lestrée, too, was unstoppable. Playing a deck built around the cheap-to-cast but hard-hitting creatures in red, green and blue, red's direct-damage spells and the best 'broken' (*Magic* slang for overly powerful) cards in black, he had an extremely consistent, fast deck. Where Dolan played individual copies of cards with narrow applications, Lestrée packed his deck with four-ofs – the maximum permissible number of a card in a deck, apart from basic lands – to give himself the best chance of always drawing the cards he needed. For the time, it was very solid deck construction and would crash up against Dolan's approach in a mouth-watering final. Says Rosewater, who along with Chris Page would transcribe the final for *The Duelist*, "The deck was very fast and very consistent. And Bertrand clearly was one of the best (arguably the best) in the world."

Playing a best-out-of-three match, Lestrée quickly imposed himself. In game one, his deck worked like a dream, pumping out a stream of fast creatures that rushed the helpless Dolan. Dolan was able to slow the onslaught with the *Legends* enchantment Kismet, which forced Lestrée's cards into play already tapped and thus unusable for a turn, but it was not enough. The Frenchman was able to burn his opponent to death with the combination of cards that had sparked such frenzied debate on Usenet a year previously; Channel, plus Fireball. The former is a green sorcery spell that lets its caster trade in life points for mana. The latter is a red sorcery that does as much damage to an opponent as its caster spends in mana. The pair usually suffices to inflict a fiery death on an unwitting opponent.

Dolan shrugged his sizeable shoulders and carried on unperturbed. He trusted his deck, which he had tuned with members of the Pi Kappa Phi fraternity during a stint in Ann Arbor, Michigan, studying Japanese earlier in the summer. Built for the long haul, it contained plenty of cards to keep Dolan alive until he locked up the game with one of his favourite cards, Stasis, a blue enchantment which forces players to skip their untap step. Ivory Tower, an artifact from *Antiquities*, would gain Dolan life to take the game long and Library of Alexandria would help him draw extra cards. In game two, Dolan was able to get his Library online and overpower Lestrée. In the deciding game, Dolan got both Library and Ivory Tower out, and was able to land a Stasis. Having neglected to pack a Strip Mine or two – the best answer to Library of Alexandria at the time – Lestrée could do little to sever Dolan's lifeline. Despite his blistering start to the final, the maverick Frenchman was eventually forced to concede in the 20th turn of game three. Rolla beat Paris and *Magic* had its first-ever world champion. It was not simply a moment for the annals – but a moment that created the annals.

Magic suddenly had a history. In 12 exhilarating months, Wizards had gone from basement dwellers to world-beaters (they even had a real office now). A legion of players had fallen in love with a revolutionary game. And the world championships had conferred glory on a hastily assembled but tightly knit community. As Mark Rosewater would later write, *The first Worlds had a lot of strikes against it, but it still stands out in my head as one of the golden moments in* Magic *history. It was raw and unorganised but in many ways it was the beginning of a very important facet of the game.*

Everyone could sense the potential that Magic *had for tournaments, but the first World Championships brought it all to an emotional boil [...] Players really cared. Everyone seemed to get that this was the beginning of the road.* Clearly, celebrations were in order.

CHAPTER NINE
Sermon on the Mount

By LATE 1993 when *Magic* came out, the international business landscape was undergoing convulsions that would shape the millennial age. The foundations of the much-trailed knowledge economy were being laid at an ever-more rapid pace. The inkling was stirring, that unorthodox business practices and innovative products placing a premium on intellectual technologies would rule the information age. Not far from Wizards, in Redmond, Washington, Microsoft had recently launched Windows 3.1, which helped steer PC-users away from MS-DOS to a world of dragging-and-dropping, copying-and-pasting and writing with real fonts. The first ever web-browser, Mosaic, developed by the National Center for Supercomputing Applications at the University of Illinois Urbana-Champaign followed shortly after. And online service providers like The World and Compuserve had begun taking the internet out of academia and the military, into homes and businesses, heralding the advent of the dot-com era.

In amongst this foment, a bunch of very smart guys and gals sequestered in a suburban basement had cooked up the ultimate intellectual product. Wizards had successfully monetised the ideas pouring out of Richard Garfield's over-clocked gaming mind with a genre-busting card game. By tearing up the rulebook and subverting conventional business wisdom, they had created a truly revolutionary product and a phenomenon very much in tune with brainier times. Quite incredibly, considering their complete lack of experience, they had also managed not to screw it up. "It was our ignorance that made the game good," says Jesper Myrfors. "We were too stupid to know what we 'couldn't' do." Like cartoon characters running off the edge of the cliff, legs spinning in mid-air, Wizards knew they could not look down. And, says Myrfors, by getting the game to market in the face of considerable adversity, they somehow made it to the other side of the gorge.

As the money started rolling in and the market for *Magic* exploded, life for Wizards' handful of employees was challenging, but also an unmitigated blast. Suddenly, they had the means to do what they had always dreamed of doing – to make fantastic games – and had proved what could be achieved by following their creative instincts. Everyone had pitched in ideas, energy and time and, lo and behold, a hit had been born. Why change a winning recipe? Peter Adkison was happy to ditch all notions of traditional hierarchy and figured that great ideas could come from any part of the company. Indeed, he wanted to create a new kind of company where the geeks – once banished to the backrooms by shoulder-barging alpha males in shimmering pinstripe – were running the show. Having grown up in a low-income family (his father was an army chaplain), Adkison admits he had an innate distrust for accountants, lawyers and strident capitalists. He was determined to do things his own way.

By the time Wizards moved out of his basement into offices in Seattle suburb Renton, a month or two on from *Magic*'s release, the company had grown from 5 employees to 22. By May 1994, that number had swelled to over 50. With a recruitment policy Lisa Stevens dubs the "nearest warm body" hiring approach, the company ranks were filling with anyone Wizards could get their hands on. It was a heady time, and like a benevolent over-geek Adkison ushered new members of his flock through the door to a promised land of beanbags, table football, and other assorted high-jinks far removed from the traditional work world that Adkison hoped to turn on its head.

For many at the office – essentially a rag-tag collection of previously maligned 20-somethings, suddenly banking large pay-cheques for working on their hobby – that meant as much sex as their newfound status would procure. Rules were for squares anyway. And sleeping with your co-workers seemed as good a way as any to spread consensus, the value at the heart of Wizards' ad hoc company culture. As John Tynes, who joined the company in spring 1994, would later write, *Wizards was a big horny summer camp and we were starring in the teen sex comedy of our fevered dreams.* The fleshy frivolities would last until *Magic*'s first birthday.

*   *   *

THE ENTIRE WIZARDS staff made the trip to Milwaukee for Gencon '94, a team-building exercise combined with a sort of glorious homecoming. Where a year before they had been peddling cards to a sometimes sceptical crowd out of a ramshackle booth, this year they were the convention's star attraction. The game had infiltrated every corner of the show and after four days of gruelling competition, even produced its first world champion in Zak Dolan. *Magic* was being feted by the gaming industry and punters alike and the mood in the Wizards camp was buoyant. Gencon capped a mind-blowing year and Adkison wanted to reward his staff with a show of generosity. Not one to do things by halves, when the show wrapped up, he chartered a bus and packed 30 or so willing employees off to the mountains for a weekend of unbridled hedonism in a rented ski lodge.

Given the sweaty-palmed state of semi-arousal some of the company had been in all year, it is perhaps no surprise that one late-night drinking session at the lodge turned into a titillating candle-lit game of 'Truth or Swill'. A number of the well-lubricated Wizards crew dropped their inhibitions and egged each other on to reveal ever-more risqué details of their sexual proclivities. Mischief-maker-in-chief Adkison was happy to join in and with the night well advanced and all present somewhat sozzled, the munificent leader spilled the beans about his sex life to his assembled employees. Where once that would have meant a handful of lifelong friends, this was a different congregation. Despite Adkison's honest and big-hearted belief that he could share anything with his fellow journeymen as equals, things had been changing at the company without him realising. The hangover would prove a real stinker.

During the game, one recently recruited female employee called Carrie slipped out, shocked and uncomfortable at hearing her boss reveal his most intimate secrets. She took her concerns to the other managers and, rather than awaken to the kind of back-slapping he might have hoped for, a bleary eyed Adkison found himself on the end of a painful dressing down, led by Wizards vice president Lisa Stevens. For all Adkison's brilliance in corralling a group of friends together to make *Magic*, he had misjudged just what a different beast a fully-fledged company was. Trying to push at every boundary possible, he had over-stepped a very serious one and would have to face the consequences. The ski lodge game of Truth or Swill was the high watermark of Adkison's attempts to revolutionise corporate culture. His real strength would prove to be fixing what he broke, to ensure Wizards could live on long enough to shake their heads knowingly as a wave of similar start-ups repeated their mistakes, kicking off their shoes, burning brightly, then imploding in their hubris. But in the short-term, it was a rude awakening: "That night was the loss of innocence," says a rueful Adkison today.

WHEN WIZARDS TRAIPSED dejectedly down the mountain, they left the wildest heights of their rebellion against professional norms behind them. The journey downhill was bumpy. Stevens, to whom the complaints from the drunken game had been addressed, felt keenly her responsibility as an officer of the company on the board of directors to protect the shareholders' investment. For as much as she had loved the company's rollercoaster journey, she knew that the ground was shifting beneath Wizards' feet. What had been acceptable when they were just a group of friends making hardly any money was very different to the situation they were currently in. Now, they were raking in seven-figure sums thanks to the faith investors had put in *Magic* when it seemed like a crazy pipe dream. Stevens could not help remembering that a janitor from Boeing, for example, had her life savings riding on *Magic*'s success – and felt that the company now stood at a major crossroads.

Despite her personal friendship with Adkison and overall indifference to whatever fun anyone wanted to get up to on their own time, she called the company lawyer for advice. He was unequivocal: "You need to bring this to the board and you need to make a big deal out of it. Because, if you don't follow certain rules and regulations, you could face lawsuits that could cripple the company and destroy the investment of your shareholders." Stevens had little alternative but to convene a chastening meeting with Adkison and all the major shareholders, where a choice was laid down: to continue as a group of friends who were just having a good time, or to transform Wizards into the most successful company it could be. To a man, the shareholders voted for the latter option, which meant Wizards had to be run more professionally. But it changed things irreversibly for the band of gamer-friends who been there at the start: "It was now a job," says Stevens. "From that point on, we worked for a company and not for ourselves."

For some – like John Tynes – it was the end of a perfectly valid dream, a betrayal of ideals, a selling out to corporate America. But it was not something Adkison did with any relish. The expectations on him from all quarters were huge and he was buckling under a complete lack of business experience: "For me personally, it should have been the best days of my life after *Magic* came out, but they became the worst days of my life," he says. "1994 and 1995 were hell. Everybody was mad at me, it felt like, all the time. I was continuously in a situation where retailers were pissed about allocations, distributors were pissed about slow shipments, employees were pissed about who they had to work for and so on." The company's growing pains mirrored Adkison's own. Without the example set later by the quirky companies which emerged from the dot-com boom, it was almost impossible for the Wizards boss to know how to combine his iconoclastic instincts with successful business practices. He was in many ways the older brother to the internet start-ups who would follow in Wizards' wake. He railed against the rules and got into trouble. But by doing so, he also altered the expectations for his younger siblings and smoothed their paths considerably.

Fortunately for Adkison, however traumatic it might have been at the time, the Truth and Swill incident could have been far more damaging. Though Stevens says that Adkison felt at the time, "… that the company died for him that night," it was in truth more of a rebirth for all concerned. Adkison, increasingly surrounded by qualified managers as the company exploded, realised he was going to drown if he could not decipher their jargon. And, he says, enrolling on an MBA course in 1995 had an almost instant effect on him, inspiring him, restoring some bruised self-esteem and eventually granting him the skills to lead Wizards forward as the successful company its shareholders believed it could be. The most radical of Adkison's initial plans for the company – like the very flat hierarchy – soon fell by the wayside, ultimately to the relief of many.

"It worked when it was small," says Myrfors. "It worked when everyone knew each other. But when you start to hire from the outside, you get personalities involved in the mix that you're not prepared to deal with. And when there's that amount of money at stake, you also get a lot of leeches and hangers-on." There was, says Skaff Elias, "A lot of *Animal Farm* going on." Even Richard Garfield says he cringes when he thinks back to those early days – because the implications for the quality of his game were very real. "The thing was, [a flat hierarchy] completely invalidated people who were experienced," he says. "You had people who didn't like or didn't play *Magic* making design decisions with equal authority to people who loved it and had been there since the beginning and had played games all their lives – and that just doesn't make any sense."

With that in mind, Garfield and Elias made it their business to create a functioning research and development department to ensure a steady flow of *Magic* cards, whatever madness seemed to be swirling around them. Others tried to set a good example, like Rick Arons, an early manager recruited by major Wizards' shareholder John Jordan. Arons is today executive vice-president of Pokemon USA and modest about his role at Wizards. But Elias credits him as among the game's most important figures for the part he played in transforming the company culture, tackling whatever briefs came his way with diligence and good grace; never criticising or correcting the work-shy or inexperienced, but setting up his teams to work efficiently and harmoniously. Magnanimous and shrewd, he would later prove vital in setting the game on a new course to ensure its survival, in the face of company-wide scepticism.

What he, Garfield and Elias all acknowledge though is that, whatever his mistakes, Adkison was the man who got himself and Wizards back on track. Humility, perseverance and gut instincts honed on lengthy campaigns in the gaming catacombs, redeemed Adkison. His vision had slipped into excess at times, but not all of it was bad. Adkison was able – in a way that presaged other knowledge-economy trailblazers like fellow Seattleites Amazon, for example – to hone in on what really mattered in a fast-evolving cultural and commercial landscape. He was smart enough to perceive how business would be shaped by the flow of knowledge within companies, between companies and back and forth to customers down the rapidly proliferating cables of the nascent internet. Firstly, he recognised the importance of the output of his genuinely creative staff and put R&D at the heart of the company. He trusted in Garfield, Elias and the other playtesters the company recruited to its staff to sustain a high-quality product. Secondly, he did everything possible to make Wizards a customer-facing company, attuned to the needs of gamers everywhere. Arons says Adkison did not even call them customers. To him, they were an extension of the gaming circles he had spent his life in; his 'friends'. He wanted to make sure the company maintained a dialogue with them just as it had when it had listened to concerns about *Arabian Nights*' pink card backs. Like it had when Chris Page and Dave Howell had gone online to answer rules questions in the days after *Magic*'s launch. Like Adkison had in fact done when reaching out to potential game designers on Usenet before *Magic* was even conceived.

That meant hiring an army of what Wizards called 'net reps' to handle all manner of customer service queries online – from where to buy the game, to interactions between certain cards not covered in the game's still sketchy rules. It was what the idealistic gamer in Adkison wanted – to create not just customers, but a community. And while Truth or Swill was camaraderie taken too far, the bonds Adkison helped establish between company and fans endure to this day. Designers are regularly recruited via an online talent search, endless tweets are fired back and forth between Wizards staff and players, and consultation on all manner of rules changes lights up message boards. It is the kind of personal relationship other companies have desperately tried to contrive with their customers over the past 20-odd years and testament to Adkison's innate smarts. In many ways, Wizards was dot-com-era Silicon Valley *before* Silicon Valley and all the more significant for its success in outgrowing its early flirtation with unbridled geek-topia. Accordingly, world domination was just around the corner.

CHAPTER TEN
Scriptures and Shrines

OVER TWO DECADES on from *Magic*'s birth, it is hard to imagine a world where Usenet *was* the internet. Where writing a book did not feel somehow anachronistic. Or, where information was hard enough to come by, that it would be slowly digested, savoured on the mind's palette and then shared with selected members of a social network, known, back then, as 'friends'. Today, information (at least in most democratic regimes) is one big, jolly free-for-all. Knowledge, a vast soup of noughts and ones, is pervasive. Vigilant devices in our pockets, on our wrists and in our glasses chatter to the cloud. And yet, it might all be cobblers, a distorted feedback of Wikipedia mistakes, Photoshopped news pictures, conspiracy theories and memes. Perfect access to imperfect information. The media sphere is so busy and deafening, we can barely make out what is important to us. But, thanks to Tim Berners-Lee, we have it all at the tips of our fingers. With filters, search engines and peer recommendations we slog through it all, dodging fake Viagra, mail order brides and magnanimous benefactors in Uganda. It *is* great. But time was, life was a little simpler.

When Richard Garfield assembled the Delta card file – the final list of cards spawned from playtesting that would become the *Alpha* printing – he did not even reveal to the playtesters what the final rare cards would be. He wanted *Magic* players to exist in a world of imperfect information. That way, the potential for wonder would exist at every turn. Mystery would enrich his game, just as it had done for early adopters like rec.games.board poster Michael Smith. But the scarcity of information only fed curiosity. The same Smith who had at first revelled in discovering his opponents' cards, was the guy who a few weeks later collated a complete card list online. *Magic* was so fascinating and so new, that the hunger for information about it was huge. The potential for learning about the game, understanding it and sharing experiences seemed infinite. *Magic* was a sky full of stars yet to fall into familiar constellations; a universe to explore and savour, card by beautiful card.

Anticipating the clamour for information somewhat, Wizards took a gamble and printed up an eight-page flyer called *The Duelist* to hand out at Gencon '93. It was not much – a couple of news articles, a guide to putting together your first deck – but it was the first stone laid in a material *Magic* culture, an acknowledgement of a gut instinct felt by those who had encountered the game at its inception: here was something not only worth playing, but also worth discussing. That instinct proved to be correct. And the great *Magic* talking shop was open for business.

By the time I got my sticky adolescent hands on cards in New Zealand, in late 1994, *Magic* was already a game too big to be beyond easy cognisance. Over 1,000 different cards had been printed and the game had a past, as well as a present, not easily accessed. Booster Packs of the product – even of the current set, *Revised Edition* – were extremely scarce and the supply of older cards on the far-flung islands was miniscule. Somehow, what should have been a hindrance to enjoying the game – like missing half the tiles from a *Scrabble* set – only added to *Magic*'s mystique. It was no role-playing game. But it did present its own world to explore, with quests to undertake (the hour-long slog in the backseat of someone's parents' car to the nearest game store in Auckland, for example), which all came as a welcome refuge from the pains of adolescence, homesickness, spots and fancying terrifyingly cool girls.

If *Magic* had reached us in New Zealand, it was because it had exploded beyond all expectation. It had outstripped not just the confines of a gaming hardcore, but also outgrown the small pool of early internet users. Richard Garfield had no need to fear – the vast majority of players in those early years were un-networked and for them, *Magic* was still a world of imperfect information. Indeed, it was a deeply thrilling world on some visceral level that only youthful discovery can be. For us, the printed word was still the first port of call for information. Along with Wizards' official mouthpiece *The Duelist*, two other magazines quickly became canonical: *Scrye*, launched in June 1994, and its louder, brasher cousin *Inquest*, which came out a year later. Their success was largely down to card lists published in the back of each issue, detailing every *Magic* card in existence, along with its current (by print standards) value on the secondary market. It was these price guides that allowed us to get an idea of what was and what wasn't a good trade. However, the lists did not explain what the cards actually did – all that most new players could do was run their fingers longingly underneath cards, whose evocative names and staggering prices sent them into convulsions. Card lists would be snatched out of friends' hands, for the thrill of consuming the knowledge first, fastest, most completely. Of possessing it. Recalls Rich Hagon, now one of the game's foremost personalities, "Even in the late nineties, I can remember literally trembling as I read *Scrye* and looked at these card names: Bazaar of Baghdad, City of Brass... You didn't even know what they did – but you were desperate to find out." Unlike a computer game, though, there was no cheat code, no surreptitious way to unlock clues. Just burning, unrequited desire.

The *Scrye* price guide was a mammoth piece of work, esoteric in its beauty and as impenetrable to the uninitiated as the latest stock prices in the *Financial Times* or *Wall Street Journal*. It was the brainchild of the magazine's first editor and publisher, Joanne White, who had been introduced to *Magic* by Peter Adkison at Origins in 1993. White already had a role-playing magazine in her stable, but immediately saw the potential for a publication about the fascinating new game and the genre it could spawn. *Scrye* was born just as *Magic* was going nationwide and the scramble for cards was reaching its peak. And while eager readers may have scanned the pages for news and strategy, what really kept them coming back was the sprawling price guide which, uniquely, listed a low, median and high price for every card in print. It was a sophisticated snapshot of the *Magic* secondary market and one made possible by White's nous, diligence and eye for detail. Her price guide was a living one: between each issue (printed sporadically at first), she would send out copies of her guide to retailers to mark up with the prices they were selling single cards for. She would then input all the returned data into a Byzantine spreadsheet to calculate the three price points for each card. Retailers were paid for their input and the budget for the price guide easily matched that for actual written contributions. It was a mind-boggling undertaking, but one that established the magazine as the number one tool for *Magic* traders everywhere. *Scrye* was stuffed into rucksacks or sat, heavily thumbed, on the shelf of every games store. Even photocopied price lists did the rounds and would be diligently consulted in the middle of any complex trade.

The Duelist, meanwhile, as Wizards' official publication, could never include a price list. To do so would leave Wizards on tricky legal ground, as denoting an official value to individual cards in their randomised packs would essentially turn *Magic* into an unlicensed lottery. Instead, the title grew quickly from an eight-page pamphlet into an all-singing, all-dancing magazine, which could provide players with *Magic* information straight from the horse's mouth. With unrivalled access, high production values and an official stamp of approval, it was the Maybach of *Magic* magazines and set the standard in editorialising the game's rapidly crystallising culture. Lisa Stevens recruited a journalist named Kathryn Haines (who originally knew nothing about the game) to head up the magazine. Despite her lack of expert knowledge, Haines deployed solid editorial instincts to provide readers with a fantastic breadth of stories: spotlights on local scenes, interviews with artists, a regular column from Richard Garfield and strategic pieces on the emerging science of deck-building. All helped give readers around the world a sense of belonging to a wider community – just as role-playing magazines had done for Wizards' founders. *The Duelist* was also in a position to address players' questions about the game (particularly issuing official rulings on problematic cards and clarifying blind spots in the game's rules themselves) and could recruit contributors from its readership. Both these aspects re-enforced Wizards' customer-centric approach. While pastimes and passions have always been for people who want to belong to something, *The Duelist* helped cultivate the sense that there was something meaningful for *Magic* players to belong to.

A wider part of that was the establishment of a *Magic* slang that seeped into articles across the board, reinforcing the growing identity that players were adopting for themselves. John Jackson Miller, who would become

Scrye's second editor in 1999, says the birth of *Magic* argot was vital to the community's emergence. The terminology used to discuss the game was popularised by the triumvirate of magazines on the market before internet use became widespread. Pet nicknames for decks, like 'burn decks', featuring red direct damage spells, and 'weenie decks', featuring swarms of (often white) small creatures, dotted the texts in *Scrye, The Duelist* and *Inquest*. From there, they became part of the lingua franca in classroom back rows or in comics or games stores. "Somebody had to coin those terms," says Jackson Miller. "They came from the hobby, into the magazine, then went back out to the wider world." In so doing, they helped knit together the disparate local *Magic* scenes coalescing the world over into a more homogenised movement. Many adolescents learning the game in countries like France (where I finished secondary school) and Germany (where I live today), could bandy around *Magic* patter in English before they could order a coffee, ask directions or book a hotel room – the practical stuff their teachers were trying to impart on them. *Magic*'s vocabulary was a badge of belonging. It helped nurture the thrall the game held players in, vocalising what it meant to be suddenly, hopelessly obsessed with it. At the same time, it furthered theoretical understanding – as language always does – of the subtle forces at work within the game.

IF PLAYERS HAD anything to talk about at all, it was because *Magic* had arrived at the cusp of the internet boom rather than in its very midst: it had been conceived as a physical product rather than as a video game or indeed as a smart phone app, as it might have been today. What that did mean is that every player opening Booster Packs with the relish of a puppy tearing open a pillow needed opponents. For many, that meant visiting a game store or one of the comic stores rapidly adapting to stock the new product.

Before editing *Scrye*, John Jackson Miller edited a trade magazine called *Comics Retailer*. His stint in charge of the title began in November 1993 – a precipitous time for the industry. Comics were coming off the back of a booming year, one vastly and artificially inflated, which did not augur well for the following 12 months. As well as a swathe of distributors pumping out sales to a dizzying number of stores in North America (the number taking *Comics Retailer* jumped from 3,000 in 1990 to 11,000 in 1993), a wave of serial investors had infiltrated the hobby to suck up what value they could. Jackson Miller dubs them 'locusts' and believes they started actively buying up comics in the early 1990s following the collapse of the sports card market. This created an unsustainable bubble in the industry. And, when it burst in 1994, the locusts would move on to pastures new. A certain collectible card game fell into their sights…

What all this means, though, is that in late 1993 when *Magic* was released, comic-store owners were in a unique position: On the one hand, they were nervously looking ahead to a crash that would only be a matter of time in coming. On the other hand, they were liquid enough after a strong 12 months to take a punt on a potential new earner – something their customers were already clamouring for. At the time, for example, Brian David-Marshall was working in the marketing department for a chain of comic stores in New York. As he was also a gamer, he would field questions about that hobby, too. It quickly became apparent to him that his customers were hungry for one product above all: "Someone literally grabbed me, shook me and said, 'Where the hell can I find *Magic?*'" he says. "I was like: 'Holy crap! We need to get this!'"

Thus, clever comic-shop owners began to diversify. Using the cash flow provided by a meteoric comics glut, they took a bet on a product they thought might keep them in business when superheroes lost their lustre. Some cleared space in the back of their shops and set up tables for *Magic* players to play on. And, eventually, even *Comics Retailer* changed its name to *Comics and Games Retailer*. As comics nosedived in 1994, *Magic* was the lifeblood that allowed a number of stores to stay alive. "I think a lot of retailers insulated themselves by buying *Magic* then marking up the single cards," says Jackson Miller. "Suddenly, you began seeing display cases full of cards appearing in comic stores around North America – and I believe that *Magic*, in 1994, saved at least 500 shops."

IF YOU AREN'T looking for the shop, you'll probably miss it. Sure, you might notice the group of gangly youths hanging around outside to get some rare natural light, smoke a cigarette and imbibe a fizzy drink. But most likely, you will put your head down, quicken your step and skirt around them. I can't blame you. It's easier that way. Easier than wondering what they might be doing at this address, just outside the town centre where the rents are cheaper, the units a little rundown and where the high street's franchise invasion has shunted the few remaining independent shops. A glance up at the window will leave you none the wiser: rows of sun-faded boxes, perplexing and gaudy point of sale, dusty paraphernalia… what does any of it mean?

This is a typical game store. And, for better or worse, it is many *Magic* players' natural habitat. On almost any day of the week, they can come here to play, to trade, or to stock up on dice, card sleeves, deck boxes, playmats and all the other assorted gubbins which compose a *Magic* player's kit. These little shops, often run by one or two people, sometimes a couple, are the foundation upon which the *Magic* community is built. Here, a curious kid will shell out his or her hard-earned pocket money to buy their first cards – and, hopefully, return a few weeks later, armed with the makings of a deck and in search of an opponent. These places, often badly lit, poorly decorated and ripe with the funk of late-night gaming sessions, are where players come to practise, learn new skills and deepen their knowledge of a relentlessly challenging game. They are ramshackle and intimidating, akin to the specialist record stores parodied in Nick Hornby's *High Fidelity*; shrines for reverent *Magic* players in search of enlightenment. But they are also a place, increasingly, I can understand you walking by.

Often, in fact, I have to brace myself before entering, slipping between the figures hovering at the door and summoning my civility to nod to the owner behind the counter and its cascading wall of glittering *Magic* Boosters. It is a very different world in there. One that I suppose part of me thinks, I should have outgrown by now. This is a space that exists away from the society I have grown up to be a part of, which espouses some values as adult and relegates others – particularly 'play' – to juvenile status. When I rationalise and remind myself that I need not espouse those same values; that *Magic* is about more than play and that play in and of itself is not necessarily bad, I am fine. I can settle into some kind of ease with my hobby. But my rational mind is always in a tussle with my deeper programming. And in the game store world, at least in that initial step through the door, that plunge through the water's dark surface, it is my instincts that grab the upper hand. Here I am, they say, leaving the world I tried very hard to belong to again after the upheaval of my teens. Here I am, they say, stepping willingly back to the margins. Here I am, ducking into the shadows, shame still a monkey on my back.

There was a time I could love these places and their strange psychic energy unambiguously. My first pilgrimage to one was to Pendragon Games in Auckland, soon after learning to play. The journey quickly became a regular trek, undertaken every Saturday that someone's parents could be talked into the drive down Highway 1 to the nearest thing New Zealand has to a gleaming metropolis. They were cramped journeys, with us packed four to the backseat, but they went by in a blur. After a week of playing only at school, where the opponents were always the same, we would anticipate excitedly what cards we might be able to trade for with the Pendragon regulars – or indeed what cards they might deign to show us from their heaving folders packed with seductive older cards we had never had the chance to procure pack-fresh.

Pendragon itself was located in a basement at the bottom of Queen Street, Auckland's main shopping thoroughfare. Decked out like a dungeon with faux stonework and accessed via a narrow set of black steps, it was an evocative place to play fantasy games. You could barely tear my best friend Simon and I away from it. All day long we would stand at the one main table in the store – previously used for tabletop games but now firmly in the hands of the *Magic* players – slinging cards until our ride home beckoned. In all those hours and hours of playing, I cannot remember once drinking a glass of water or going to the toilet. Our only break would be a lunchtime dash to the nearby Baron of Beef for a steak sandwich and curly fries. We played and played and played – innocent teenagers swept up for the first time in a scene bigger than ourselves and excited at being able to contribute to it, even only as cannon fodder for the more experienced players stalking the crepuscular space.

These are places that many (especially those undergoing their own teenage transformation) still love and I can see why. Abstracting the fact that the crowd is almost exclusively white and male, the individuals composing it are usually decent enough people. The same thing goes for the owners. These are people who are led heart- not head-first into the business. They sacrifice evenings and weekends to stay open for gamers. Provide coffee and snacks. And in Berlin, land of cheap rents and big spaces, they even often provide a toilet, which they must clean every evening once it has been liberally sprinkled with gamer piss. This is not an endeavour driven by dreams of financial success. These are people who care about the community and who relish their leading role within it.

But, just like the library at Mahurangi College was, these shops are turf. The tangible space a community has carved out for itself and which it is loath to surrender again. Here, there is safety in numbers. Reassurance in peers who look, act and speak the same. And a comfort to looking inwards rather than out through the cluttered windows. Hiding in the shadows, these places preserve the community's cosiness, without holding it up to scrutiny or opening it up to others whose differing values might enrich it. Maybe I'm getting old, but it is a myopia that, to me, seems self-defeating. *Magic* is competing in a cluttered marketplace for the public's entertainment budget; up against bars, gigs, the cinema, you name it. And no longer the wide-eyed teenager lurking at Pendragon, I cannot pretend I want to spend my Friday night in most game stores. The physical environment is a symptom of its inhabitants' insecurities. In gloomy back rooms, *Magic* cloaks itself in stigma.

How do you encourage a community to look outwards though, when it is so accustomed to lurking in the margins? Greeted with a grunt, as you step into your average game store today, it can feel like a very distant goal. In fact, it took sewage leaking through the roof back at Pendragon Games for us to leave the place. Even when it moved to an anonymous inner-city mall and lost much of its soul, we were still stalwarts at its gaming tables. In fact, it is entirely possible I spent every weekend of 1995 there until I left New Zealand for good in early 1996 for another new start in France. It was a scene being repeated all over the world at the time. *Magic* players were discovering something they had never had before: a home away from home. And, it turns out, they didn't want to leave it.

By 1994, comic-store stalwart Brian David-Marshall had (perhaps fearing more customer dust-ups) dived head first into *Magic* and was organising tournaments for New York players as fast as he possibly could. Hundreds of players were coming out to play the game and, he says, it was all he could do to get them to leave whatever rented venue he had found to house them in, once the final rounds had been played. "We were even getting charged extra money," he says. There had to be a better solution.

In 1995, together with business partners, David-Marshall founded what would become the ultimate *Magic* shrine – a place far-off gamers like myself could only dream about. Called Neutral Ground, it distilled the early experience of comic and games stores into a new format, dubbed a 'tournament center' by the founders. Instead of being a small mom-and-pop store with a space cleared for a table or two, it was a 2,500-square-foot space in the Midtown Manhattan loft district, packed out with tables. Up on the ninth floor, accessed by a rickety lift affectionately nicknamed 'the elevator of doom' by regulars, it was not somewhere likely to pick up passing trade. This was a destination, a resort, a sanctuary: a gaming space with a store attached, rather than the other way around. Neutral Ground quickly became the centre of gravity for the finest players on America's East Coast – some of whom would sleep on benches at the nearest station rather than going home, before rocking up the next morning to play again.

For David-Marshall, it was the realisation of a long-held dream. As a child of the *Dungeons & Dragons* generation, he had been shunted back and forth between friends' houses as and when their parents got sick of the gaming teenagers under their feet. He had played at food courts and malls. But he had never had a safe all-ages environment in which to do what he wanted to do most: play games. Neutral Ground, open every day bar Christmas and Thanksgiving, filled an unspoken need for hundreds of players in a similar boat – old enough to be allowed independence, but not yet welcome in many of the places adults go to socialise, especially in the US with its draconian drinking laws. As such, it quickly became a hub for a whole community of people who would never have met – or indeed may not have had a community to call their own – if *Magic* had not existed. With a roof over their heads and a language of their own, a more self-confident generation of gamers was stirring.

Meanwhile, the influence of Neutral Ground and of the plethora of comics and games stores equipping themselves with tables would be significant, not only for *Magic* but for gaming as a whole. Previous iterations of gaming –

successively war-gaming and role-playing – had been time-consuming and difficult to set up, either because of the number of pieces required or the number of players needed. But *Magic*'s rapid gameplay and visual appeal helped lay the groundwork for another revolution in gaming which would follow on its heels: the rise of the 'German-style' boardgame. According to John Jackson Miller, by putting in place the infrastructure for *Magic*, retailers had inadvertently developed the perfect space for showing off a new wave of board games that began with the release of *Settlers of Catan* in 1995. All shop owners had to do was to lay them out on their new in-store tables, unpacking all the high-quality and beautifully illustrated components in front of a captive audience of lunching *Magic* players looking for a change of pace. A new market – and new marketplace – was born. *Settlers of Catan* has since gone on to sell over 15 million copies worldwide and has been huge in shifting hobby gaming ever more towards mainstream acceptability.

Wizards of the Coast, meanwhile, acknowledges the central importance of physical game stores to *Magic*'s continued health. Helene Bergeot, director of organised play and trade marketing at *Magic* HQ says, "Store-run events are actually the key drivers for growing the *Magic* community." She has overseen the implementation of more and more in-store events, notably the hugely popular 'Pre-release' tournaments which take place a week before the official release of each set and give excited players their first chance to get their hands on the new cards. Whereas previously Pre-releases were run on a regional level for hundreds of gamers at a time, they have since 2012 become firmly entrenched in local neighbourhood stores. Brian David-Marshall says this has been the single biggest boon for the game in years: "It makes people want to open stores, it hones people in on where the stores are in their area and more importantly, if I go to a store 15 minutes from my house and I meet you or someone else who lives in the neighbourhood, we might say, 'Wow let's both come back on Wednesday and play Commander [a popular casual format]. That sounds awesome!'" Although David-Marshall sold Neutral Ground in the early 2000s to pursue a career writing, commentating and designing games of his own, he has never lost sight of the lessons he learned in that Manhattan loft. "I talk every day to people I met there who have become part of my life," he says. "The social aspect is tremendously important to *Magic* and bricks and mortar stores are crucial in fostering that." However alien, elitist or plain unappealing many of them may look, game stores exist as a portal to a community that is, at its core, good. It needs people like you, though, to make it better. So next time you see gamers lurking outside their favourite haunt, try stepping in, instead of around. It is a leap of faith we can take together.

CHAPTER ELEVEN
I'm Bad, I'm Nationwide

WHILE MAGIC HAD launched very much to a traditional, hardcore gaming public, haunting the hallways of convention centres in faded black T-shirts with their long-suffering elf maidens in tow, the game also fell into unexpected hands. Like many genre-busting products before it, it seemed to combine numerous elements in a synthesis that perfectly captured the zeitgeist and attracted a legion of disparate fans. The same startling newness that hooked me propelled the game initially to overground craze status. Its various facets appealed to the curious-minded from different backgrounds: traditional gamers were attracted to *Magic*'s mechanics, certainly, but there were also those attracted to the game's art, like comic book fans, or those attracted to its collectability like trading card devotees or the increasingly visible post-modern collectors for whom pop-cultural ephemera were just as valuable as Penny Blacks. Like *Dungeons & Dragons* had done a generation before, *Magic* hit a nerve in the public consciousness that catapulted it – at least in its first flush of success – from dingy-game-store staple to legitimate mass phenomenon. By 1997, Wizards were even running television adverts for the game with the (admittedly less-than-sexy) catchphrase, "All you need is a deck, a brain and a friend."

It was the kind of pep talk I was giving myself, as I prepared for another move around the world. After two years of struggling to adapt to New Zealand, my family decided to return to Europe. *Magic* was the one souvenir I would take with me from my time in the Antipodes. My cards crossed the ocean, shipped in a metal container with all the remaining possessions we had, including cardboard-clad furniture that had been left unwrapped and lurking under our tiny wooden house in New Zealand. There had been too much of it to fit inside; an absurd sign of how life had shrunk from better times, receding rapidly into the past.

France would be our new adventure. My parents had always imagined they would one day join the British exodus to rural Normandy in search of the good life. While the circumstances were now very different, the move held at least a latent appeal. It would not be easy financially, emotionally or linguistically. But it was something that appealed to some of us. I admit, more so to me, who had been learning French in school for years, than to my two little sisters. I, at 15, could at least harbour vague fantasies of louche Left-Bank loitering in some smug Parisian future. My sisters on the other hand found themselves in the situation I had been in when we left England – ripped out of schools they were settling into; leaving behind friendships that were becoming meaningful; heading to a country they had no affinity for. To say it was difficult for them would be an understatement.

After a bleak winter in 1996, shuttling from rented house to rented house, our funds, hope and familial ties were all strained to breaking point. After trawling every notaire's office in north-west France though, we eventually found a big old Norman farmhouse to call home. It was reassuringly solid after our New Zealand rabbit hutch and the furniture fit inside it at least. There was space enough for all us to have our own bedrooms, space enough for the cats (Tigger and Mrs Miggins, the other Kiwi souvenir we brought with us) and space enough for us to recover slowly as a family, gathered round a pulsating stove in the one room we could heat.

It was located less in a place and more in a time. Some-when pseudo-medieval. An alternative 1996, shaped by a careening, off-course DeLorean. The hamlet we landed in was 50 per cent mud, 50 per cent peasants. It stank of slurry and mystery carcinogens from burning black plastic. The entire community was held together with bailing twine and the weather was rain. It did not seem like fertile ground for a craze I imagined had entranced the world.

At school, none of the kids I pushed my broken French upon had heard of *Magic*. A country so strangled by the conservatism of its republican dogmas has no room for genuine youth culture. Instead, the utilitarian blob of concrete I attended when I first arrived was full of wannabe adults into crap facial hair, leather jackets, tacky identity bracelets, snogging, cigarettes and mopeds; a pastiche of the provincial French lives they would grow into if they didn't get the hell out of town – the life I might live if I didn't get the hell out of there, too. I shuddered. And told myself it would all be very different when I was rapping philosophy with the other cats at the Sorbonne. In the meantime, I could only feel an odd twang of nostalgia for playing the game, day in, day out in New Zealand. Or imagine the game's surging popularity in America, the epicentre of the card-quake that had rocked me and whose distant tremors were being felt in communities up and down the land.

FIFTY MILES NORTH of New York City lies the wealthy Westchester town of Bedford. It is a place where affluent professionals, often from the media and entertainment industries, set up family homes at a comfortable distance from the five boroughs' madding crowds. The prevailing political winds in Bedford and the cluster of villages that surround it are liberal, the inhabitants are well-educated and, for the most part, suburban serenity rules OK.

In 1995 though, that tranquillity faced a mighty challenge as *Magic* arrived from the city like an urban pigeon blown off course. It landed in local playgrounds and quickly caught the attention of Bruce Dennis, the superintendent of schools in the Bedford district at the time. Dennis was in charge of operations at seven schools, spread out over 57 square miles and sat as chief executive on the citizen-elected board of education. On his beat were five elementary schools, including kids from kindergarten age through to 11-year-old fifth-graders; one middle school for children in grades six to eight and finally a high school catering to pupils up to the 12th and final grade. *Magic* was the latest craze, as popular in those playgrounds as it had been in mine in New Zealand, and in particular, it had captivated Pound Ridge Elementary School and Fox Lane Middle School. There, siblings of different ages who played together at home, showed off the awesome new game to their friends during the day.

A knock at Dennis' door from one of the parents of the *Magic*-playing children soon followed. The parent in question wanted Dennis' permission to set up a *Magic* club on school premises, which would be supervised on a voluntary basis by parents of the kids involved. The idea was to make sure the *Magic* kids had a safe environment to play in, at no burden (hiring someone to oversee the club, for example) to the school district itself. Dennis' own 11-year-old son had recently picked up the game so, being no stranger to it himself, he gave the club the go-ahead. Kids could take part with parental permission, and their *Magic*-playing would have to be kept separate from anything curricular. Dennis acknowledged the game might not to be to everyone's taste and that some of the artwork might be labelled disturbing by certain parents, but he felt that overall, it was harmless fun. "It was a game with a lot of mathematical properties in it," he says. "And the kids who tended to be drawn to it seemed to be the very bright kids who engaged in those kinds of things." As long as kids had to opt into the club, he saw no harm in allowing *Magic* to have a home on school grounds.

It was not too long before another knock – rapid, percussive and persistent – followed on his office door. This was the rapping of one Mary Ann DiBari, a local attorney and former nun, who was raising two grandchildren she had taken over custody of from her daughter. Her grandchildren attended Dennis' schools and she had heard from them about the *Magic* craze sweeping the land. Now, she had urgent concerns she wanted to address to the local schools boss.

A placatory Dennis convened a meeting to give DiBari's concerns a fair hearing. The parent who had helped set up the *Magic* club attended, as did an education board member who was a psychologist. DiBari came, too, flanked by a psychologist of her own. "This game," she told the meeting, "is dangerous, harmful to children and misogynistic. Bedford's schools should not be associated with it in any way." Unsurprisingly, her psychologist backed her play.

A shrewd and experienced educator, Dennis asked for a day or two to mull over DiBari's concerns. He returned with a decision that stunned all involved. "Bedford was a somewhat liberal community which abhorred censorship of any kind and would not take kindly to someone trying to restrict children's access to a particular pattern of thought," says Dennis. Nonetheless, in a move that took DiBari by surprise and startled Dennis' friends and colleagues, he declared a 30-day moratorium on the playing of *Magic* on school grounds. He was, said upset parents on the pro-*Magic* side, "caving into a whacko." But the Bedford schools boss thinks it was the best decision he ever made. It was up to him to take any concerns about safety at his schools – in this case backed up by a professional opinion – seriously. His analogy was simple: if someone told him the drinking water was unsafe, he would not just glug it and say, "Well it tastes fine to me." No. He would switch it off at the mains and have it rigorously tested. And that is exactly what he proposed to do with *Magic*.

Dennis contacted Wizards of the Coast and explained the situation Bedford Schools District found itself in. The game's makers were sympathetic to his plight and supplied him with three complete sets of their product (much to the delight of his son who had never seen some of the cards before). Dennis then distributed the sets to three different child psychologists with a list of questions. Dennis wanted to know if there was anything about the game's images or content which would render it dangerous to school-age children, despite its playing on school grounds having been limited to kids with explicit parental permission.

In the meantime, he had to deal with significant disquiet among local parents. Those with *Magic*-playing children were deeply unhappy at Dennis' actions. Others, although not invested in the game itself, had seen little in Dennis' three-year tenure to suggest he would capitulate to what they saw as a conservative, religious agenda. As pressure grew, Dennis remained calm: his decision had been strategic. And it was vital that he could put forward a solid case to assert the school's right to allow the playing of the game to continue.

One by one, the three psychologists reported their findings to Dennis. And one by one, they gave the game a clean bill of health. Armed with the results, a relieved and vindicated Dennis reported back to his bosses – the seven-man, elected board of education. At a public meeting, he announced he could now safely recommend the continued playing of *Magic* on school grounds, under supervision and only by children given parental permission to do so. It was not the decision that DiBari had been expecting. Having been delighted at the initial ban, she now turned furiously on Dennis and let slip her real agenda. Clutching a bible in one hand while poking Dennis in the chest with the other, she issued an ominous threat: "I am going to bring you down," she said, "as the superintendent who promoted Satanism in Bedford schools!" Not quite realising what he was getting himself into, Dennis replied with a cocksure quip. "Well," he said, "give it your best shot!" War was declared. And *Magic* was on the frontline.

FRANK ZAPPA'S RIPOSTE to would-be censors was concise and to the point: "I wrote a song about dental floss," the irreverent guitarist once said. "But did anyone's teeth get cleaner?" Nonetheless, Mary Ann DiBari was convinced that *Magic* wielded a real and menacing influence over its players. "In the game there was [the] Demonic Tutor with a pentagram on him and black leather and many other cards with an upside-down sword and a swastika," she told media supportive of her cause. "The card game was an initiation into Satanism."

Determined to make good on her promise to oust Dennis, she then formed a group called the Association Against the Seduction of Children, along with her friend Ceil DiNozzi. Together, they managed to rally a small number of followers to their cause. Dennis estimates that a dozen or so (extremely vociferous) locals banded to the Association out of 45,000 people in the school district. But DiBari could count on the support of a wider conservative religious movement. That included *The 700 Club* (a prominent evangelical TV show), the Catholic Lawyers Association (an ambiguous group with no connection to the arch diocese), plus an array of pastors, pundits and partisan online outlets. All in all, it was an almighty stink – and, in September 1995, the crusading association hit national media headlines with a public meeting in Pound Ridge, where they denounced *Magic*.

Around 300 people attended and police were called in to control the crowds. Actress Glenn Close, whose daughter was a pupil in Bedford District, even came out to show her support for the embattled educators and lent the event an A-list edge. The game's supporters and detractors took to the microphone to air their concerns, while reporters from media including the *New York Times* scribbled frantic notes. Nothing sells papers like a good 'Posh schools promote Satanism' scoop. DiBari kicked things off accordingly: "*Magic: The Gathering* is steeped in the hidden language, imagery, signs and rites of at least 30 satanic cults in this country," she said. "Moreover, it is a codification of the beliefs, practices and perceptions of the new Satanists of today. There are inducements in *Magic: The Gathering* to engage in destructive, cruel cult practices." Outsiders to the district piped up in her support, including characters such as the pastor Steven Kossor, publisher of a newsletter for all those, 'concerned about public education in America.' As he would later write, the scenes he discovered in Pound Ridge disturbed him greatly: *Upon arriving in Pound Ridge, I immediately noticed the street signs. A white arm, with a finger pointing, names each street. The only problem is that there are TWO fingers pointing on every street sign in Pound Ridge. The index finger and the pinky are both sticking out. For those of you who don't know occult symbolism, that's how you make the sign for the HORNED BEAST or SATAN...* (Emphasis his own).

In the face of such zeal, it took brave school kids to defend their hobby. One fifth-grader battled his nerves to announce in a quivering voice, "I play *Magic*, and I don't want to sacrifice anybody or anything." Unfortunately, that testimony fell on deaf ears. Mary Ann DiBari continued what Dennis described as, "a full-frontal assault against all aspects of our school district curriculum." She had co-opted *Magic* as the thin end of a wedge. Her attacks on *Magic* became the launch pad for an attempted hijacking of Bedford schools' curricula. Soon, DiBari was calling for prize-winning children's books to be banned, attacking the schools' drug and alcohol education programmes and slamming poetry-writing exercises given to children. Dennis resorted to inviting a Roman Catholic priest, who had previously performed exorcisms, to Bedford's schools, to vet the libraries and make sure they were free of malicious demons.

After a lull in hostilities during some of the 1995–1996 school year, Dennis was served with a court summons in October 1996. It alleged that he had violated 113 of the plaintiffs' (DiBari was lead plaintiff) first and fourteenth amendment rights. The litany of complaints included *Magic*, but also featured bizarre and extreme objections to a variety of practices at Bedford schools. The ensuing legal battle took its toll on staff morale, cost the school district $500,000 to fight and made unlikely *Court TV* stars of Dennis and the district's attorney. At a community meeting organised in the wake of the summons, 1,000 people came out to show solidarity for the under-siege superintendent and protest against the would-be censors riding rough-shod over the community's values. "It's interesting to note," says Dennis, "that during a considerable time that this lawsuit was in place, the president of our board of education was himself a Presbyterian minister. I happen to be Jewish. And the area was itself a largely Christian, Roman Catholic community. The notion that a community such as that would be able to get away with anything of the sort that she alleged was kind of preposterous." Thankfully, after a traumatic five-year trawl through the US legal system, even a very conservative judge could only find for the plaintiff on three of the 113 allegations. An appeals court overturned even these points. And, says Dennis, that was when DiBari "crawled back under her rock." She had failed in her spurious quest to bring down the *Magic*-supporting superintendent.

Despite his clash with the Association for the Seduction of Children, Dennis never cursed *Magic*, although the temptation when he was fielding 30 or 40 phone calls a day for much of 1995 and 1996, must have been hard to resist. Instead, Dennis says that Wizards of the Coast were extremely cooperative at every turn, despite Bedford never seeking financial or legal assistance from the company. That said, although healthily detached from the case, Wizards did look on with heightened interest at the scenes that played out on the other side of the country.

While it was clear *Magic* had reached new and uncharted territories, the artistic freedom its aesthetic had been founded upon could clearly become a hindrance to wider success. With national chains on the brink of stocking the product, allegations of spreading Satanism were the last thing Wizards needed. As the game's *Fourth Edition* came out, all cards referencing demons were dropped and an offending pentagram was clumsily removed from the card Unholy Strength. For a seven-year stretch from 1995, DiBari and co, while not successful in sterilising Bedford's schools, put the willies up Wizards. No more cards referencing demons were released in that time, just in case we all turned out to be little card-playing Damiens. To *Magic* players' credit, they proved they had better things to do than sacrifice goats: like contribute to a community that was springing up around their favourite game and, in some unwitting way, play a part in the wider cultural shifts that would, as of 2002's *Onslaught* expansion, make demons an acceptable part of *Magic* again.

CHAPTER TWELVE
The Deck

As MAGIC CHATTER rose in volume – in stores, in magazines and, for the most savvy of players, on Usenet boards like rec.games.trading-cards.strategy – the slang bandied around by its players grew in significance. *Magic* language reinforced their commonality and helped to define them as a new and distinctive group. While much of it was banal – pet names for specific cards, for example – some of it was becoming increasingly analytical as players fumbled for terminology to describe what was taking place in their games. In 1995, one such term sprung from the work of pioneering internet writers Paul Pantera and Rob Hahn – a phrase that had been hovering seemingly on the tips of *Magic* players' tongues worldwide. When it was finally uttered it became immediately axiomatic and is still used today by players who sense its meaning in their bones. It was a term that at its birth elucidated something players had been trying to grasp in their burgeoning understanding of the game's strategy. Which formed, and was vocalised, because it had to be; forced into being by perhaps the most important stack of cards ever shuffled in the game's history. While the term itself was the deceptively simple two-word blend, 'card advantage', the deck which inspired it was anything but. It came to life in the California sunshine, fattened on the vine to lip-smacking complexity, just down the road from Stanford University.

PALO ALTO NESTLES in the northwest corner of Santa Clara County, all concrete and tennis shoes atop land that was once orchards. On hot days, of which there are plenty, residents say you can feel the ghosts of those departed trees and the tangible absence of the shade they once provided. One tree in particular does remain: a handsome 1,000-year-old redwood in nearby parkland named El Palo Alto, the 'tall stick' after which the city is named.

Palo Alto is also prime Silicon Valley territory. Its inhabitants are some of the most wealthy and best educated in the United States and work in their droves for Apple, Google, Facebook and the other grandees of the internet age. Before those concerns colonised this slice of America's West Coast though, the brainpower incubating at Stanford University and some of the nearby University of California campuses was sinking its considerable talents into other pursuits. Zak Dolan, the inaugural *Magic* world champion, pursued post-graduate studies at Stanford, for example. But his achievements were eclipsed by another Palo Alto local who played a pivotal role in *Magic* history. His radical approach to the game defined an era. And his creations propagated rapidly through the local area before, appropriately, firing the nascent online culture around *Magic*. He went from local hero to world-renowned innovator, made famous by the possibilities of the internet technology being developed all around him. His name was Brian Weissman and he was *Magic*'s first celebrity.

In 1994, Weissman was a sophomore at UC Santa Cruz, 35 miles to the south of his hometown Palo Alto. An angular, athletic guy with dark hair and sunken ice-blue eyes, he had a competitive streak that had been nurtured by high-school team sports. As a student, that same drive had made him a fixture of the Bay-Area tournament scene established around the seminal early 1990s video game *Street Fighter*. One weekend, though, on a regular trip home to see his girlfriend, he stumbled upon a new fascination that immediately stirred his competitive – as well as creative – juices.

At a friend's birthday that January, *Magic* made its first appearance in Weissman's life. A mutual friend, who had himself just picked up the game, had managed to find two *Unlimited Edition* Starter Decks as a gift for the host – and, to ensure a good game, had brought along his own newly acquired cards, too. The decks were divvied up and a splinter group from the party camped out on the floor to play the new game. Weissman watched from the edges, impatient for his friends to finish up. But, after an hour or so, it became clear he was waiting in vain. In time-honoured fashion, he decided that if he couldn't beat them, he had better join them, and sat down to try the party-crashing card game.

The enthusiasm in Weissman's voice today when he recounts his first game of *Magic* is something golden; confirmation of a halcyon past each *Magic* player treasures, hoping quietly it is shared by others. Perhaps before we had online statuses to update, it was an experience we never got to trumpet with the same exuberance we might have today. But no matter how great or how modest a *Magic* player, everyone got started somewhere. Everyone wrestled complicated cards, fuzzy rules, and a head-scratching new way of gaming. Everyone felt a spark. "It was almost 20 years ago," says Weissman today in his rapid-fire patter over the phone from his Seattle home, "and I remember it vividly."

For most *Magic* players who picked up the game in its very early days, only one thing mattered: size. Big gnarly creatures were the order of the day – the bigger the numbers in the bottom right hand corner, the quicker you could reduce your opponent's life from 20 to zero. Strategy such as it was, wasn't particularly more complicated than that – either play lots of cheap-to-cast small creatures to overwhelm your opponent, or steadily build up your mana over a number of turns to summon harder-to-cast, big creatures which could kill your opponent in a couple of attacks if left unchecked. The visceral thrill of calling into battle fearsome monsters attracted many to the latter tactic.

One of *Magic*'s most ubiquitous big monsters in those days was Craw Wurm; a six-to-cast, 6/4 green Creature. It did nothing flashy – other than kill your opponent in four turns (four attacks, one each turn, of six damage) unless destroyed, removed or blocked. As a card printed at common, it was also a card many players came across when opening their first packs or playing the game with friends' newly born collections. It may not have been much, but Craw Wurm was instantly 'gettable' to all new players. And, like many others at the time, Weissman tapped his six mana and slapped one down on the floor with relish during his first game. Enchanting it with a card called Flight was his next move and created a formidable threat. As the name suggests, the card Flight grants a creature the 'flying' ability. Such a creature can usually only be blocked by an opposing creature with flying, thus making it more likely to attack unimpeded and deal its damage to an opponent. Things were looking good for Weissman. His opposite number, though, was holding him at bay and building up a threat of his own: the powerful green creature Gaea's Liege. Gaea's Liege can tap to transform any land in play into a green-mana-producing Forest. Then, when it attacks, its power and toughness become equal to the number of Forests the defending player controls. As more and more are transformed by the Liege's special ability, it becomes an ever-more dangerous creature, ready to swing in with the fatal blow.

Gradually Weissman's opponent took control of the game. First, he destroyed Flight so that he could block the Craw Wurm. Then he began turning Weissman's lands into Forests, one by one. Despondently, the *Magic* debutant glanced at his hand. Barring one random green card, it was packed with blue cards, which he would never be able to cast now. All his blue-producing Islands had been transformed and he was staring down a potentially huge Gaea's Liege. The outlook was bleak.

As expected, the Gaea's Liege swung at Weissman, swelled to 12/12 having turned a dozen of his lands into Forests. If Weissman were to block with his Craw Wurm, it would die and leave him facing a lethal Liege the following turn (the Wurm can only survive four damage and deal six, insufficient to kill the attacking Liege when blocking – or to survive itself). It was looking dicey and Weissman was ready to quit – until he considered what that one random green card in his hand was; an inconspicuous spell by the name of Fog.

A green instant, Fog could be played at almost any time in the game, including during Weissman's opponent's turn. It could also be cast with the Forests that had otherwise thwarted Weissman's plans. As his opponent attacked eagerly, sensing victory, Weissman responded by tapping a single Forest for one green mana and casting Fog. His opponent grabbed the card. *Creatures attack and block as normal, but none deal any damage*, it read. The Liege went from being a game-winning threat to useless: it would not deal its damage but having attacked would still remain tapped and unable to block. On his turn Weissman dutifully attacked with his Craw Wurm and finished off his stranded opponent. "So," says Weissman gleefully, "I won my first ever game of *Magic* with Fog and from that point on I was hooked." It would not be the last time in his *Magic* career that Weissman turned defence to his advantage.

*　　*　　*

STILL STOKED FROM his first *Magic* experience, Weissman returned to Santa Cruz and excitedly showed the game to his friend and fellow *Street Fighter* player, Matt Wallace. Weissman had bought three Starter Decks of *Unlimited Edition*, but in doing so had blown his student budget. Wallace, though, had a little more disposable income, a car and the same competitive streak as Weissman, all of which were necessary for the pair to procure more of the ultra-scarce gaming cards.

"The store where I bought my original cards was called Gamescape in Palo Alto," says Weissman. "For whatever reason, when it was extremely hard to find *Unlimited* cards anywhere, this one store had them. The rumour was that the owner of the store was close friends with one of the original guys at Wizards of the Coast and therefore could get cards for the store." It is tempting to imagine Peter Adkison stopping off at Gamescape on his epic drive to Gencon four months previously – if he did, he unwittingly aided Weissman's rise to the top of the *Magic* pile.

In any case, Gamescape (sadly now closed) was in an enviable position and exploited it fully. Each day, before they opened for business they would open a display box's worth of *Unlimited* Boosters – 36 15-card Booster Packs each containing one rare card, 3 uncommons and 11 commons and lands – and sell the individual cards for a flat fee on a first-come, first-served basis. Rares and uncommons were displayed in a ring binder while commons were sorted in a box and left to be picked over by the card-starved clientele. It was rudimentary compared to today's secondary market, but punters flocked to the store in their droves. "People would line up outside waiting for it to open," says Weissman. "You could buy any rare from the binder for $2 and any uncommon for $1. It didn't matter what they were. That included all the crazy cards – all mint edition. I clearly remember going in and seeing the binder full of Moxen and actually passing them up for stuff my primitive neophyte's *Magic* brain thought was better, like Lord of the Pit."

Today, a mint condition *Unlimited* Mox – 20 years out of print and counting - costs over $1000 from a major retailer. Lord of the Pit costs around $10, but summed up everything that made *Magic* exciting: it was a black card in an era when various forms of heavy metal ruled our teenage lives. It was a 7/7 flying, trampling demon, which you had to appease each turn by sacrificing your own creatures. It was a high risk, high reward card that oozed dark fantasy flavour – and precisely the kind of thing that gave the Association Against the Seduction of Children fits. It was immediately impressive to early players who overlooked the subtle but devastating power of the Moxen. Lord of the Pit's overt fantasy stylings hooked players from the word go, even if it was the game's subtle mechanical complexities that kept them hooked. In that sense, Weissman was no exception.

Just as he had with *Street Fighter*, the Japanese language studies major immersed himself in his new favourite game and began to explore its nuances. Richard Garfield's baby was still a mysterious game – not everyone knew quite what cards actually existed, nor how the rules' finer points worked, nor indeed what, if any, rules covered deck construction (other than the 40-card minimum mentioned in the first small rule book squeezed inside Starter Decks). *Magic* was wild – and only with the formation of the Duelist's Convocation, Wizards' official tournament sanctioning body, in late 1993, had any guise of standardisation been imposed on the game. Richard Garfield had from the very beginning envisioned *Magic* tournaments for his intellectually challenging game and the DC (later the DCI, with an 'I' for international) was the organ that made tournament play possible. Still, information only trickled out of Wizards, via *The Duelist*, via early internet channels, via word of mouth. Until players heard for sure that what they were doing was 'wrong', they were happy to experiment. "The genie was out," says Weissman, "and people were discovering things."

After building a towering mono-black deck using four or five Mox Jets and the power of several Demonic Tutors (a sorcery which lets its caster search for any card in their deck and put it straight into their hand), Weissman started to build a deck strictly out of artifacts. Inspired by the second *Magic* expansion *Antiquities*, which provided many cards which interacted with the artifact card type, Weissman soon had a 300-card stack built around generating enormous amounts of mana with some of the new set's additions to the *Magic* card pool. The Urza lands (which could produce more than a single mana) and Candelabra of Tawnos, an artifact that could untap lands, became its mainstays. With this he battled on an almost daily basis against his now equally *Magic*-obsessed friend Wallace (wielding a blue and white deck) on the sticky table-tops of the UC Santa Cruz Recreation Center.

The pairs' formidable creations, though, would not fly in the emerging world of DCI-sanctioned tournament play. For their first official competition, the two friends had to jettison some of their favourite tricks (the Moxen were, for example, restricted to one of each sort per deck) and learn some new ones. Weissman ditched his artifact deck and returned to a black-based deck, splashing a little white and green to help deal with opposing enchantments and artifacts, something black cards do not do well by themselves. But, combined with powerful cards like Icy Manipulator, Royal Assassin, Meek Stone and Mind Twist, the deck still packed a mighty punch: just as Weissman had won his first-ever game of *Magic,* he rode his new slimline stack to victory in his first-ever tournament, too.

It was a spur to the competitor in him and proof that he and Wallace were on to something in their approach to the game: "It wasn't just me and Matt beating up on the local casual gamers," says Weissman. "People had come from the Bay Area over the hill to Santa Cruz to play in the tournament and I managed to win it. So that was really a defining moment and validated what I wanted to do with the game." Flush with success, Weissman redoubled his efforts to crack *Magic* and fine-tuned his approach via epic gaming sessions with Wallace. Crucial to the way the pair understood the game was their decision to alter the rules to suit their tastes for drawn-out battles: instead of playing each game from a starting total of 20 life, they decided to play with 40 life each. This had the effect of completely warping many of the game's fundamentals, effectively halving the power of all the creatures, for example. Aggressive, cheap creatures, like the ones Bertrand Lestrée would ride to a runner's-up place in the World Championships that year, had no place in the pair's games. They were completely outclassed by the expensive creatures the pair could cast with their well-developed resources. Similarly, the pair realised that with such high life totals, they could use life points as another resource, one that would afford them the time to reach the complex late-game that they both enjoyed, where they could cast powerful game-ending creatures and would win after a dramatic back-and-forth. Inadvertently, the pair had hit upon an entirely new paradigm and it was one in which Wallace's blue-white deck seemed to consistently come out on top.

*　　*　　*

As MAGIC FEVER took hold all over the US, the tournament scene exploded around Weissman and Wallace. The *Street Fighter* buddies smelled blood and attempted to distil what they were learning from their titanic tussles into a tournament-legal deck for a forthcoming event called Mana Fest. Mana Fest was the biggest tournament in Northern California at the time and approximately 500 people were expected to attend. The thrill of competing against such a vast and high-quality field drove Weissman and test-partner Wallace on – and forced them to look at why Wallace's blue-white deck, given enough time, was proving unbeatable.

As Weissman's mana-driven artifact deck ran out of steam, the blue-white deck was leaning on a particular group of cards to grind out victory. The first was the blue instant Ancestral Recall, which for one blue mana allows its caster to draw three cards. The second was blue sorcery Braingeyser, which lets its caster draw as many cards as he or she spends in mana. The third was the blue creature Sindbad, which could be tapped to draw a card, and the final key component was a land from *Arabian Nights*, Library of Alexandria. As well as tapping for a colourless mana, it could be tapped to draw its controller a card if he or she had exactly seven cards in hand.

Many players had in isolation enjoyed playing with these cards or noted how each of them had a fun or powerful effect. But what the pair of UC Santa Cruz students, locked in long and gruelling games against each other, were able to do so effectively was to identify precisely what these cards had in common: all of them allowed their caster to net cards. Ancestral Recall (also one of the so-called 'Power nine') does so most obviously, giving a one-shot benefit of three cards, for the paltry cost of a single blue mana. Just like Black Lotus or the Moxen, it breaks one of the game's fundamental rules: at the start of each turn, a player draws a single card from his or her library (or deck). By casting Ancestral Recall and drawing three, a player can essentially skip forward the development of his resources by three turns. Perhaps not the mana laid out on the table in front of him or her, which Weissman's artifact deck was able to generate in spades. But the less obvious resource that the pair were beginning to perceive as vital to success: the contents of one's hand. The more cards in hand you have (seven being the starting total and maximum hand size allowed at the end of a turn), the more options you have. All of the above cards help deliver the resource of cards in hand in one way or another. Permanents (cards which stay in play unlike sorceries or instants) like Sindbad and Library of Alexandria can even do it over a number of turns, building a gradual, but often-unbeatable advantage for their controller. It was this phenomenon, this 'card advantage', that Wallace and Weissman latched on to as crucial to victory. Their discovery would change *Magic* strategy forever.

In the meantime, with Mana Fest edging closer, Weissman hit upon the idea of combining a favourite tool from his black deck with Wallace's blue and white cards: Mind Twist. Mind Twist can be cast for one black mana and any number of other mana to force an opponent to discard that many cards. If drawing cards was so strong, the pair reasoned, the inverse must also be true. With Mind Twist, a player can again impose superiority of cards in hand, boasting a full grip with which to kill an opponent stripped of defensive options. It was another huge stride forward for the pair's deck-building and, as the tournament approached, their theories began to fall neatly into place. There was just one hitch.

"The problem," says Weissman, "was that we wanted to play a deck with four copies of Library of Alexandria, which wasn't restricted at the time [it would be restricted to one-per-deck in May 1994] and we wanted to play four copies of Mind Twist. But between us we didn't own eight of those, so we flipped a coin to determine who would get to go and represent our brains trust at the tournament. Matt ended up winning the coin toss and we put together a deck that we actually called 'The Deck.'" Born out of necessity, its singular name has gone down in *Magic* history.

The first iteration of The Deck was a blue-black-white deck built on a core of cards which generated card advantage (such as Mind Twist and Library of Alexandria), permission spells (which stop an opposing spell as it is being cast) such as Counterspell and Power Sink, flexible removal in the form of Disenchant, mana acceleration in the form of Moxen and Mana Vaults, and extremely powerful game-ending creatures: four Juggernauts, gleaned from Weissman's artifact deck, and four Mahamoti Djinns, a giant blue flyer that had been backbreaking in Wallace's blue-white deck. This combination of cards allowed The Deck's pilot to control the game – by countering opposing spells or destroying opposing threats – until the late-game state where those powerful creatures could be cast and ridden to victory, just like the long grinding games the pair had playtested together. Similarly, if The Deck's pilot drew Moxen and Mana Vaults in their opening hand, he could accelerate to a proxy of that late-game state where they had plenty of mana in play and could cast a backbreaking Mind Twist, creating a similar state to the one Weissman had experienced in those long games when he had run out of options as Wallace sat opposite him, replenishing his hand. So long as the pilot could reach that state, life total became fairly meaningless: defend, destroy, counter, control and contain. Only the final life-point of the controller's 20 actually mattered, the pair reasoned. Stay alive long enough and the sheer weight of card advantage packed into The Deck would do exactly what it had done in all the pair's games together: simply, inevitably win the game. While not perfectly streamlined, weighing in at 64 cards – four more than the newly minted minimum deck size of 60 cards – and containing a few whimsical additions like Chaos Orb and Argivian Archaelogist, it was a deck of unprecedented focus and unusually attritional qualities. Mana Fest had never seen anything like it. Accordingly, says Weissman. "Matt just annihilated the field. The Deck destroyed everybody."

It would be the zenith of Wallace's *Magic* career. A few months later, he dropped out of college to take up a job at a company called Netcom, one of the first internet service providers. As real-life commitments took over, he ran out of time for *Magic*, leaving Weissman their collective card pool and the responsibility to develop The Deck further. Weissman was happy to oblige, fine-tuning the potent pile of cards as the latest set *Legends* was released in June 1994. *Legends* brought with it a host of powerful new options for The Deck at just the right time: on 1 August 1994, after a brutal showing at 1994's US National Championships, won by Bo Bell, one of The Deck's staple cards, Mind Twist, was restricted to a single copy per deck by the Duelist's Convocation. It was time to innovate again.

Weissman's tinkering quickly yielded results. One by one, local ringers fell to him, and soon he began to dominate all of the area's regular tournaments. The Deck was ready for a bigger test, and in February 1995 it would face one in the form of a giant tournament called Dundracon. In preparation, Weissman turned The Deck into a sleek card-advantage machine, the like of which no one had seen before. The most notable refinements were the inclusion of Disrupting Scepter, which can be activated in its controller's turn to force the opponent to discard a card; Mana Drain, an upgrade on the standard Counterspell; and Moat from *Legends*, an enchantment which prevents all creatures without the flying ability from attacking.

What Moat amply demonstrates is how card advantage can be leveraged not only by drawing extra cards or forcing one's opponent to discard them. If an opposing deck is playing a dozen creatures, bereft of the flying ability, with which they intend to kill their opponent, all those dozen creatures are nullified by Moat, a single card. With a Moat in play, each time Weissman's opponent drew a creature, he was in effect drawing a blank card, thus conceding card advantage. As long as Weissman could protect Moat with his suite of counterspells, he could sit back and defend until his advantage became overwhelming. Even the only creature Weissman selected for The Deck aided that plan: Serra Angel, a 4/4 flying creature that does not tap when it attacks.

At the time, Serra Angel was one of only four creatures in the entire game that did not tap to attack – and the only one with flying. The significance of this ability was that Serra Angel could both attack (soaring over Weissman's own Moat) *and* remain untapped to block opposing attacking creatures. With an offensive and defensive function rolled into one, she was perfect for The Deck. And, Weissman realised, she was only needed to finish the job off. Instead of playing a horde of creatures, Weissman would play all the elements he needed to control the game, until his opponent had been fully contained. While others were still obsessed with churning out creatures as quickly as possible – just like the Craw Wurms they had learned the game with – Weissman could see that this was unnecessary. The Deck would simply answer all threats thrown at it and draw out the game until its advantage became insurmountable. Only then were his Serra Angels needed at all. So, flying in the face of all *Magic* wisdom at the time, he included only two in his list of cards – the only creatures in his entire deck.

At Dundracon, over two days of intense duelling, Weissman went on to lose only a single game (each match comprising up to three games), ultimately claiming victory over a mono-red deck centred around the powerful enchantment Blood Moon in the final. It was a watershed moment for *Magic*. The radical, near-creatureless Deck had swept all comers (and prevailing *Magic* notions) aside. It immediately sparked frenzied discussion amongst open-mouthed onlookers, including a number of Wizards staff, who rushed to speak to the 20-year-old at the finish. As Jim Linn, East Coast playtester and by then one of the Wizards employees in attendance later wrote, *It was the first time I think the Magic environment had seen a deck like that. People were just amazed at it – I was amazed at it; I couldn't believe it was so successful.* Within a month or two, everybody in the Bay Area was playing a version of Weissman's deck, while others in the *Magic*-playing universe tried to decipher its contents. It earned column inches in *The Duelist* and some of the very first virtual column inches, too. In short, it was a game-changer. In recognising the fundamentals of the early *Magic* environment and breaking all the rules to design a deck capable of beating nearly everything thrown at it, Brian Weissman solved *Magic*'s first 'metagame', creating the optimal deck for the conditions the game was played in at the time. The Deck, though, was not simply a one-off pile of cards bringing fleeting success. Its design philosophy was so penetrating, so honed in on the mechanics which made *Magic* function as a game, that it would become the game's first 'archetype' – a deck design that would be replicated time and time again as new cards and new environments appeared. By almost any measure, The Deck earned its definite article. And soon, as its fame spread on new media channels among a fanatical *Magic* crowd, its creator Weissman was elevated to legend status.

CHAPTER THIRTEEN
Plug Me In

IT IS AN irony of history that the last great paradigm shift in analogue gaming should have been made possible by the digital medium Usenet. Without the internet and the connection it forged between Peter Adkison and Richard Garfield, there would be no *Magic*. But it is also possible that without *Magic*, the internet itself would have looked very different from the one we know today. The rise of one did not simply help fuel the other. Instead, the two technologies (and the communities they spawned) cross-pollinated in a fertile digital swamp, creating a common history that cannot be sliced in twain. As soon as *Magic* was released in 1993, it was plugged into the internet and set off an outbreak of online discussion among its early audience, many of whom, as students or technologists, had access to Usenet at university or the forward-thinking companies that employed them. Indeed, a year into *Magic*'s lifetime and even *The Duelist* was pointing people online in an article entitled 'Electrons are your friends'. *For cool net access, you'll need a computer and a modem*, warned author and long-serving Wizards employee Dave Howell. He then went on to explain how users could send emails directly to the company, who were embracing the medium as a way to build bonds with their customers, or their 'friends', as Peter Adkison called them. Howell also listed the Usenet groups where the game's hardcore had found each other and singled out rec.games.trading-cards.magic.strategy as the hub of the new *Magic* community.

Because *Magic* by its very design was a game of endless choices, every choice its players did make – from deck selection, to deck design, to actual choices within games – was a potential theme for debate. The initial result on Usenet was a deafening cacophony, as players struggled to grasp which aspects of the game boasted genuine significance. Before, indeed, players realised how they could talk about those factors, as the language needed to define the phenomena they were encountering settled into place. It took Brian Weissman's cerebral approach to deck construction and the higher level of analysis it demonstrated to open the eyes of *Magic* players who had been working on pure instinct. Up until The Deck landed like a monolith amongst monkeys, Usenet was a jumble of pet decks being posted online by their creators, news and rules discussions, tournament adverts and so on. But when a friend of Weissman's, Sun Microsystems employee Paul Pantera, popped up to extol The Deck's virtues, it served as a lightning rod for serious *Magic* players everywhere. One of those inspired by the electricity surrounding The Deck was Usenet lurker Rob Hahn.

WHEN HAHN BEGAN reading about The Deck, he immediately sensed that *Magic* discussion had reached a new threshold. Instead of simply posting a list of the cards he was playing, Weissman – who had little online access and relied on Pantera to represent him – explained *why* he had chosen those cards, outlining the concept behind the design and the synergies between the cards. So many of Weissman's choices were counter-intuitive to early *Magic* players, that without his results, without the analysis he was propagating via his discussions with Pantera, his deck may have been largely dismissed by casual observers. A card like Swords to Plowshares, for example, played a huge role in The Deck, allowing Weissman to remove any creature completely from the game (rather than it simply dying and being sent to the graveyard zone, where it can be revived by numerous effects) for the cost of a single white mana. The card's drawback – that it gave the creature's controller life equal to its power – had led to the card being dismissed by many early players who visualised the game as nothing but a race to reduce the opponent's life total to zero. Weissman, however, looked past that and saw the startling efficiency of the card within his strategy. Remove a threat cheaply – live on to fight the long game – and eventually lock the opponent down completely. Once that had been achieved, it didn't matter how long it took to kill with his two

Serra Angels. His position was a virtual checkmate, his victory inevitable. In that sense, says Hahn: "The Deck was fundamental in showing the level of complexity *Magic* could reach."

Perhaps not a player or deck-builder on Weissman's level, law student Hahn did, however, possess excellent analytical skills and a love of writing. As discussion around Weissman's deck blossomed and his contemporaries began to discuss their decks more cogently, Hahn began to perceive over-arching strategies that those talking online were failing to adequately distinguish. Late one night in the autumn of 1995, a determined Hahn sat down at his trusty Mac SE and began drafting what would become a seminal *Magic* document; a Usenet post that would decisively crown the internet as the medium for cutting-edge *Magic* discussion. Borrowing a martial arts analogy, he called his piece 'Schools of Magic' and rattled it off as the midnight oil burned down. Satisfied with his work, Hahn posted it on Usenet and stumbled to bed. The next morning, he awoke to find 300 emails in his inbox.

Hahn's breakthrough was his clarity in identifying the different resources that decks, or groups of decks, were leveraging – or denying – to cement their wins. The Weissman School, for example, was focused on drawing cards and denying cards in the opponent's hand to create overwhelming 'card superiority' as Hahn dubbed it. The Handelman School (named after Garry Handelman, another Bay Area player searching for a way to beat the omnipresent Weissman Deck) focused on quickly disrupting the opponent early on, then playing and protecting powerful creatures, a strategy that dominates the game's tempo. Decks in the Chang School (after Warren Chang), included in Hahn's second draft of 'Schools of Magic', attacked the opponent's mana to prevent them casting their spells. These were, wrote Hahn, deck 'archetypes' – strategies that went beyond a single deck with a single mix of cards and rather highlighted the fundamental areas in which games of *Magic* were won and lost. *Magic* was like a pie that could be carved up into different pieces and in trying to present these pieces together, Hahn was helping to reveal the whole pie to players for the first time. "I think what I was trying to do," he says, "was define the metagame in a real way, which I didn't feel had been done until then. The idea of the metagame had been discussed – but no-one had put it all together and said, based on the cards, based on the environment, based on the rule set: here it is."

A metagame can be loosely described as a game stretching beyond the conventional rules of a particular game, for example deciding to win exactly three matches of *Magic* at a tournament. Or playing *Jenga* blindfolded. Or attempting to build more hotels than your best friend in a game of *Monopoly*. 'The metagame' then, as described by Hahn, was a synecdochal use of the term, co-opted by *Magic* players: one of the infinite metagames open to *Magic* players became seen – and talked about – as *the* defining metagame. Namely, in a game of unprecedented choice, what cards should I choose to play with? Or, more specifically, what deck should I play with at a given tournament if I want to beat the other decks in attendance? Thus 'the metagame' became in most *Magic* parlance the term used to describe the ensemble of decks one could expect to face, as well as the interplay between them. It is, admittedly, confusing – but it was even more obscure before Hahn put flesh on the theoretical bones being tossed up in the Usenet ether. Here, suddenly, was a snapshot of the state of *Magic* strategy. It was a giant step forward in understanding the game and a hugely influential piece of writing. Mike Flores, one of *Magic*'s most successful columnists, says, "Rob made me think about and look at the game in a much different way. He enriched my experience of *Magic* and inspired me to start participating on the Usenet boards."

FLORES WAS NOT the only one leaping feet first into the now vibrant online *Magic* community. As ever more players joined the conversation at rec.games. trading-cards.magic.strategy, the limits of the newsgroup medium were being sorely tested. As Flores puts it, "I personally was becoming disillusioned by the signal-to-noise ratio." Hahn, meanwhile, was wrestling with his 'Schools of Magic' document, having to rewrite it each time a new development occurred and then post a new version on Usenet. As new posts accumulated, it would be pushed ever further down the newslist and hundreds of players trying to find it would email him asking him for a copy. Unthinkable as it might seem now, there was no way for Hahn to hyperlink to his text: each correspondent had to be answered in turn and the 'Schools of Magic' content painstakingly copied and pasted into a reply. It was a chore Hahn had never anticipated when he wrote his brilliant *Magic* article. So, when an IT specialist by the name of Frank Kusumoto emailed him about a pioneering new project he had in mind, Hahn was relieved.

Kusumoto was a *Magic* enthusiast with an intriguing day job. In late 1995, when he contacted Hahn, he was working for the FBI and Department of Defense. His specific remit was to organise the tide of human intelligence (as opposed to signals intelligence, from satellites and so on) that the US Navy received. He was, essentially, in the business of spies and something like the IT department's tinkering 'Q'. The challenge Kusumoto faced was making the vast quantities of information on fleet movements, maritime operations and smuggling that operatives sent in accessible to analysts. In his search for the right tools to do so, he was keen to explore the possibilities of a new programming language called Hyper Text Markup Language or HTML, the code that would facilitate the shift from newsgroups to the website-centric internet we know today. "I want to try using this new-fangled HTML thing to build a *Magic* website," he told Rob Hahn. "And, if it works for *Magic*, maybe it will work for the Navy, too." Hahn's 'Schools of Magic' would be the first text that Kusumoto posted to his website and would be joined by a handful of Kusumoto's own writings. The experimental website would be called the Dojo, decided Kusumoto, and he would be its self-styled sensei. In wonderfully hammy kung fu-ese, the wise and enigmatic leader invited visitors to the Dojo to 'study and grow strong'. They did. In rapidly spiralling numbers. And before long, the Dojo was renowned as the finest *Magic* school in town.

Initially, Kusumoto's plan was to curate the best posts from Usenet and present them – with the help of the new website format – in a way that made the information more accessible. But very quickly, he had to revise his expectations: not only would he have Usenet to sift through, but players also started emailing him articles directly. Not just strategy pieces arrived in his inbox but opinion pieces, too – and says Kusumoto, once he had accepted the first, "the floodgates were opened." In his first couple of months running the website (hosted on 1MB of free space from service provider Netcom), Kusumoto clocked up dizzying internet bills as the dial-up tariffs of the time creaked with the weight of traffic surging from his home. With its handpicked content, rapid and accessible flow of information and collaborative, open-source approach to deck innovation, the Dojo slowly but steadily became

Magic's centre of gravity. As the game became more focused on competitive play (which it would in 1996, following a major strategic decision by Wizards of the Coast), so the Dojo took on ever more importance and its users and contributors became ever more prolific. Its editorial strategy, says Kusumoto, fell naturally into place: "To be an advocate for fair play and for the average tournament player."

Nonetheless, the site had its controversies, particularly regarding its approach to innovation. One of its key features became a section entitled Decks to Beat – a more naked way, in-keeping with Kusumoto's desire to make information more accessible, of presenting the tournament metagame. In it, were the latest decklists gleaned from tournament winners. Were you to have any chance at your local competition, you either needed to 'metagame against' these decks (design one which beat them) or, more likely, copy them. The idea at the time, that anyone would 'net-deck' – build, card for card, a copy of a deck listed online – was abhorrent to many players, who had lovingly collected every card and crammed them into their decks depending on taste or trial and error. The Dojo's Decks to Beat section was deemed by many to be the death knell for creativity, when it fact, it was anything but. Aping the kind of open-source thinking being promoted in savvy R&D departments all over the land, it actually accelerated learning by squeezing out whimsical (and often plain bad) decks, focusing minds and refining deck-building theory. It was, in effect, the logical conclusion of the process started by 'Schools of Magic' and a standard that all *Magic* players today have become accustomed to. With the tournament scene exploding, it became a vital time-saver to serious *Magic*-card slingers who could focus their efforts on playing, practising and experimenting – brewing up decks against a clearly defined metagame. To this day, looking up the latest winning decklists online is the number one pastime for many players and in that respect, the Dojo was streets ahead of anyone else. As Pete Hoefling, the owner of major online store and content provider StarCityGames.com puts it: "The Dojo laid the framework for what every *Magic* site is today."

Crucially, many of the biggest *Magic* writers, including many still active today, were able to make their name because of sensei Kusumoto's discernment. By taking on an editorial role (personally proof-reading and posting over 20,000 texts in his stint at the helm), Kusumoto fed the notion of celebrity and authority within the *Magic* world. Instead of drowning in Usenet postings, authors with something to say found themselves singled out and celebrated on the Dojo. Names like Brian Weissman and Robert Hahn were joined by a string of top tournament players all finding a voice for themselves, as they battled to be the best in the land: Brian Kibler, Jamie Wakefield, Eric Taylor, John Schuler... their names quickly earned a place in the *Magic* canon. The latter is even largely credited with inventing the form of *Magic* writing known as the 'tournament report', a blow-by-blow account of a player's performance at a given event. As its inventor, he earned the right to subvert it, too, and sparked outrage with a fictional report called 'How I won mid-Atlantic Regionals with my Song of Blood deck'. The Dojo was, in short, a springboard for innovators – both players and writers – and allowed many to go on and earn money from their writing as outlets competing for talent sprung up in the Dojo's wake.

Hahn himself was recruited in 1997 by Wizards' Mark Rosewater to become his assistant editor at *The Duelist*. It was Hahn's dream job – and he happily took an enormous pay-cut from his role as a corporate lawyer in New York to join the magazine in Seattle. But as good as the content the refreshed team produced was, the Dojo had permanently changed the *Magic* media landscape. Instead of singing the praises of 'cool net access', *The Duelist* staff were having crisis meetings on how to address their plummeting subscription numbers. The magazine's big problem was the 90-day turnaround between issues, which was being made to look glacial by the Dojo's Decks to Beats section, updated after tournament results poured into Frank Kusumoto's inbox every weekend. Like many (if not all) print titles, *The Duelist* suddenly found its rationale for existing undermined. In response, says Hahn: "there was serious discussion at Wizards about buying the Dojo." Wizards eventually decided it would be more healthy to have a strong, independent voice talking about *Magic* and focused their energies instead on creating content for their own website. Could Hahn replicate the Dojo for Wizards, they asked him. They even had a budget in mind for him to do so: $6 million.

Wait a minute, thought Hahn. *If you're willing to spend $6 million to create another Dojo, there must be somebody out there willing to fund the existing Dojo as a company.* And certainly, with venture capital being thrown willy-nilly at internet start-ups in the first dot-com boom, there was. Hahn got on the phone to Kusumoto (by now burnt out by editing *Magic* articles) and offered to buy up a controlling stake in the Dojo. Kusumoto agreed and the Dojo was reborn as the Psylum Dojo, an ad-supported website with Hahn as its boss and Mike Flores (at first an intern) on its staff.

For a time, the site continued to flourish and in 1999's Flores-penned article "Who's the Beatdown?" published one of the game's most important texts. In it, Flores described how when similar decks faced each other, understanding which deck was the aggressor and which was the controlling deck in the match-up was decisive for victory. He explicitly enumerated a thought process for determining the role each deck was playing and the consequences it had for the pilot of each deck. After 'Schools of Magic' had drawn the lines of the metagame, 'Who's the Beatdown?' enunciated the effect that knowledge should have on strategic, in-game reasoning. It taught players that understanding what decks they would be facing had an impact not only on deck design, but also on the decisions made within a game. As such, it was the next quantum leap in *Magic* theory, again made possible in both execution and propagation by the internet's connecting power. Flores signed off with the haunting maxim: *misassignment of role = game loss*, a warning so lucid it sounds like a life (not just a *Magic*) lesson. It is one still discussed in every card shop or tournament on the planet, while the phrase 'Who's the Beatdown?' has been pronounced in every accent possible. Flores' article permanently altered the thought patterns of *Magic* players everywhere, helping unite them into a supra-national, sub-cultural group.

Unfortunately, the internet still suffered its Babel moment. And while language was not the ultimate reckoner, hubris on a biblical scale was. As sites funded by opportunistic venture capitalists failed to monetise, the dot-com bubble burst spectacularly in 2000. The Dojo, despite a final rescue attempt with a sale to the USA Networks-owned Sci-Fi Channel, eventually imploded. Its tatami mats were rolled up and put away. Its shoji were slid shut for a final time. And its loyal band of students were ushered out of its shomen to study and grow strong at the host of websites that sprung up in its wake. There would never be another Dojo. But each and every *Magic* site today owes a debt to the genius of sensei Frank Kusumoto.

*　　*　　*

To say that the Dojo's influence was limited to *Magic* websites, though, would be to sell short its groundbreaking design. It was in fact part of a tangible effect being had by *Magic* players on the very fabric of the early internet. Two factors were crucial to the sway *Magic*'s online community was able to have. Firstly, their simple weight of numbers; the fact that, before anyone else, they were a genuinely coherent online community. Sociologists studying the early internet today look at two groups – online role-players and newsgroup communities and, as Skaff Elias points out, in the Usenet days, *Magic* traffic trailed only pornography and weather boards in its volume. As *Magic* players explored their obsession online they created links between local shop-based scenes that otherwise would have taken years to form, harnessing the new technology to become a distinct and visible group. In so doing, they heralded the internet's ability to thrust previously small, underground scenes into the light by dint of greater numbers and coherency. As the primary identifiable group online in the mid-1990s, they also became a de facto proving ground for the viability of the forms of internet use that others would go on to adopt. One key example was the heavy presence of *Magic* card auctions on Usenet, a hugely popular way of buying and selling cards at the time. Says Elias, "A friend of mine wrote his economics PhD at MIT [Massachusetts Institute of Technology] specifically using *Magic: The Gathering* to collect data about auction formats on the internet. Today, he kicks himself because he didn't found or invest in eBay." The same phenomenon was echoed in the name of the notorious Bitcoin exchange, MT.Gox, so called because it began life as a platform for trading "MTG" (*Magic: The Gathering*) cards. Even addictive hook-up app Tinder owes a debt to the proliferation of collectible card games – its designers say its pioneering swipe interface was inspired by sorting through stacks of cards.

The whole premise of the Dojo meanwhile, was that the amount of information being generated by *Magic* players was so great, that it would be a valid testing ground for technology destined for wider applications. For that reason, says Flores, "Frank Kusumoto is the second most important person in the history of *Magic*, after Richard Garfield. He had this skill that other people did not have at the time: the organisation of information on websites so that it could be consumed by everyday people." In that sense, Kusumoto was inventing the way the internet would be used with every keystroke of code he wrote for the definitive *Magic* website. To boot, the Dojo would lead the way in what would become the buzz concepts of the first dot-com wave – user-generated content, content aggregation, driving traffic to centralised locations which could then be commercialised... "Literally, the evolution of the internet is there and you can see it in the Dojo's early iterations," says Flores. "Here Frank was, working for naval intelligence and just inventing this thing that other people came to adopt in many other areas."

That they did so, had much to do with the early *Magic* community's second defining characteristic: its composition at the time. Take Rob Hahn for instance. He discovered the game in 1993, whilst working in the IT department of a Wall Street hedge fund. One lunch break, leafing through an IT industry magazine, he stumbled upon an article detailing a new craze that was sweeping the computer industry up in Seattle, at Microsoft and beyond. That craze was *Magic* and it was being rapidly embraced by and popularised amongst members of the tech workforce (including Paul Pantera at Sun Microsystems). The same developers who were building the World Wide Web's infrastructure were also scouring it for information pertaining to their hobby. Says Hahn: "It's entirely possible that people from Microsoft or Netscape looked at the Dojo and said to themselves, 'Hey, this is a really smart way of organising information on the internet. Maybe we'll use that somewhere.'" *Magic* and the internet were linked from birth and developed in startling symbiosis. Neither ever looked back. Serendipitous timing thrust them together to their mutual betterment. And, with the virtual wind in its sails, *Magic* powered forward into uncharted territory, along a new course plotted by Wizards of the Coast.

CHAPTER FOURTEEN

Play the Game, See the World

MAGIC'S EARLY EXPLOSION into the public realm was not without its fallout. The revolutionary product's vertiginous rise created tumult radiating from punch-drunk Wizards of the Coast, via starved supply chains, all the way down to players, who were either hopelessly in love with a product they couldn't buy or, as in Bedford Schools District, assailed by meddling do-gooders. When Peter Adkison says that 1994 and 1995 (after a glorious 1993) were the worst years of his life, he can be forgiven his lament.

Having unleashed an unprecedented product, Wizards had no off-the-shelf business model they could rely on to ensure its success. And, as revenues rose, the fear that mismanagement might kill the golden goose began to build. Wizards' inexperience had helped create an iconoclastic product, but now it risked creating another discarded collecting fad; a *Garbage Pail Kids* for the 1990s. As John Jackson Miller had noted, the 'locusts' who had speculated on sports cards and comics were already turning their attention to *Magic*. A horde of hustlers, flipping boxes of sets like *Legends* at a huge mark up, or cracking open the product and selling the single cards to desperate players, were beginning to create a dangerous *Magic* bubble. The problem for Wizards was: how long would their players stay interested in a product that was spiralling out of their price range? Black Lotus, printed only 22,800 times in *Alpha*, *Beta* and *Unlimited*, was racing towards the $100 mark by the end of 1994 and was emblematic of the dangers *Magic* faced. If the *players* turned away in disgust, the 'collectible card game' would be left to fend on the market not as a game, but as a pure collectible. That would leave it susceptible to the fatal boom and bust nature of such a commodity. Something had to give.

ASK MOST PLAYERS of a certain age what the worst set in *Magic* history is and the response will almost certainly be *Fallen Empires* (1995's *Homelands* runs it a close second, though). Released in November 1994, it is stigmatised in part for its relatively weak cards and fiddly gameplay which introduced rafts of counters and tokens to the otherwise pared-down elegance of the *Magic* battlefield. But really, *Fallen Empires*' lacklustre reputation hinges on one simple fact: it was the first set that was printed to demand. As such, it did not immediately go up in value. For that reason, ask Wizards employees of a certain era – including Richard Garfield – what the most important expansion in *Magic* history is and the response will almost certainly be *Fallen Empires*. "We had to take the reins away from speculators and collectors," says the game's creator. *Fallen Empires* was the beginning of that process.

Whereas previous sets had been woefully under-printed, including *Fallen Empires*' predecessor *The Dark* (at 62 million cards), this time Wizards set out to fulfil all the orders streaming in from distributors. Their hope was that by increasing supply, they could begin to deflate the bubble building up in their product. This would be like a controlled explosion of a lone suitcase on a station platform. A chance to defuse a dangerous situation at the time of the company's choosing, rather than let a sudden destructive blast rip through the market. There was, however, one slight blip: retailers, unaware of Wizards' plans, had vastly exaggerated the orders they were placing just to be able to get *some* of what they assumed would be another scarce *Magic* release. John Jackson Miller, from his time at industry publication *Comics Retailer*, knows of one store who, in the hope of securing 50 boxes of the hotly anticipated set, due out in the run up to Christmas, ordered 550 of them. With Wizards ready to print more cards than ever before (four times as much as *The Dark*) every single one of those boxes shipped, costing the store tens of thousands of dollars and ultimately putting it out of business. A controlled explosion this wasn't. *Fallen Empires* began crashing the market, assuring it of its dubious place in *Magic* history. The following year's *Ice Age* and *Fourth Edition* were also deliberately heavily printed to consolidate the process. Indeed, by the end of 1994, Wizards had already printed their billionth *Magic* card and at that point stopped making print-run data public.

BURNING THE SPECULATORS before they could burn *Magic* was only one half of the equation, though. There was still a risk that *Magic* fever could run its course and that the legion of players who had picked it up in its first flush of success might get bored, down tools and move on to another game. Lisa Stevens had hedged against that as best as possible by buying up as many licences for established intellectual property as she could, to delay the entry of a powerfully branded competing card game to the market. That advantage would only hold for so long though. A new approach to the product, a new proposition for its players – and not its hoarders, flippers and hustlers – was needed. It was former Philadelphia stalwart and now full-time Wizards employee Skaff Elias who found it.

By 1995, the ruddy, bearded Elias was Wizards' brand manager. In reality though, he had far more on his broad shoulders at the frantic company headquarters. From helping establish the R&D department, to designing cards himself, to business development and product management, Elias had fingers in almost every Wizards pie. So dedicated was he to *Magic* (and so run off his feet), that he could often be found asleep under his desk when the lights went out on another madcap day. There was no going home at a time in the game's development Elias describes as "extremely precarious".

One question in particular plagued Elias: how could a player justify spending hundreds of dollars on Wizards' product for any more than a year or two? While the answer up until that point – from all quarters – had been, 'Because the cards keep going up in value', Elias could see that this was unsustainable. So, with that in mind, he began to spend his long evenings researching what games had remained commercially successful for long periods. The more Elias read, the harder it was to ignore not only the staying power of classic games like chess, bridge and poker, but also the models embraced by professional sports.

Little over a year before, Zak Dolan's triumph at the inaugural World Championships had shown the central role that competition held for many

Magic players. Within Wizards meanwhile, the fastest growing area of the company was the fledgling organised play department, as more and more players signed up to join the Duelists' Convocation International (DCI), the game's official sanctioning body. But just like everyone at Wizards at the time, DCI boss Steve Bishop and his team were struggling to get to grips with *Magic*'s mind-blowing scale. Even officially sanctioned tournaments, complying to the DCI's early deck-building and organisational rules, were shambolic. Unfortunately, there was very little understanding at the top of what went into producing a good competitive event. These early tournaments were, says Elias, nothing short of "disasters", run by a willing but inexperienced team who were simply in over their heads. It was something that Elias could see was a huge problem: "The tournaments were being run by a bunch of people who had never played games competitively before and the structure of early tournaments reflected that."

Furthermore, by the beginning of 1995, tournament play such that it was, was in danger of stagnating. The environment was ruled by the Power Nine cards (including the now $100 Black Lotus), all of which had climbed so high in price that a worrying two-tier field of haves and have-nots was emerging. How long would it be, wondered Elias, before the have-nots simply stopped turning up to play altogether? Drastic action was required to redress the situation by scaling back on which cards would be allowed for tournament play. But how could that be done without incurring the wrath of the tournament 'haves', in many cases players who had helped make *Magic* a success from day one?

The solution that gradually swam into Elias' focus was a tournament series that would not only turn *Magic* from an ephemeral collectible into a perennial game, but one which would provide a positive value proposition for switching to new deck construction rules. His idea was to found a professional tournament circuit, or 'Pro Tour', backed to the hilt by Wizards financially, played with cards everyone had access to and which would cement the primacy of playing over collecting. Elias' Pro Tour, he hoped, would create a new level of investment – both intellectual and monetary – in the game from its fan base. It was a truly radical proposition. And, at its inception, one that almost no-one believed could work.

* * *

JUST OVER A year into Wizards' frantic expansion, the company's staff was still largely composed of 'nearest warm bodies', brought on board to plug holes wherever possible. As former employee John Scott Tynes would write years later in an article for Salon.com entitled 'Death to the Minotaur', *If you were a Seattle gamer in 1994-95, you had to be wilfully incompetent not to get a job at Wizards.* In particular, says Tynes, the city's black-clad goth community was heavily represented at Wizards HQ, complete with a *dramatically heightened sense of outrage to perceived slights or efforts to sell out.* Elias, who had railed against the inefficiency of the current tournament organisers on the one hand and now wanted to propose on the other a hardcore, cut-throat competitive vision for *Magic*, fuelled by big bucks, seemed in for a losing battle. Still, he was convinced that his idea for a professional tournament series was the best way to ensure the game's survival. He was also convinced he could count on the support of at least one ally: Richard Garfield.

Early on in *Magic*'s dizzying rise, Richard Garfield had already reached the decision that the game should be a product for its players rather than its collectors. His faith in the quality of his game was absolute and it was his hope that it could join the pantheon of great, enduring games, with players respected for their skill and intelligence. He was also well aware of the dangers facing the game if it were simply to muddle on in its current state – popular, but for how long? Although he was initially reticent when Elias put the idea of the Pro Tour in front of him, worried that it would make the game too serious, he came round to the idea as the analogies to the classic games he wanted to emulate became clear (bridge, poker, chess... all featured competitive play at their apex). Similarly, reasoned Garfield, the existence of professionalised sports had not wiped out the grassroots; quite the opposite in fact. The NBA and casual basketball, for example, could co-exist quite happily and, thought Garfield, without the NBA to aspire to, there would probably be far fewer people shooting hoops on their local court. Remembering that he had always wanted to see games elevated to the same level as sport – albeit as sports for the mind – he sensed *Magic*'s chance to make a lasting mark on the cultural landscape. If Wizards played their cards right, they would gain far more players than the factions they might lose.

Garfield, though, for all the sway he held in the organisation, was not the sort to kick up a fuss or criticise the currently mediocre state of tournament play. Elias had to go on building alliances within Wizards to get his idea off the ground, even with *Magic*'s creator onside. His next port of call was Peter Adkison, who could immediately see the strength of Elias' vision. Having witnessed how *Fallen Empires* had burst the *Magic* bubble, he was fully aware that a new conception of the product was required for it to move forwards. Injecting cash into a professional play programme not only put the onus on *playing Magic* but also sent out a positive riposte to naysayers claiming the *Fallen Empires* crash was the beginning of the end for Wizards. "I loved the idea and made the changes in the organisation necessary to make it happen," says Adkison. "But there was a point in time where out of 100 or so employees, only four of us believed in it."

The fourth was Rick Arons, the executive who had been slowly but surely spreading professionalism from his desk like ripples in a pond. Sure, he liked to walk around in his socks, but he had a keen mind for business development and possessed the authority, tact and dedication to steer Elias' idea through the initially sceptical Wizards environment. A huge sports fan, Arons could grasp the potential a professional tournament circuit had, not only for elevating the quality of *Magic* play, but for legitimising it in the eyes of the general public: "Your grandma might not know what *Magic* is," he says. "But she'll understand what a $10,000 cheque is."

IT WAS SEDUCTIVE logic. And the razor-sharp Seth Matlins recalls it with glee as he details his experience with Wizards of the Coast in 1995. Sipping coffee on the other end of the phone line, on a sunny Los Angeles morning, he says with admiration, "When I first met Wizards of the Coast, no-one would have expected *Magic* to reach its 20th anniversary. But they planned for it."

Matlins is a marketing guru who in 1995 was working for ProServ, the second most powerful sports marketing company in the world, behind IMG. While IMG had been built up around the commercialisation of golf, ProServ was built up on tennis, with Arthur Ashe and Stan Smith as its first clients. Its expertise lay not only in representing athletes, but also in broadcasting and television production. In 1995 though, they were in a phase of diversification. The first rumblings of television's declining efficacy were being felt in the industry, cable was gaining traction and viewerships were beginning to fragment. That meant ProServ were open to new ideas. But still, when they took a phone call from Rick Arons at Wizards of the Coast, it came as something of a surprise. What was *Magic* anyway? It did not take long for Matlins and his colleagues at ProServ to find out. They were immediately impressed by the rigour and scope of what Arons had to tell them. The feeling was mutual and Matlins was brought on board as part of a shadow government emerging at Wizards HQ.

A second group working on tournament play started up – not wholly in competition with the existing unit, but not wholly in concert with it either. In keeping with Peter Adkison's *laissez-faire* attitude, Elias, Arons and co were free to work on an idea a majority of the company still felt would ruin the game. But what alternatives did they really have?

Matlins remembers some outlandish options being discussed as a responsibility to Wizards' shareholders. Should, for example, the company sell out while the *Magic* brand was at its hottest and build the *Magic: The Gathering* theme park? Certainly, it would be a way to cash in on the game if it really was nothing but a fad doomed to die out in the near future. But in their heart of hearts, not only did Garfield, Elias, Arons, Adkison and Matlins not want that – they also had immense faith in the product. Even Matlins, in no way a gamer or typical fantasy fan, could see how powerful *Magic* was: "The core premise was great," he says. "You have to give credit to the fundamentally brilliant IP [intellectual property] and gameplay, while the collectible quality of the game undoubtedly added value. Nobody wanted to sell out – so the question became: how do we step outside the traditional lifecycle for a game, which runs about 18 to 24 months, burns really hot for 12 to 16 months, then hits a decline?" The group even briefly considered whether a play could be made to attain Olympic status for *Magic* as an intellectual sport. If nothing else, it would be an impressive PR stunt.

Increasingly though, the idea of a big-money professional circuit became inescapable: 'The $1-million *Magic* Pro Tour,' had a ring to it and was an offering that put many sports at the time in the shade. It would, the group hoped, prove compelling to *Magic* players and frankly anyone in earshot of the phrase. It would galvanise the game's grassroots – from local shops upwards – giving players something to aspire to, rewarding the very best with a platform upon which to shine. This was a chance to affect real cultural change. Everyone involved realised that the Pro Tour could legitimise and remunerate *Magic* players' skill and creativity, so that they might earn a similar status to the high-school quarterbacks or valedictorians out there: "It was important for us to reward people for their efforts and to give people a sense of self-esteem," says Elias.

Vitally, it would also smooth the transition required to level the tournament playing field between the haves and have-nots. "The second purpose," admits Elias, "was to 'bribe' the players. I hate using that word, but we wanted to show them that we would reward them for playing the game with only cards printed in the last two years – a new tournament format that we would call Type II." The game's old-school players could certainly continue playing with cards from the game's entire history at Type I tournaments (the format now known as Vintage) – but the brunt of Wizards' official prize support and promotional focus would go to a format that provided equal opportunity to all players, no matter how long they had been playing the game. The Type II format (today called Standard) would feature cards currently in print over a two-year period and would rotate as and when new cards were published, with outgoing sets replaced by the new printings. This would keep the format fresh and constantly challenging, much like Garfield had originally imagined. *Magic: The Gathering*, remember, was originally to be available for a year before being replaced by a completely different *Magic: Ice Age* product – only the necessity to rush expansions out to the game's early adopters had changed that plan.

The creation of the new format was a huge and controversial schism that would relegate Type I to *Magic*'s margins. But in conjunction with the Pro Tour, it finally provided Wizards with a model for sustainable sales. "They had a vision for what Rick referred to as the 'metagame,'" says Matlins. "His analogue was a pinball machine with all the names of the high scorers on it." As long as the rewards of triumphing in this vision of the tournament metagame were high enough, players would now have every reason to continue to buy new *Magic* cards. It was a brilliantly holistic vision and precisely the business model Wizards had been looking for. The Pro Tour itself would be laid over an infrastructure similar to tennis, namely a ranking system based on the Association of Tennis Professionals' rankings, where players ascended by beating those ranked higher than them. It even harked back to the 'ladders' for card games like hearts that Garfield had run for his Maths Department colleagues back in his University of Pennsylvania days. And, as one of his columns in *The Duelist* magazine in the spring of 1995 revealed, he was fully on board with the idea. *Recently, I claimed that I could make any game popular if I could build a good ladder around it*, he wrote. *Each player [on a ladder] has many different chances for success. When a player moves up even one rung from the bottom of a ladder, he has achieved a kind of victory.* That same aspiration would be the bedrock of *Magic*'s future as an enduring, perennial game.

IT MIGHT NOT have been much, but its consequences would be seismic: a tiny news story, tucked away in the bottom left-hand corner of page 10 of *The Duelist* issue number eight, from December 1995.

PROFESSIONAL POSSIBILITIES FOR MAGIC TOURNAMENTS

The first in a series of professional Magic *tournaments is in the early planning stage at Wizards of the Coast. Members of the* Magic *team have been scoping out sites in the New York City area and hope to put together an initial event by early next year. For more information, contact Wizards of the Coast Customer Service at (206) 624-0933.*

WHILE THE SELF-EFFACING manner of the Pro Tour's announcement almost certainly hints at the internal scepticism at Wizards of the Coast, the master plan was now public knowledge. John Jordan, the company's biggest shareholder, was onside and preparation began in earnest for the first big-money event – one that would have to prove the viability of Skaff Elias' radical idea.

As the news story in *The Duelist* says, the venue for the first-ever *Magic* Pro Tour would be New York, in a converted loft near Greenwich Village. With no qualifying system in place, the best-known players around the world were canvassed by Wizards and invited to intend. Bertrand Lestrée, for example, the runner-up to Zak Dolan at the 1994 World Championships, remembers receiving a Fed Ex package while on work placement in the UK. He had stopped playing *Magic* six months previously, but as he opened the courier's parcel to discover a letter from Wizards telling him they would fly him to New York to play in the game's first ever-professional event, all expenses paid, his interest in the game was suddenly rekindled. His case proved in microcosm the allure of playing at the top level, for high stakes, and getting a holiday thrown in, to boot. Fittingly, the Pro Tour's slogan would for many years become 'Play the game, see the world!'

Other players heard about the impending event – to be held on the weekend of 16-18 February 1996 – by word of mouth. While Wizards had a rough idea of the big names they wanted to play at the tournament, the other slots available needed filling – and were awarded on a first-come, first-served basis to anyone who called up and asked for one. A total of 347 players would make it to the Pro Tour and would be split into a Junior and Masters competition according to age (a distinction which would be later scrapped). Despite a snowstorm delaying the start of the tournament, there was a palpable sense in that New York loft of a new era beginning. Richard Garfield himself kicked off proceedings with words that summed up what a watershed moment it was: "The reason I take games seriously is because I consider them the intellectual counterpart to sports," he told a wrapt audience of fans. "I would love to see games raised to the stature of intellectual sports." The concept was a fine one, but Elias, Matlins and the other Wizards and ProServ staff in attendance could only cross their fingers and hope that the event would prove their big-money gamble correct. Certainly, as far as the players were concerned, this was a thrilling new arena to compete in. One 17-year-old player in the Junior portion of the competition, a Neutral Ground regular called Jon Finkel, could barely contain his emotions. Today, he says that first Pro Tour was like, "being in a school football team that gets to play a game at Wembley. It was clearly a bigger stage."

As the rounds progressed, that feeling began to spread to the organisers, too. By the semi-finals, with thousands of dollars on the line, the play had ratcheted up to a new level of intensity – and everyone in attendance had been swept up in it. There were no bleachers or close-circuit television as there would be at later events for the crowds of eliminated players to watch on. So they scrambled as best they could on to nearby tables and chairs to lean in and get a view of the play as it was unfolding. The tournament rules had not been fully ironed out yet, so the players were allowed to play out their matches without a time limit. As the semi-finals stretched out, the atmosphere became electric – and it was then that the organisers were convinced they were on to something. Matlins recalls being bowled over by the intensity in the room. "What you saw was passion, engagement, interest – and if I remember correctly, you could even hear 'Oohs' and 'Ahs' from the crowd at various plays," he says. "That was the moment I went from knowing the Pro Tour made sense, to believing it made sense. I wasn't a *Magic* player and I'm not today but in that moment you could palpably feel the connection of an audience to the play of others and for a sport, that's fundamental." For Elias, seeing Matlins' reaction was the proof of concept he needed – sure, *Magic* was exciting to gamers. But when a non-gamer was as awestruck by the unfolding excitement as all the *Magic* players in the room, the Pro Tour's entire rationale was vindicated. This was sport; it would produce drama, birth heroes and legitimise not only its big-money heroes – but also all the wannabes striving to be like them. "It was astounding," says Elias.

By the time American player Michael Locanto triumphed against Bertrand Lestrée in a gruelling final to become the first ever Pro Tour champion – winning a cheque for $12,000 in the process – *Magic* had changed forever. Not only did its players have a reason to be proud, but Wizards, too, could reflect with self-confidence on an excellent business decision. It was, says Peter Adkison, their first. "Up to that point, *Magic* had been big and amazing because Richard was smart and creative," he says. "This was the first time we made a really smart business decision rather than simply getting lucky, and it took us to the next level as a company." The core believers at Wizards had been fully vindicated. And, as the shadow organised play unit absorbed the existing one, fears about the game's future abated. "Unequivocally," says Elias, "this saved *Magic*."

CHAPTER FIFTEEN
Which Way Home?

SCRABBLING AROUND FOR somewhere to play *Magic* at all in rural France, the Pro Tour passed me by. Tournaments were something I was only vaguely aware of and I had been told, in hushed tones, that if you didn't have a Black Lotus, you may as well stay at home. Instead, my focus was on trying to create that place called home, with the game that had served me so well in New Zealand. At first, my parents drove the one sister I had coerced into playing and I, to a tiny video game store in a nearby town called St Lô. But on its one small table, surrounded by soulless shelves of carts and discs, mumbling in schoolboy French to the local ringers, it was hard to recreate the Pendragon days. The shop changed hands. The table disappeared. And, with little love lost, we had to seek out a different town to play in.

Au revoir St Lô. *Bonjour* Avranches; a small, austere, hilltop commune. A Sherman tank lurked on an imposing roundabout in its middle. General Patton broke through the German lines in the battle of Normandy here and, well, that's about it. Still, it was here, on the Wednesday afternoons France reserves for catechism, that we would come to game, in a tiny narrow room with ill-fitting furniture above a theatre that was a dull, dead building at that time of day. Sure, there were good people there. Guillaume. Christophe (whose copy of the *Magic Encyclopedia* I should probably return after 17 or so years). But it wasn't a community of gamers with folders full of old cards and cool bands to tell us about, in the way the Pendragon elders had been. Instead, it was kids of the same age, quarantined in their awkwardness in that uncomfortable out-of-the-way room that was always, always the wrong temperature. It proved hard to get close. I couldn't be myself in French yet and nor could my sister. We had little common experience with the *Magic* club's other players. And we weren't sharing anything day-to-day that transcended our clumsy bi-lingual gaming; anything we could point to and laugh about, in the way we might have done with Simon Hope and his *Magic*-playing sister. It didn't feel great. It wasn't a scene. And without much engagement in whatever tournaments might have been happening nearby, my interest began to slip.

It makes sense then that, looking back, my fondest memories of playing *Magic* in France are domestic. That the best times came not in a frustrating outside world, but in trying to create a safe, familiar one suspended in it. The high point really came one long, yawning summer holiday. It was a hot season, like all the best ones in memory are. The sun had baked the local mud into fine dust swirling on the breeze. The nearest *anything* was 15 minutes drive away. We couldn't drive. The torpor that consumes teenage souls set in.

To fight it, my sister and I hit upon a way of keeping ourselves amused. For hours on end we would mix the hundreds of unloved junk cards we owned together into big piles, from which we would randomly pluck components for a deck. First some creatures. Then some spells. Then some artifacts. It was a very primitive form of what today gets called 'cube drafting', where players assemble their own personal selection of cards to build decks from with their friends. We didn't have any clever notions like that. Just stacks of duff cards that we wanted to rediscover in a private space carved out from the sighing stone house we called home. The simplicity of it all let us reclaim the game as something personal even as, in the outside world, it started to grow into something we weren't able to get a handle on. That something was more structured and serious. It held no meaning for two deracinated kids looking for a calm centre to the universe in the gentle, repetitive rhythms of play. The sun poured in through an open window. We sat on a thin rug on uncomfortable floorboards, with the sound of BBC Radio Four and my dad's footsteps coming through the ceiling from his studio above us. And somehow, with communication reduced to sibling code rather than a treacherous foreign language, we found peace.

It took another 15 years or so, but my sister and I did play each other again, in the same house, one Christmas after she had rediscovered the game with her partner. Sitting up on Christmas Eve, chucking down cards on the dining room table, till long past the hour Santa should have visited, we found another moment's peace. This time though, we were adults bringing our world home, using the game like a trail of breadcrumbs to lives that existed well beyond the length of the driveway, up to the road, leading away from the village we had once hated. Sitting up, with parents asleep, we were changing the meaning of home with every card we laid on the blue oilcloth, every crunching attack, every laugh and clink of glasses. This was our chance to express identities which had outgrown whatever that place had once been. No longer were we prisoners of its isolation, escaping it with a game as best as we could one long-lost, weary summer. We were there on our own terms. Grown up. Free. And for that reason, those Christmas *Magic* games are the most memorable I've played. I look forward to repeating them as the years tick by and we all make homes of our own.

What we never repeated was our bedroom-floor, junk-drafting summer *Magic* marathon. We probably realised even then that we were saying goodbye to the game, eking out from it what pleasure we still could, having realised that the game no longer fit the world we found ourselves in. Soon, I was hitting 18 or 19 and the desire to explore beyond the driveway and beyond *Magic* was too strong for me. I had been returning to England in the summer holidays to work and see old friends, rather than playing card games. That taste of independence, of earning a little cash, meeting new people (including girls) confirmed to me that there was more out there. More than the confines of the local Lycée and staring across benches at break to the popular set I couldn't quite belong to. More than the inevitable clashes with my parents about being a miserable adolescent with no ambition. More than half-heartedly swapping and playing cards in a cramped room above a sleeping theatre. A shoebox full of *Magic* and memories stared at me from the mess on my bedroom floor, asking me what I wanted out of life. I wasn't sure. But I sensed I needed change. Reluctantly, I fired up the chirping modem that had made its way into our house and joined an online auction site. Underground Sea, Birds of Paradise, Shivan Dragon, Hypnotic Specter, Demonic Tutor; one by one, I sold my few valuable cards and left behind a hobby that I told myself was juvenile. The proceeds of my fire sale went towards driving lessons instead. I was about as skilled behind the wheel as I was at *Magic*; that is to say, not very skilled at all. My moustachioed instructor, with his bi-focals, tracksuit and clipboard despaired. But after many, many laps of that tank in Avranches, I finally learned to pilot a car. The keys to the humble family Citroën were mine. Adulthood beckoned. And *Magic* was left trailing in the dust.

CHAPTER SIXTEEEN

Heroes…

THE SCENES AT the first Pro Tour had demonstrated the vicarious pull *Magic* could exercise on spectators gathered in hushed ranks around the action. But as my fading interest showed, there were still challenges to creating aspirant Pro Tour players on a wider scale.

One thing the game needed was for role models to emerge, who could be celebrated in the game's media. But Wizards were worried that finding heroes in among the Pro Tour ranks might prove a little harder than plucking the star player from a championship-winning sports team or PR-ing the front man of a rock band. The game was still largely the preserve of a games-store demographic – one earning some deserved time in the spotlight thanks to the Pro Tour – but would compelling, charismatic, confident celebrities reveal themselves from a previously maligned group? And what if the game itself proved less skilled and more luck-based than its creators believed? That would not only undermine the notion of professional *Magic* as a competitive 'sport', but, if Top 8s (the direct knockout rounds) featured a different line-up of fortunate players each tournament, how could any stars of any staying-power hope to emerge?

While a generation of brilliant minds would answer the question of the game's skilfulness, the first question was not something Wizards would leave to chance. Stars are not born, they reasoned. They are made. Heavy coverage would be given to the Pro Tour players in a new supplement to *The Duelist*. Called *The Sideboard*, after the supplementary 15 cards players can swap in and out of their decks between tournament games, it would focus entirely on competitive play. The holy grail of coverage though would be television – and here Seth Matlins' experience proved crucial in negotiating a deal with ESPN2 to show potted coverage of the *Magic* Pro Tour. While Wizards could not convince ESPN2 to go the whole hog and broadcast a reality show built around the Pro Tour competitors, the early Pro Tour broadcasts which dotted the network's schedules went some way to cementing the status of the new professional *Magic* caste. By buying up time on the channel, says Rick Arons, Wizards were sending a message to all their players: "Hey, we know you're serious about this – and we are, too. We're going to bring legitimacy to the game." It acted like a call to arms to *Magic* players and it was one they would wholeheartedly embrace.

When camera crews began conducting vox pops of the first Pro Tour fields, they asked players whom they most wanted to play against. One by one their interviewees would reply with the name on everyone's lips, the player who at the Pro Tour's inception was regarded as the world's best. He had won US Nationals in 1995 (as well as two Type I tournaments on the same weekend), under the watchful gaze of Skaff Elias and R&D's Mark Rosewater. His methodical play and consistent results helped allay their fears that winning *Magic* tournaments was purely down to luck. For his peers meanwhile, he was *the* man to beat. His name was Mark Justice and he came from Salt Lake City in Utah.

Justice, already in his early twenties when *Magic* came out, owned a chain of sports-card and comic book shops in the city. Like many similar shop-owners he was keen to diversify when the outlook for his current wares became grim. *Magic* was the lifeline he stumbled upon, and with the help of a deep pool of nearby players, he quickly immersed himself in it. When local tournaments started to appear, Justice became hooked. He is by his own admission a competitive guy – and *Magic* became a proving ground for the young man raised in the Mormon faith.

What Justice discovered during his first forays into competitive *Magic* was much more than a battleground upon which to demonstrate his talents. He also found himself surrounded by a vibrant community, who were opening his horizons – despite the sideways looks they attracted from the Salt Lake mainstream. "There was definitely a nerd stigma to *Magic* back then, but it didn't matter to me," says Justice. "The people I was meeting were smart individuals who I enjoyed talking to about far more than just *Magic*. If these were the geeks – I wanted to be associated with the geeks." It was a huge leap into a new world for Justice, who had grown up in a nearby small town steeped in traditional faith-based values. While he had grudgingly complied with those, here was a community he genuinely felt something in common with, a visceral kinship that would greatly impact his identity. His *Magic* nickname swiftly became the 'Stormin' Mormon', but if anything, the game was Justice's sanctuary from qualms about the faith he had been raised in. Here was a chance for him to shed the fetters of his religious upbringing. And he would do everything he could to earn this smart and secular community's embrace.

What the clean-cut young man from sheltered Salt Lake did not realise, though, is just how much everyone on the Pro Tour wanted a piece of him. Not just rival players, but Wizards, too. This, they figured, was their would-be champion. Justice had a string of big wins under his belt (as well as Nationals in 1995, he also helped the US win the team portion of the 1995 World Championships) and could demonstrate how skilful *Magic* was to the game's widened audience. He also seemed to boast the maturity and composure to be an advocate for the Pro Tour. His sixth-place finish at the first-ever professional event in New York sealed Wizards' belief – Justice would be the face of their intellectual sport. "In hindsight," says Justice. "I wish that had never happened."

THE CREATION OF the Pro Tour had an instant impact on standards in the game. Suddenly, here was the justification players needed to practice and improve. It was the green light – or greenback – that said it was OK to pour time, money and passion into a hobby built on brains rather than brawn. With rewards as great as many sports and crucially rewards that were quantifiable to the man on the street, the Pro Tour was cathartic for the brainy kids sat at home on Usenet rather than slogging it out on their local sports field. As Peter Adkison puts it, "We created a lifestyle opportunity for a young generation of *Magic* players, fresh out of school, to be professionals." No-one wanted to pass it up.

The most tangible knock-on effect was a steep rise in collaboration between players. The second Pro Tour would be held in Los Angeles (earning a full-page announcement in *The Duelist* this time) and would be fed by Pro Tour Qualifier tournaments or 'PTQs'. This framework allowed players to focus their efforts and strengthened the *Magic* community as players travelling from PTQ to PTQ began to make lifelong friends, bound together by a common goal. Teams began to coalesce in California, Boston and at Neutral Ground in New York. The Dojo hummed with activity as players strived to understand the decks dominating the new metagame. And Usenet members shared in the highs and lows of its community heroes as they battled for a place on the Pro Tour. Robert Hahn wrote a seminal tournament report after winning a PTQ feeding Pro Tour LA, that not only brilliantly translated the elation of scaling new heights, but inspired others to try harder, play better and, in the case of Mike Flores, to write about their exploits in the game. *It's five in the morning and I'm up because… well, I'm alternatively tired beyond belief and filled with adrenalin,* began Hahn. *It's a weird state of existence. I just thought I would post a little report on my experience earlier tonight (actually, last night by now) as it was my first time winning a large (250+) tournament. This may get long, so bear with me, or skip on to the next thread…* No-one did. Instead, they lapped up the ecstatic account of Hahn's PTQ triumph and through him lived out a little of their own dream to reach the professional ranks.

HAVING PLAYED IN regional events in Southern California, Justice gravitated towards his friends there to further his game. Along with Mark Chalice, Henry Stern, Mario Robaina and a core of Californians, Justice became part of the most impressive early team roster in *Magic*, the Pacific Coast Legends. The Legends, like the other teams forming, became R&D departments for the players, where the sharing of ideas and information proved critical in evolving the understanding of deck technology and in refining strategy. Says Justice, "Some of the decks that we created early on, on our own, were very primitive naturally, compared to the sophistication of modern decks. Collaboration played a major role in not only developing the game but strengthening the community as a whole."

While it did not reap immediate dividends for Justice at the second Pro Tour in Los Angeles, his collaboration with the Legends was part of a process of travelling and growth that left him wide-eyed. Even today, Justice has only fond memories of the people involved in the Pro Tour's early stages. Not just his team-mates and the opponents desperate to beat him, but the Wizards employees who became integral to the Pro Tour caravan. Skaff Elias was the "wise sage" of the Pro Tour, says Justice, an even-handed and fatherly figure who became a mentor to the youngsters playing the game and seeing the world for the first time. Justice has good memories of Mark Rosewater, too. As Wizards continued to try and afford their would-be champion exposure, Justice was asked to help provide colour commentary of the Pro Tour Los Angeles final – a face-off between two New England rivals, Tom Guevin and towering arm-wrestler Shawn 'Hammer' Regnier. Justice and Rosewater had no official commentary booth and were instead rammed into a phone box together to analyse the four-and-a-half hour match. "It was fascinating, though," says Justice. "Hammer absolutely mentally destroyed Guevin." At one point Guevin had to excuse himself from the final to throw up in the bathroom, so intense was the enmity between the players on the biggest stage in *Magic*. Hammer, unsurprisingly, won that one.

But despite all the good times, storm clouds were gathering on the horizon for Justice, as he ventured ever further from his roots back home.

WHILE THE EARLY adopters of Usenet and the Dojo may have been gradually pulling the *Magic* community tighter together, as if tugging on the laces of a corset, the world remained a stubbornly big place in 1996. While it might seem parochial for an American company and American community, producing and playing an American game, to rush to celebrate a local lad as, 'the best player in the world', a little myopia was to be forgiven in less-connected times. Although *Magic* had begun its translation into other languages since the release of an Italian *Revised Edition* in 1994, who really knew what brilliant players were incubating in card shops in Japan, Germany, France or Sweden? The Pro Tour was a way of finding out – and Wizards had done their best to invite foreign players, like Bertrand Lestrée, to the inaugural event. By the time qualifying was up and running for the third, in Columbus, the PTQ programme had become far more cosmopolitan – and the players gunning for Justice's unofficial crown increased in diversity.

Olle Råde was a willowy, 17-year-old Swede with striking, shoulder-length blonde hair. He had taken a year out of school to do a work placement at a local game store in his native Gothenburg, having inherited a love of all things card, board and dice-based from his dad. Råde senior was a journalist by day, but a gaming aficionado by night, who sat on the jury of a Swedish gaming-industry prize. His son, who had taken up *Magic* with the release of the *Revised Edition* 18 months previously, now had enviable access to cheap Booster Packs and a steady stream of opponents to practice against. During quieter hours in-store, Råde was honing his skills and, having read excitedly about the Pro Tour in *The Duelist*, was determined not to miss the first local PTQs.

Sweden's early *Magic* scene was strong, as evinced by Leon Linback's third-place finish at the very first Pro Tour. Along with Lestrée, he was one of only two non-North Americans in the Top 8. Although not known personally to Råde, he was an example of just what local players were capable of. The practice Råde was getting in against the card-slingers wandering into his shop each day then, was of the highest quality. Råde could soon hold his own and demonstrated as much at one of the local PTQs in the run up to Pro Tour Columbus. Playing a mono-black deck designed by early innovator Adam Maysonet around the powerful card-advantage engine Necropotence, he reached the finals, together with a friend. That qualified both players for the far-flung tournament, so the pair decided to split the airfare portion of the prize. Råde then twisted the arm of his local store (where he had worked unpaid all year) for the other half. Then, he readied himself – as much as any 17-year-old readies themselves for anything – for a trip to a far-off land to play cards.

Råde made it to Columbus unscathed, but the same could not be said for the rest of the Swedish contingent. Severe delays forced them to miss the start of the tournament, leaving the teenager, on his first trip to America, battling in the Masters section by himself. The fearless young Swede had chosen to play in the older age bracket, rather than the Juniors, to be with friends now stranded in an airport somewhere. With a dose of Scandinavian stoicism, Råde shrugged his shoulders and got on with playing *Magic*, just as he did every other day of his life. After a friendly opening match against Canadian Peter

Radonjic, he began to relax and decided to enjoy his American adventure, whatever happened in the tournament.

Despite losing his opener to Radonjic, Råde settled into an unflappable rhythm and began to rack up wins. He lost only one further match that day and made the cut for the tournament's second day. As the 'Little Viking', as he was immediately dubbed, continued to do well, his expectations started to grow. Having hoped to make day two – and done so – Råde began wondering if he could perhaps win a little money. As the wins continued on day two, he began to wonder if he could win enough to buy a copy of his then favourite card, the pricey *Arabian Nights* rare Juzam Djinn. Then, as he lost only once more in the regular Swiss-pairings portion of the tournament (where players are matched against opponents with identical records), he began to believe he could win enough to buy four Juzam Djinns – he was on a roll!

By a stroke of luck, so was his first-round opponent. Råde ended up playing Radonjic three times in total during the course of the tournament as the pair's fortunes became intertwined. Råde lost on day one, beat Radonjic on day two and then faced the Canadian again in the semi-finals. The quiet teenager won through here, too, to reach the final, but cemented a friendship that has lasted to this day. Råde's biggest take-away from the tournament, though, was something more tangible. Smashing everyone's expectations, the Gothenburg teenager beat Sean Fleischman in the final, to become the first non-American to win a Pro Tour. He received a cheque for $22,000 in the process, a slight disappointment to the young player who had imagined he might somehow be awarded the cash immediately. The Juzam Djinns would have to wait for his return to Sweden, where his slightly concerned parents were also waiting for news of just what he was up to.

"For some reason, I just forgot to call home," says Råde, who also admits he was less than crystal clear to his parents about where he was going for the weekend. "I don't think my mum even knew that I was in the US!" he says. Eventually, the Rådes called up Wizards of the Coast to explain that they thought their son might be playing in a big tournament – and could they perhaps find out how he was doing. "He won!" came the reply – a great shock for the worried but very proud parents. When Råde returned home to face the music, having celebrated with a big meal in the US with the Swedish players who did eventually make it to Columbus, he found himself feted by his family and friends. In fact, a summer news drought meant that he even made it on to the front page of the newspaper where his father worked – as the young Swedish star taking on the world's best, in a global gaming phenomenon.

ONE MONTH LATER, the 1996 World Championships – now incorporated into the Pro Tour calendar – were held at Wizards headquarters in Seattle. Anticipation was suitably fevered in the build-up and many expected Mark Justice to claim the title that would rubber-stamp his status as the best on the planet. The invitation-only tournament pitted 125 players against each other, using a skill-testing mixture of three different formats, for the chance to win $26,000 – as well as bragging rights and a place in the rapidly expanding *Magic* history books.

As the tournament shook out, Justice did maintain his impressive form, reaching the final against an unknown Australian player by the name of Tom Chanpheng. This would, most assumed, be a walkover for the home-grown hero, who turned up to play the match in a suitably grandiose three-piece suit. But fate had other ideas for Justice, who most observers believe threw away the finals.

Råde, meanwhile, had also kept up his streak and had reached the semi-finals to finish fourth. The high finish meant he accumulated further ranking points for professional play – so-called 'Pro Points' – which, together with those he had earned in winning Pro Tour Columbus, propelled him to number one in the professional standings at the end of the first-ever Pro Tour season. Much to his surprise, he was awarded *Magic*'s inaugural Pro Player of the Year Award, a title he hadn't even known existed. It earned him Pro Tour invites and travel and accommodation for the following season, which meant he would extend his break from high school by another 12 months (not that his supportive parents minded) and garner a little more of the stardust being sprinkled on the newly famous ranks of *Magic* pros.

In contrast, Justice, having reached the finals, had done just about enough to maintain his stellar reputation. But with competition intensifying and pressure building (some self-imposed, some not) to be top dog of the new *Magic* landscape, Justice was at a crossroads. The direction he took startled everybody.

CHAPTER SEVENTEEN

...and Villains

MORMONISM IS A Protestant sect whose guiding doctrine, the *Book of Mormon*, was written by 19th-century prophet Joseph Smith Junior. Smith claimed to have found buried golden tablets containing the book's text with the help of angelic guidance and translated and transcribed their meaning into his work. His followers grew in number, but facing persecution in their native New York, were forced to relocate. At each turn, they faced yet more confrontation, until, following Smith's death in 1844 at the hands of a mob, a large number settled peacefully in Utah. There, they gave birth to sons and daughters and raised them in their faith, until one day in 1970 a boy named Mark Justice was born to them.

In accordance with Mormon teachings – in particular a commandment called the Word of Wisdom – Justice grew up abstaining from substances that could pollute his body, including tea, coffee, tobacco, alcohol and illegal drugs. Similarly, he married young and within the faith, as recommended by the Mormon Church's teachings. But something was eating away at Justice and though he did his best to conform to his family's, and to his community's, expectations, he could no longer believe in the teachings that ruled every aspect of his life. One day, when he showed his young wife his new hobby, *Magic*, she was distraught. "Mark," she told him. "You have brought the devil into this house."

Magic may not have been the cause of Mark Justice's problems, but it appears to have been a catalyst. This wonderful game, so gleefully mastered by the wholesome man from Salt Lake City, provided him with a tantalising glimpse of a community to which he wanted to belong. But at the same time, it placed him under pressure he was woefully ill-equipped to cope with. The certainties he had been brought up on began to erode at a startling rate. "As *Magic* was occurring," says Justice, "that whole world of mine shattered." Stepping out of the confines of his strict upbringing seemed to light a fire in Justice – as if he were suddenly consumed by a realisation that he had been cheated. That the values he had been brought up on had somehow hindered rather than helped him. As if he had, until then, been living out his life as someone he was not. Wrecked by the disharmony inside him, there was only one path left open to the raging Justice. He had been brought to a precipitous point by his meteoric rise. Now, to dig out who he really might be, he began to tear down the person everyone thought he was and who he was sick of being. As the Pro Tour really kicked into gear, Justice says, "I began to self-destruct."

Concretely, that meant a painful divorce that would represent Justice's break with the Mormon faith. At the same time, he was travelling ever further afield to play *Magic* – and trying to win not cash, but acceptance and self-esteem in the process. Wizards had made no secret of their desire to see him do well – and although the Pro Tour was the only thing Justice felt he could rely on for structure at the time, the need to perform was also sapping his desire to play. Instead of playing for the love of competition, he felt like he had to do well, to justify the faith others were placing in him. He says he was naive at the time and thought being the face of the Pro Tour would be great. But quickly that turned into a nightmare as the public spotlight revealed the extent of the personal problems he was having. The wide world and its temptations provided Justice with the tonic he thought he needed to soothe his woes – but it also provided him the means to fulfil his subconscious desire to tear himself apart. Beneath the glare of the cameras, the other players, the fans watching at home, and of the Wizards staff who had placed their hopes in him, he began to indulge in ever-greater quantities of drugs and alcohol. By the end of the first Pro Tour season, he was perched at the top of a slippery slope. His fall would be long and excruciating.

*   *   *

As MUCH AS Wizards wanted a hero like Justice to front the Pro Tour, they were also aware of the value a good villain can have when it comes to selling a compelling sporting narrative. While they might have been conflicted about whether they should go out of their way to create one – in the manner professional wrestling might, for example – they eventually accepted that should a bad boy appear on the scene, they would harness his reputation for their promotional needs. What they might not have expected, however, is just how bad that bad boy would be – and how gleefully he would take to the role of Pro Tour villain. If Mark Justice appeared – at least outwardly – to be the Luke Skywalker of the piece, Mike Long would be its Emperor – ambitious, fiendish and larger-than-life.

WHAT APPEARS TO have driven Long on, was a burning desire for the kind of status that Justice enjoyed in *Magic*'s early years. He, too, wanted to be regarded as the best on the planet and, as it transpired, he was not afraid to put noses out of joint on his quest for recognition (if not adulation). He was by all accounts a brilliant player and a wildly creative deck-builder. But he quickly polarised Pro Tour fans with a brand of gamesmanship *Magic* has scarcely seen since. Long was not alone in taking advantage of ill-defined rules for tournament behaviour and less-than-rigorous policing by the volunteer judges who were still learning to get to grips with high-stakes *Magic*. But at times he veered into excess, in a way that would forever besmirch his reputation. He was eventually banned by the DCI for one month in 2000 for failing to present a sufficiently randomised deck, but had also aroused officials' suspicions on two previous occasions. First, at the US Nationals in 1998, he was found with a key card from his deck in his lap. Then, at Pro Tour Los Angeles in 2000, he was given a warning for improper shuffling. Fellow players complained bitterly about his behaviour and the inexperience of the judges on hand.

While others who prospered in the grey areas of early professional *Magic* did so discreetly and slipped out of the game with their reputations intact, Long was so happy to revel in his bad-boy image that every move he made was scrutinised for skulduggery. Besides, it was hard to miss him. Often, he would sit with his feet perched on his chair, rocking back and forth (perhaps surreptitiously leaning forward for a sneak glance at his opponent's hand), babbling endlessly in a loud voice, shouting to people across the room – in short, doing everything he could to get inside the head of the player across the table from him. If he could ruin their concentration, it was easy to snatch a win.

Long quickly became a compelling part of the Pro Tour – someone fans and detractors wanted to watch in equal measure – and who unquestionably made tournaments more exciting. Even Justice, who makes no secret of the animosity that existed between the two at the time, concedes that Long played a vital role in hooking *Magic* fans to the Pro Tour. "Competitive events are better when Mike Longs are part of them," he says. "Having people to root against creates passion. And although I don't think he was much fun to be around on a personal level, he was wonderful for *Magic* in those early days."

Numerous early pros were guilty of subtle transgressions, be it fiddling with the dice they used to track their life points, sneakily drawing or concealing an extra card, or leaning in close to an opponent's hand to deduce its contents from minute printing differences on the cards' backs before opaque protective sleeves became commonplace. But it was the nonchalance with which Long greeted rumours of such behaviour that created his legend. While everyone was busy trying to see if he was cheating, he could apply his excellent play skill to win against a distracted opponent. In essence, Mike Long was playing a game that extended far beyond the cards laid out on the table, a liminal one, pushing at the boundaries of the acceptable because it was inherent to his own vision of gaming. He appeared to derive as much satisfaction from playing with the assumptions and laws of the community as he did playing the game (of *Magic*), which opponents thought they were sitting down to play with him. He was, simply put, winning at his own personal metagame. And *Magic* fans, as well as the Pro Tour organisers, lapped it up. "I am the world's number one Mike Long fan," says Skaff Elias, before comparing him to baseball's notorious Ty Cobb, a player once described as, "daring, to the point of dementia."

The high point of Long's career came in April 1997 at Pro Tour Paris, the first Pro Tour to be held outside the United States. Long was playing a complex 'combo' deck of his own design. The idea of a combo – or combination deck – is, as the name suggests, to assemble a combination of cards that together will outright win the game. Instead of having, say, a variety of answers to an opponent's threats like a defensive control deck, or trying to overrun an opponent with a swarm of quick creatures like an 'aggro' deck, combo decks tend to have a very clear and linear plan – to draw or find the cards they need to win, while protecting them from opposing disruption. Long's deck for Pro Tour Paris is largely credited as being the first combo deck with the necessary resilience to win big tournaments, where the high variance in combo strategies often reveals itself over the course of so many rounds: for every game you assemble your deadly combo and just win, there will be other games you draw all the wrong cards and, being such a linear deck, cannot meaningfully disrupt your opponent in the meantime. Long's deck, built around the enchantments Squandered Resources and Cadaverous Bloom, aimed to generate incredible amounts of mana before killing its opponent with Drain Life, a black sorcery whose potential as a finisher had first been exploited by playtester Charlie Catino during *Magic*'s earliest days at the University of Pennsylvania. If fuelled by enough black mana, Drain Life can kill an opponent in one fell swoop – much like a black Fireball.

The deck, dubbed 'Pros-Bloom' because it also used blue spell Prosperity to draw cards, was testament to Long's deck-building genius. Accordingly, it swept him to the finals where he faced none other than Mark Justice. In a quirk of history, Justice was playing a deck he had borrowed from Long in the queue to register for the event. With his divorce ongoing and his home life falling apart, he had had to be talked into attending the event by Wizards' Mark Rosewater. Packing zero cards for the trip (and with absolutely no preparation under his belt), he originally intended to take a trip to Paris at Wizards' expense and find solace hanging out with his Pro Tour friends.

He might not have counted Long among that group, but nonetheless, they decided to split the winnings for first and second prize before playing the final, with an extra $500 to go to the eventual winner. While that meant Justice played in a relaxed and sometimes slapdash manner, it did not detract from Long's desire to win at any cost. Here, after all, was his chance to topple the man whose crown he desperately wanted, by beating him in person, regardless of their deal, something viewers or readers at home would know nothing about.

With Justice lulled into believing that the final would be played out in relatively casual fashion, Long went for the jugular, deploying his typically audacious gamesmanship. His deck was constructed in such a way that it would win, once the combo had been established, by casting Drain Life. But because the actual kill card was only needed right at the death, Long included only one in the deck. Rather than draw redundant copies when they were not needed, Long relied on card-drawing effects to grab the singleton copy only once all the other necessary combo pieces were in place. This was a risky design choice and unusual for the time. And it caught Justice off-guard.

In game one of their best-of-five final, Long miscalculated as he attempted his one big killer turn. Forced to remove Drain Life from the game to generate mana with his Cadaverous Bloom, Long's plans fizzled and he was unable to assemble the rest of his combo. But, because he had willingly ditched his Drain Life, Justice was tricked into thinking Long must have more than one copy in the deck.

Having noticed Justice's mistake, Long toyed with his rival in the remaining games. In game two, as Long began to assemble his combo, he summoned all his braggadocio to convince Justice it was not worth their time for him to go through the required iterations and – yawn – conclude the tedious business of actually killing him. Wouldn't it be better if Justice just conceded so they could move on to the next game? Justice did. And the incessantly babbling Long smirked at his free win.

Later, before game four, Long went even further. In a breathtakingly audacious move, he switched the Drain Life out of his deck into his sideboard. He now had no way to kill Justice. But having seen the ease with which he had drawn a concession from his opponent, he thought he could do it again. This time though, Justice raced to a win, to set up a deciding game five. Here, Long put his kill card back into his deck and set up his combo. As he was doing so, he showboated, flashing the Drain Life to Justice. He then took an agonising amount of time to play out his win, gradually revealing the entire contents of his deck to show Justice that all along, he had had just that one killer card. It was an excruciating end to the final and a sadistic conclusion to the pair's rivalry. Long was crowned Pro Tour Paris champion.

While Justice says that, with the money already split, he was not playing with his usual rigour, Paris was symbolic of a worrying change in mindset for the would-be champ. Upon his return to the US, he moved up to Seattle to freelance for Wizards and escape his crumbling home life. In effect though, he was giving up on *Magic*. "I moved to Seattle about a month after Pro Tour Paris," says Justice. "After that, I never attacked the game with the same seriousness again."

Instead, attracted to the hedonistic party scene based around Seattle University, Justice sunk his efforts into a relentless charge towards the bottom. Imbued with a misguided sense of his own indestructibility – gleaned from his early rise in *Magic* – he emptied bottle after bottle of booze into himself, began playing every tournament fried on acid and topped it all off with the occasional cocaine binge. It was a giant 'fuck you!' to the Word of Wisdom, but a miserable descent into the black for one of the *Magic* community's smartest and most engaging personalities. "There was no limit to the amount I would drink," says Justice. "I wanted to be drunk. I don't know if I was an alcoholic during this time – or how you might define it – but I had a problem. And with drugs on top of that, I was spinning out of control."

Justice's self-inflicted nosedive soon led to him aping the worst kind of behaviour in the *Magic* big leagues. One notorious incident took place at Grand Prix Atlanta in March 1998. Grand Prix were the second-tier of *Magic* tournaments in Wizards' organised-play pyramid, large open events where Joe Public could duke it out with the pros for the top prizes on offer – including cash, Pro Tour invites and Pro Points. In Atlanta, though, Justice was less than the hero fans might have been hoping to come up against. Blasted out of his mind on cocaine and no longer listening to the rational part of his brain, he made a decision he regrets to this day – and which tarnished his reputation forever.

In the Draft portion of the tournament, where players take turns to select cards from Booster Packs passed around a table of eight players until they have assembled enough for a deck, Justice drafted several copies of a powerful creature called Muscle Sliver.

Muscle Sliver gives all other 'sliver' creatures +1/+1. As the bonus is cumulative the more copies of the card you have in play, its impact is improved the more of them you have. Ideally then, a deck playing with the card would play as many copies as possible. The deck Justice registered to play with at the conclusion of drafting contained an impressive four. When a judge checked his deck, however, he noticed that one of the four copies of the card was clearly from a different print run to the other three. Justice claimed he had indeed drafted four copies of the card but accidentally thrown one away. He told the judge he had then bought a replacement from one of the traders in the room to replace the one he lost. The judge asked Justice if he would come with him and search the trashcans in the room to prove his story – and when Justice declined to, he was disqualified for cheating. With Justice refusing to fess up to his crimes, he muddled on with a cloud of doubt hanging over his name for the rest of his playing career, one that has been enough to keep him from ever being selected by *Magic*'s great and good for the Hall of Fame. Since the Hall of Fame's inception in 2005 both he and Long have remained its most notable exiles.

What really happened that day? Speaking publicly about the incident for the first time, Justice says he had become disinterested in Grand Prix. To him, they had become as meaningful as playing at the kitchen table. Filled with chemically assisted cockiness, he was following no-one's rules but his own. "I remember drafting three Muscle Slivers," he says. "And whatever triggered the idea, I just thought it would be really fun to have a fourth." He approached a local card dealer at the event to buy a fourth and it is this dealer who, in all probability, alerted the event judges to Justice's purchase. Certainly, it seems the player was beyond caring, beyond even trying to hide the deceit. He cheated, and was caught fair and square. The halo hovering over him when he had arrived at Pro Tour New York two and a half years previously was shattered.

"Looking back at that incident, I think it shows just how unhappy I was with myself on a lot of different levels," says Justice today. "I was not making good decisions in any area of my life. And I paid the price for that." For one, that means forever being mentioned in the same breath as Mike Long when cheating allegations are discussed – something that Justice dislikes but accepts comes with the territory. Having shown himself capable of cheating once, all of his *Magic* achievements have been cast into doubt. And though he has no way to defend himself, he has learned to live with the *Magic* community's aspersions. Today he is a father. And would rather explain to his children what mistakes he made and why, rather than covering anything up.

Those mistakes persisted for a while. And one by one, Justice burned nearly all his bridges in the community that had meant more to him than anything. The most painful aspect for Justice would be leaving the Pacific Coast Legends and the friendship of players like Mark Chalice, with whom he had conquered so many early tournaments; shared so many wonderful experiences. Wizards, too – despite trying hard to give Justice advice and to help him out of his funk – eventually could take no more of him and stopped offering him work. Justice says he was acting like a jerk. He was no longer an asset to the company. The rise to the top of *Magic* and his fall from those dizzy heights cost Justice everything. Looking back, it still fills him with sadness. "My one last word of wisdom," he says, "is for anyone who gets caught up in the making money, the competitive thing: the relationships you build in those times are far more important than the wins and losses that occur. Always try and climb the mountain, always try and win any tournament you enter, but doing so at the expense of the relationships you have built will leave you with regrets for the rest of your life."

A little over a year on from Grand Prix Atlanta, Justice left Seattle and began drifting around the US. When his money ran out, he crashed finally, blissfully to rock bottom. He was a penniless former hero, burned out and broken. It was a full-stop at the end of a turbulent passage in his life, that saw him overwhelmed by the freedom he had found for himself. He had desperately torn down the world around him, throwing out the good with the bad in a drunken rage and substance-fuelled hubris. It was the bitter end of a card-slinging Icarus. He has not played *Magic* since.

CHAPTER EIGHTEEN
The Best There Ever Was

As Olle Råde had shown, there was no shortage of candidates willing to take up the mantel of 'best player in the world,' in those early, formative Pro Tour years – especially once it slipped so decisively from Mark Justice's troubled shoulders. Still, it was a source of anxiety for Wizards to see the Pro Tour as famous for its bad boy antics, unsporting behaviour and meteoric burnouts as it was for its skill or exemplary heroes. While the game's professionalisation brought with it the inevitable side-effects of letting a bunch of young guys (because it was predominantly guys) off the leash, flying them round the world and throwing money at them, what it initially failed to produce was a generation of 'professionals' in sprit, rather than just name. For that, a little time was needed – for players to reach their prime who had grown up within the new structures and strictures of high-level organised play. For whom the Pro Tour naturally existed as the pinnacle of the game – rather than as a brand-new proving ground for the settling of scores between local scenes or, in some regards, between *Magic* players and a society from which they had felt outcast. Before they could – thanks to the Pro Tour's prize money – prove the value of being smart.

It was something that one young man – no more than a boy really, when the Pro Tour began – had always struggled to prove. He grew up feeling marginalised, awkward and lonely and was brutally bullied for his fiercely burning intelligence, puppy fat, thick glasses and untameable hair. His mother was a maths teacher and his dad was a computer programmer and together they had raised him to be as agile with numbers as they both were. Too agile for the students he found himself in class with. Too clever sometimes even for his teachers' tastes. Growing up, he felt perpetually like a fish out of water and today uses the word 'pariah' to describe his younger self. In 1996, he played in the Junior portion of the very first Pro Tour. By 1998, he was Player of the Year. By 2000, he was World Champion. His name was Jon Finkel.

FINKEL SPENT MOST of his childhood in New Jersey, with his mum, dad and sister, steeped in a brain-boosting home environment. His cerebral parents coached him intensely and encouraged him to speak his mind. While that might have been a perfectly legitimate parenting recipe, it soon found its limits once Finkel hit puberty. School went from being somewhere where the bright and brash could thrive, to somewhere where the quiet and conformist prospered. In the world of American secondary education, their role was to provide the perfectly mundane backdrop for the athletically gifted to stand out from. It was not an enriching environment for a smart aleck – however smart he may have been. In fact, it quickly became hell for Finkel as the cold shoulder from classmates mutated into physical beatings, day after miserable day. Before long, the young Finkel had started to pile on the pounds, grow his hair into a thick matted mess and disguise himself in baggy, black clothes, in a frustrated outward attempt to embrace his painful otherness. But it did not help. The bullying continued (in one episode his tormentors even urinated on him) and before long, he was playing sick in a last-ditch attempt to avoid the humiliating, hateful schoolyard. "To this day," says Finkel, "I don't have a single friend I made at high school."

In late 1993, Finkel's father Mark was transferred in his job at the British Oxygen Company to work in Woking in the UK. He took his family with him across the pond to the strange and unfamiliar island. While it might have offered a reprieve and a fresh start to the young Finkel, any hopes he had of walking into an environment more forgiving of his eccentricity were quickly dashed at his new (and very posh) school, the local branch of TASIS – The American School in Switzerland. The 15-year-old newcomer, uprooted and alone, was made to feel 'welcome' with variations on the same taunts he had hoped to leave behind on the other side of the Atlantic. Not long after arriving, he found himself sat at the back of the classroom, scribbling a list in his notebook entitled, *10 reasons to not commit suicide.*

Thankfully, though his list might not have been overflowing with entries, Finkel did find one very important one. One evening, while riding his bike home from school, a faded storefront caught his eye. In a moment of serendipity, the depressed but curious Finkel dismounted for a closer look. The shop was called Fun and Games and lurking inside at the back was a group of guys not too dissimilar from himself. Hunched over a table, they seemed to be playing some kind of card game and welcomed Finkel to join them. It was the first time in a long while that anyone had extended the hand of friendship to the teenage outcast. Only too gladly, he set about learning *Magic*, the game that would change his life.

BEFORE LONG, THE lists Finkel were writing at the back of the classroom were ideas for decks, rather than reasons to keep on keeping on. He became obsessed with *Magic*'s elegant mechanics, captivating gameplay and the chance it gave him to win. Finally, he had found an outlet for people like him, who wanted to compete with their brains, rather than their bodies. The company of people with whom he had something in common was a novelty and the crowd at the back of Fun and Games made the rest of his time in the UK that bit more bearable.

When his family returned to suburban New Jersey in 1995, Finkel knew his priority would be to find local opponents against whom he could refine his burgeoning *Magic* skills. Forced to return to the school he had always hated for his final year of high school, the need to seek out card-playing buddies became urgent – and forced Finkel to a game store a train-ride away in New York. That store was Neutral Ground and it quickly became Finkel's sanctuary from the ongoing ordeal of school. So addicted to *Magic* was he by this point, that he would often crash on the benches of nearby Pennsylvania Station rather than return home, so he could be first through the doors at Brian David-Marshall's shop to play in the daily tournaments there. It did not take long for Finkel to become a fixture at the store – and make a lasting impression on its owner. "There was a time when we didn't realise how much skill was involved in *Magic*," says David-Marshall. "We would run a Sealed

Deck tournament every morning – which we thought was even more devoid of skill – and Jon Finkel won it every single time." Sealed Deck tournaments involve players opening sealed product and building their decks on the spot with the contents. In the game's early days, the common misconception was that success in the format was down to getting lucky and opening the 'best' cards, rather than methodical deck construction. "We had no idea how he was doing it – was he cheating? – so we went and watched him," says David-Marshall. "And that was the first moment we realised just how terrible at *Magic* we really were. Jon was amazing. And immediately stood out as a singular talent."

It was no surprise then, that once the Pro Tour rumbled into motion a year later, the 17-year-old Finkel wanted in. Today, he lives only a half-dozen blocks away from the venue for that inaugural tournament (the handsomely restored Puck Building). But back in 1996, it felt like stepping into a new world – one in which Finkel could prove that, whatever his physical and social clumsiness, his mental game was the sharpest out there. He duly top-eighted the Juniors section and headed home with a $1,000 scholarship in his back pocket. It was enough to convince his parents to pay for him to travel to Los Angeles for the second Pro Tour – and ultimately kick-start the career of one of *Magic*'s most emblematic players.

That career continued to burgeon in the Junior division for the first Pro Tour season until the 1996 World Championships at which Finkel stepped up to the Masters age group for the first time. As Mark Justice made his run to the finals to keep his reputation as the game's best player alive for another tournament, Finkel ambushed the field to finish ninth. It was another neat achievement for his steadily growing *palmarès* and another three grand for his wallet. The outsize New Jersey nerd was growing in stature and the Pro Tour was taking notice. Finkel was becoming some player – one whose talent for the game of *Magic* felt innate, as if the game had been perfectly designed for the strange skill set he had inherited from his parents. He was able to think brilliantly on the fly, calculate the game's probable pathways in an instant and make winning decisions in a snap. What is more, he was strangely unfazed by the Pro Tour's pressure – as if the competitive environment was what he had been looking for his whole life. "I was never very methodical," says Finkel, appraising his skills today. "But I just had very good intuition and, in my brain, a very fast processor. I'm sure I'm not always the best at thinking things through a ton – but if you want somebody to make a decision really quickly based on incomplete information, for some reason, that's what I'm good at." In Richard Garfield's creation, a give and take of information, a guessing game where each player must anticipate what cards might be hidden in their opponent's hand, it proved a distinct advantage.

Finkel's performances kept improving. In the Pro Tour's second season, spanning 1996 to 1997, he became a consistent presence at the top tables, racking up three Top-16 finishes during the course of the year (while also abandoning college to devote all his energies to the game). While things on the home front became complicated – Finkel's parents divorced and his dad forced him to get a part-time job at Domino's Pizza – his decision would be vindicated as soon as the Pro Tour's third season rolled around. Deploying all his unnerving intuition, improved maturity and mental fortitude, Finkel made his breakthrough at Pro Tour Chicago in October 1997, cracking the Top 8 for the very first time. It was a huge moment for the young up-and-comer. Here was the confirmation, in the season's very first event, of what Finkel might achieve if he put his considerable talents to work. No more the victim, he was pocketing thousands of dollars for playing *Magic* and, he suspected, the best might be yet to come.

Finkel was not alone in that conviction. Another player had noticed his performances and was sure that this was the guy who deserved a tag he was desperate to lose. That player was Mark Justice – by now on the downward spiral that would end in his ruin – a man, who could only ruefully reflect on what the label of 'best player in the world' had done to him. *Uneasy lies the head that wears the crown*, wrote William Shakespeare in *Henry IV* – and Justice had proved every inch *Magic*'s tragic king, overwhelmed by his own legend and publicly imploding under the pressure. He sure as hell did not want that to happen to his successor. And thus at Pro Tour Mainz in December 1997, as he was puking his guts up over a toilet bowl, drunk as usual, he was struck by a moment of clarity. As Finkel edged past him to use the bathroom, a bleary eyed Justice looked up at the boy he could see was ready to be the best in the world and said simply, "Jon, don't let this happen to you." It was a moment that would stay with both of them. For Finkel, it was confirmation of his destiny. For Justice, it was a moment he could think back on with something approaching pride as he tried to reconstruct his life in the following years, knowing he was capable of recognising his own debilitating problems.

With Justice's drunken wisdom ringing in his ears, Finkel continued his charge up the professional rankings. His next significant milestone came in Rio, at the turn of the year, winning a Grand Prix there in January. Then came the big one – his first ever Pro Tour win in April 1998 – back in New York, back where his Pro Tour journey had begun. This time, he was no kid, and despite the intimidation of an old *Magic* sparring partner David Bachmann, who liked to pick on Finkel as much as anyone at school had done, he won through. The Bachmanns on the Pro Tour were becoming a dying breed as players wanted not only to win – but to prove that the game was more than just cheats, loudmouths and bores. With his mother watching on, on the closed circuit TV by now being used to screen the finals to hordes of Pro Tour spectators, Finkel ended their grip on power with an emotional, cathartic win. This was a sea change on the Pro Tour – the arrival of its first 'professional', a player whose attitude and skill fulfilled that description, as much as his prize money. After the false hopes (like Mark Justice) and the bad boys (like Mike Long), here was the champion that Wizards had been hoping for when they devised the Pro Tour. The crowds in New York cheered his name with glee. This was their hero, too – 'Finkeltron', a *Magic*-playing machine, a triumphant underdog and, under that messy exterior, a truly decent guy. By the end of the season, he was raising the trophy as Player of the Year. A team victory with the US at the World Championships in the summer was the icing on the cake. Finkel really was the best player on the planet.

IF FINKEL'S RISE to the top indicated *Magic*'s establishment as an intellectual sport, played by gamers worthy of the professional tag, it seems only natural that it should also give rise to an epoch-defining rivalry. No great champion can exist in isolation. There must always be a tussle, a struggle, a point of comparison that marks out that champion's success as truly great. Sporting history throws up plenty of examples – football's endless Lionel Messi versus Cristiano Ronaldo debate, the high-octane rivalry between Formula 1's Ayrton Senna and Alain Prost, the bitter feud between Mohammed Ali and Joe Frazier, and so on. The rivalry (a gaming rather than personal one) which followed Finkel's early success had much in common with all these three examples – not simply because it defined an era, but because it could legitimately be said to define its field for all time, too. Two heavyweights, two brilliant careers, two players who will always be mentioned in the same breath when the question arises: "Who is the best *Magic* player of all time?"

Back at Pro Tour Mainz, while Finkel sidestepped the drunken Justice, a young German player by the name of Kai Budde was making his full Pro Tour debut. Budde, born and bred in Cologne, also had a maths teacher parent (his dad) and had quickly developed an aptitude for *Magic*, having discovered the game via friends. He mastered it with the help of a clique of hugely talented local players, including Frank Adler, who in September 1996 in Atlanta, had become the first German to win a Pro Tour.

Budde was a competitive young man with a burning will to win. He had originally hoped to become a professional footballer and boasted the square shoulders, set jaw and cropped hair of someone who had drilled four times a week and played every weekend, from the age of 11. But when injuries struck in his late teens and reaching the Bundesliga looked like a futile dream, he was left with a nagging void in his life. His competitive streak screamed for an outlet. And it was *Magic* that helped provide it. The game gave the methodical and driven German a new challenge when he urgently needed one. He launched himself at it with relish.

Together with his slightly older friend Dirk Baberowski, who was studying in Cologne, he began to hone his *Magic* skills. On an almost daily basis, Budde would join Baberowksi for a regular university kickabout. Then the pair would head to the local game store to work on their other sport. It was a fruitful partnership and when Baberowski won Pro Tour Chicago in September 1998, the pair knew they were on to something. Their methods, their understanding of the game and their play skill were as good as anyone's out there – and Budde knew from his testing with Baberowski that his turn must surely come. And verily it did.

As the new season kicked off in the autumn of 1998, Budde hit top gear, using a series of European Grand Prix as a springboard to the next level. He finished second at Grand Prix Birmingham in the UK in October. Then, kicking the opposition to the kerb with almost unprecedented ease, he added a whirlwind three Grand Prix titles to his trophy cabinet in the following six months. It was a startling sequence of results that represented the rise of a new *Magic* powerhouse. Budde was clinical, flattening opponents like a rampaging striker on the football pitch. He quickly earned the nickname, 'The German Juggernaut' and, despite less Pro Points being on offer at the 'pro-am' Grand Prix events, Budde's streak of top finishes fired him into sudden and unexpected contention for the Player of the Year title.

Finkel, meanwhile, was blossoming as a person and investing some of his winnings in himself. Given a burst of self-esteem by his success, he began a gradual transformation in the Jon he was showing to the world. Off went the specs for contact lenses, in the bin went the baggy black clothes and, most dramatically of all, off went a few pounds, too. Skaff Elias, mentor to the Pro Tour tyros, had encouraged Finkel to take part in post-tournament basketball games and showed him he had nothing to fear anymore from a little physical exercise. That in turn encouraged Finkel to head to the gym to begin shedding the lumbering, soft body he had been hiding away in since his teens. It was a truly cathartic time for the young champion and a sign of the change the Pro Tour could foster in the lives of its players.

As real life seemed to open up to Finkel, his hunger for *Magic* glory abated in the 1998-1999 season. He had had his head turned – by a return to his studies, by his social life and, it would turn out, by another card game entirely – and he felt, that after his glorious 1997-1998 season, he had little left to prove. Still, almost nonchalantly, he rattled off impressive performances – a Grand Prix win and two further Pro Tour Top 8s, even as Budde chased him down in the professional rankings. It was precisely the casual nature of Finkel's success that seemed to fuel his legend. Here he was, taking his foot off the gas, yet still seeing deeper into the game than many of his peers, thinking more turns ahead and identifying audacious lines of play that only he could make work. It was captivating stuff and, with a contender rising in Europe, made the Pro Tour compelling for all the right reasons.

Ultimately though, Finkel's casual brilliance could only take him so far. At the World Championships in Tokyo that summer, the German Juggernaut steamrollered into town. Playing an artifact-heavy mono-red deck built around the powerful creature Covetous Dragon, Budde slaughtered the opposition in a devastating run to the final. There, in a then record quick time of only 20 minutes, he won a one-sided best-of-five match against America's

Mark le Pine to seal his first Pro Tour victory, the World Championship title and, perhaps most significantly of all, Player of the Year ahead of Jon Finkel. It was a shot across the bows not only for Finkel, but for America and its predominant position in *Magic*. Indeed, the frenzied discussion that would build up in the following years about who was the greatest player of all time, would often take on chauvinistic overtones. It was something that needled Budde as American commentators set him new and unlikely benchmarks to have to reach to match their hero Finkel. But with his usual matter-of-factness, he surpassed them.

The seasons that followed were shaped by an exchange of victories from both sluggers, like punches shipped across the Atlantic between Joe Luis and Max Schmeling, the American and German heavyweights who captivated boxing in the 1930s. Like those two rivals, though, there was never enmity between the two *Magic* players, only respect. In many ways, Budde could not have been more different from Finkel had he tried. Perhaps because of his sporting background, Budde took preparation far more seriously than not only Finkel, but also many of the Pro Tour's hotshot Americans. It was a factor that helped Budde topple them at the business end of tournaments. The diligent German even sought nutritional advice from an unlikely source: two British friends, Ben and Ivan Ronaldson, who were real tennis instructors at Tudor palace Hampton Court in southwest London. In gloriously archaic fashion, they would send him hand-written letters containing not only advice to go easy on the caffeine, but also painstakingly transcribed metagame predictions for forthcoming Pro Tours. Budde meanwhile practiced endlessly online using a rudimentary programme called Apprentice, which allowed players to play a rough version of *Magic* against each other and test out new decks with a hitherto impossible rapidity. Other friends in the Cologne *Magic* scene would scour the Dojo and Usenet for ideas. It was a complex and, in every sense of the word, sober operation. "I never drank much alcohol, that's just not me," says Budde. "Often the Americans would start partying as soon as they had reached the Top 8, head off to anther strip bar and hit a few drinks. I would test the match-up for the final day and go to bed early and I'm sure that made a difference." Indeed it did, as Budde's Top 8 opponents often defeated themselves with tired, hungover blunders.

The numbers stacked up on both sides of the debate: Finkel bounced back with an excellent 2000, for example, winning a Grand Prix, US Nationals, Worlds and the all-star Invitational tournament. Budde riposted with a stunning 2001, which featured an incredible three Pro Tour victories in a row, a feat no-one has come close to matching. Budde also sealed a further three Player of the Year awards – from 2001 to 2003, earning over $300,000 in the process. Finkel was never far behind him – and by the time the two colossuses stepped away from professional *Magic* in 2004, they had altered its landscape forever, catapulting the Pro Tour into a golden age. In total, Finkel clocked up 13 Pro Tour Top 8s in that time, going on to win twice. Budde reached nine Pro Tour Top 8s and converted a stunning seven of those into wins – a record that is likely to stand for many, many years to come. Together, they became the drivers of *Magic*'s evolution as a legitimate intellectual sport, underpinned by the framework that Skaff Elias had dreamt up.

Their success helped re-situate *Magic* cards as something to be played with first and foremost, rather than hoarded. The cut and thrust of their rivalry at the top of the tournament rankings proved that *Magic* – despite the dose of luck occasionally involved in drawing the right cards – was a game of great skill. Its best players could beat not only their opponents but also the hang-ups they had been lumbered with growing up. The Pro Tour was giving players self-belief and an opportunity to be really, really good at something. It affected each and every player taking part. And, quietly, it helped chip away at social preconceptions, too. Once-ridiculed 'nerds' were morphing into self-identifying 'geeks', the gatekeepers of the information age. Their interests, formerly mocked, were drawing grudging admiration at work and at play. Richard Garfield's dream of sports for the mind had become a little less far-fetched with every brilliant tournament win racked up by Finkel and Budde and they became the standard-bearers for a new, more self-confident generation of brainiacs. Budde even remembers being invited as a guest on a sports programme on local TV. In the green room, a swimmer and his coach asked him what he did. When Budde explained, they scoffed. Then Budde told them how much money he had won playing cards. The smiles disappeared from his questioners' faces. The coach turned to his charge and told him, he would have to swim for the rest of his life to earn the same amount.

As Rob Hahn, who had found his own niche with the game's help, puts it: "The Pro Tour transformed a lot of young men's lives for the better. Let's face it: before the Pro Tour, we were a bunch of nerds. The last to be chosen for a sports team. The guys who were going to be picked on in school. Often, people without wealth, privilege or bright futures. But the Pro tour helped players realise not only that they were smart, but also that it was OK to be smart. Especially for younger players, that really gave them a lot of self-confidence. And the best example of that is Jon Finkel." Finkel, now a successful hedge-fund manager, says simply: "I would have been a very different person without it."

In November 2011, Jon Finkel was given a sickening jolt – a reminder of how life had been before he had discovered *Magic*. For one reason or another, the usually compulsive email-checker had gone a few hours without looking at his inbox. Upon getting home from work and flicking on his phone, he was confused by a deluge of mails from friends alerting him to an article that had been posted on design and technology blog Gizmodo by a woman named Alyssa Bereznak. A dreadful sensation of violation gripped Finkel as he logged on to check out what she had written.

In a spectacularly cynical diatribe, Bereznak had detailed a series of dates she had gone on with Finkel (whom she identified by name), having met him via the online dating portal OKCupid. Though the dates may have not been hugely significant to Finkel, they were nonetheless private – and here they were being splashed across the internet, in an article its author proudly trumpeted as 'shallow'. In it, she detailed her horror at discovering that her date was not only a *Magic* player but also a previous World Champion. How could he be so surreptitious to have left the information off his dating profile, to have 'infiltrated' his way into dates with herself and other women, she wondered. *Just like you're obligated to mention you're divorced or have a kid in your online profile, shouldn't someone also be required to disclose any indisputably geeky world championship titles?* she wrote, before blathering, *Mothers, warn your daughters!* It was bullying dressed up as hard-nosed wit – and what is more, an exploitative attempt to piggyback on Finkel's reputation, at which she expressed horror, to embellish her own. Gizmodo's somewhat geeky audience responded with a flood of comments (the story was even picked up by other news outlets, including *Forbes*, the *Washington*

Post and CBS). And, while some of those tipped over into angry attacks, the outpouring of support for Finkel was huge. Where once everyone had joined in with the school bullies raining blows on the boy, they rallied to the man's side in a moment that showed just how much the world – and Finkel – had changed in *Magic*'s lifetime. *Playboy*'s Playmate of the Year Sarah Jean Underwood even tried to get Finkel to go on a televised date with her – an invitation the *Magic* champ politely refused.

Finkel is admirably sanguine about the episode today, pointing out it could have been far worse. However his achievements might have been ridiculed by Bereznak, they turned him into someone far better-equipped to handle the finger-pointing and name-calling life is wont to doll out. "There was a point in my mid- to late-twenties when I realised I hadn't really thought anything bad about myself for a long time," says the man who at school had struggled to compile a list of reasons not to end his own life. "I'm kind of disconnected from my core ego now and if something goes badly, it doesn't impact on how I feel about myself anymore. If someone had written about me like that when I was a teenager or in my early twenties, it would have felt much, much worse." To boot, the sympathetic postings had been a powerful reminder of the strength of the *Magic* community and his place within it. A World Champ at something a striving and vacuous blogger found irredeemably nerdy, he may well be, but says Finkel, "I can't think of another community I'd rather be a part of."

Today, both he and Budde are again part of the *Magic* community, following their inductions into the Hall of Fame and the lifetime Pro Tour invites that go with it. And, although a new generation of pros with more time to practise and more to prove might be giving them a run for their money, both have top-eighted multiple Pro Tours since their return. Finkel even won Pro Tour Kuala Lumpur in 2008, with the same kind of nonchalant excellence that forged his legend, becoming the first Hall of Famer to win a Pro Tour upon his return. The rivalry between the two has given way to a friendship which has even seen the two playtest together before big events. Nowadays, they are two guys with a glorious *Magic* past between them; one that has earned them membership to their own exclusive club: the very best there ever was.

CHAPTER NINETEEN
Gordon, Plum, Spence and Eric

I HAVE NEVER played on the Pro Tour. Never won money with *Magic*. And I have certainly never threatened the status of 'best player in the world'. But speaking to Jon Finkel one evening over a trans-Atlantic Skype connection as the *Magic* celebrity decompresses in his far-off New York apartment, I can't help but feel a wave of empathy well up in me. While Finkel's story is one of extremes – from the bullying he suffered to the spectacular manner in which he overcame it – it is impossible not to feel something in common with him. There is simply, undeniably, a bit of Finkel in all *Magic* players of a certain generation. He is our champion.

Magic helped us to feel better about ourselves, more included in a world upon whose periphery we felt caught. And, even if I lay down my cards, searching for self-esteem up other roads, *Magic* was waiting for me, past twists and turns and forks and dead ends. *Magic* was a reflex. Something learned in a formative emotional context that could not be unlearned when, despite passing years, those emotions and that context would return. Even if the game might have lost some of its sheen in Normandy and I had pushed it aside in an attempt to move on in my life, it would broadside me again. Maybe moving on is itself an illusion. Maybe. Either way, *Magic* surfaced not long after I had parked up the shuddering, muddy, family hatchback for the last time and left home. My Sorbonne dreams had dissipated like the smoke from a limp Gauloise and, wanting to be closer to old friends, I headed for Blighty again.

With my *Baccalauréat* in my back pocket, I had decided to return to

England for university. But having lived abroad, I was told I would not be eligible for a student loan – the main way English students fund their courses. As my parents couldn't afford the tuition fees either, that left me with little choice but to defer my university place and earn the money for school in the only trade I had learned so far: waiting tables in swank restaurants.

For a year then, I ironed tablecloths, polished cutlery, shuttled plates, piloted the cheese trolley, carved at the *guéridon* and danced through the aisles in a Bolero jacket and bow tie; crashing, burning and collapsing into bed every night before undertaking the same performance again the next day. It was exhausting, but inspiring, too. I watched as the chefs prepared exquisite food in the kitchen and could rub shoulders with the suited-and-booted in the dining room. Most importantly, though, it was well paid. And, with every tip earned on every frantic night, the distant utopia of university edged a little closer.

Unfortunately, the intensity of catering jobs means they often have a short shelf life. Money starts to run out. Suppliers' bills begin to pile up. Payday becomes fraught. The chef starts to pin people to the wall, flashing cold steel dangerously close to warm flesh. At some point, when the Michelin inspector has passed you by, the sommelier has started drinking the profits and the staff food has, inevitably, gone to shit, the time comes to throw your apron to the ground and get out while you still can. Having quit a job in Oxford with a spikey-haired loon in the kitchen and his toxic wife front-of-house, I pitched up in Scotland in 2001 with a local friend who had also walked out. We stayed at his parents' place on the Isle of Arran for two restorative weeks, getting up late, walking up mountains, watering in local pubs and occasionally looking for jobs. Our efforts amounted to nothing. So we went to Glasgow to get wretchedly drunk instead.

This proved an epiphany to the 20-year-old me. Raised on a diet of grim provincial nightclubs playing hideous pop hits to shiny shoed Neanderthals, I was finally, gratefully, converted to the wonders of the dance floor. It happened at legendary party Optimo (Espacio), one beautiful, raging Sunday night. Nina Simone's *My Baby Just Cares for Me* poured like honey from the throbbing speakers between two crunching techno tunes. I kissed some delicious local lass. And, for a moment, I was transported to the bliss that smoke and lasers and records spinning in their judgement-free circles can create, far beyond the drudgery of daily life. On the way home, I bought Irn Bru in a big, cold, glass bottle. There was, I figured, no better place to be.

As chance would have it, Scottish firebrand and chef Gordon Ramsay had just opened up in town, too. His restaurant was looking for competent waiters, so I pitched up at the door the next day, clutching my CV. I parlayed myself into an immediate start, found a friend of a friend to crash with (an alcoholic, amateur pornographer and drummer called Plum) and was suddenly an honorary Glaswegian. The hours were ridiculous. My living conditions were terrible. (A paralytic Plum would bring home strangers to drum with before breaking down in floods of tears, normally a couple of hours before I had to start the breakfast shift. Once, he threw the wok through the kitchen window.) But the city was unlike anywhere I had ever lived; a vibrant, greasy assault on my country-mouse sensibilities.

Though any free Sunday nights were spent thrashing at Optimo, in the rest of my limited free time, I got lonely. I was shy, with what felt like too many imperfections stamped into me at the factory. I worked unsociable shifts. Didn't know anyone in the city or really how to get to know anyone. I was starting to pine for some kind of soulmate in my life, but hell, I would have settled for anyone's company other than Plum's. Drinking pints by myself, propped at the bar of Sauchiehall Street institution Nice N Sleazy just made me miserable. Maybe, I thought, I needed a hobby or something.

One split shift, I was wondering around Glasgow's studenty West End in a clapped-out daze, when a bright yellow storefront caught my eye. The shop in question was a comic and games hotspot, well-stocked in all things geeky. For whatever reason, I ducked inside, intending to buy some miniatures, paints and brushes. Perhaps, I thought, fiddling with toy soldiers for the first time in years would entertain me. It would at least be something I could do by myself; meeting people still impossibly daunting. If nothing else, it would be a shot of retail therapy on a day more cloud than silver lining.

I sidled up to the till with a packet of Space Marines and a few pots of acrylic. A large man named Spence was manning it and we got chatting about gaming. He was, it turned out, a fan of my dad's and had briefly worked with him at Games Workshop. On the spot, he gave me a 15% discount on everything in the store. My eye wondered over the shelves and spotted *Magic* cards, the game apparently still going strong after my break.

With Gordon Ramsay's cash burning a hole in my pocket, a juicy reduction on offer and any responsible notions of saving for uni jettisoned, I pounced. Spence told me they had single cards, too. And very quickly, I was back on the bandwagon, buying cards at discounted prices with the first taste of disposable income in my life. It was a rush. A nostalgic, tongue-in-cheek one at first. But as cards started to accumulate in a box next to my Ikea sofabed at Plum's, an old obsession started to fire in me. Each day off now involved a trek to Spence's shop to make good use of my discount, buying up cards I had never been able to afford in New Zealand. More than playing, I was buying myself happy. But it would do, I told myself, until I made it to the promised land of Bristol University, where everything would surely be better. Where everyone got a fresh start. And where intelligence would trump social class and other tiresome divides in a brainy meritocracy.

Exactly how many seconds it took for my vision of university as a blank slate to die is hard to say. Ten maybe. Although it could have been nine. It was the ranks of freshly polished VW Golfs barfing out haw-hawing, rugby-shirted Londoners that did it. A cosy coterie that had been to school together and probably hunted lower-class pariahs like me on horseback. Now, they were slumming it in Bristol having failed to get into Oxford or Cambridge. It was a miserable sight to greet my arrival. I lugged my stuff from the car of a family friend, with my stomach tied in knots. I said my goodbyes. Began to unpack and Blu-tacked posters to the wall. This was going to be tough. I left my door ajar, playing a Belle and Sebastian CD at conspicuous volume like a forlorn Glaswegian mating call.

I had told myself that *Magic* would be a big part of my life at university. I would use my independence and free time to trek to far-flung tournaments and become a sharper, more competitive player. Finally, I would get to grips with the *Magic* lifestyle that seemed to be bringing satisfaction to so many people – and, which at times, seemed to make me happy, too. That is, when I indulged it. When I let my guard down. When I held my cards between my fingers, forgot to wonder what anyone else might think and just felt OK with everything. I headed out of halls on that first day and went for a walk around town, trying to get a handle on an intimidating new city. At the same time, I was looking for somewhere to play and stumbled on a shop called the Captain's Log.

The Log was a shabby old place, across the road from a multi-story car park, behind a shopping centre that has now been torn down. Peeling red paint flaked from its frontage, metal grills obscured the windows and sun-faded *Star Trek* cut-outs pressed themselves against the glass like prisoners trapped in a sordid nerd fantasy. It wasn't much. But a bloke behind the counter assured me, that buried somewhere in the detritus was a table that people used to play *Magic*. Promising to return at the weekend, I started the trek back to halls and steeled myself for meeting-and-greeting.

I'm not sure how many times I played at Captain's Log before I gave up on *Magic* again. Not with the same deliberation as at school. But with a passive, almost imperceptible letting go. A shelving of cards, rather than a sell-off. For all my initial fears and despite the insecurity gnawing at me, I found a handful of great friends down the sterile, beige corridors of Wills Hall, thriving in the shadow of the hair-gelled and hand-bagged. They gave my confidence a much-needed boost. Told me to go easy on the twee, miserablist indie. And got me out into the real Bristol – a beautiful, colourful, sweat-pit of a city, writhing under a permanent fug of weed smoke and bobbing along to its own haphazard beat. Despite episodes of heartbreak, financial penury and academic underachievement, I found the sense of community I had been looking for. The next couple of years disappeared in a frenzy of dancing, binge-drinking and sexual-mechanical pursuits. And my *Magic* cards didn't get a look in.

Even after leaving New Zealand far behind, I had imagined *Magic* would be the key to unlocking friendships as rewarding as I had discovered there. That it could fill the confines of my life in the way it had done when I was a teenager, despite the horizons of that life growing ever wider and encompassing more interests. Instead, what had bothered me was that *Magic* became a proxy for really meeting people. I was never again in the position I was in, in school, to play with the people I spent the whole day with anyway. That meant *Magic* could be a frustratingly one-dimensional way of getting to know people. Of making '*Magic* friends' instead of genuine friends. That was a feeling that in France (and often later in Berlin) was exacerbated by a language barrier where the banter inherent to sitting down and gaming became too difficult to follow, yet still squeezed out the real-life topics that as an adult you hope to share with friends. Coming into university, an intensely social atmosphere, I became aware of how *Magic* could at times make me feel more isolated rather than less, by accentuating my otherness and dangling a tantalising, frustrating facsimile of friendship in front of me. Because it was defined by only one thing – *Magic* – it felt bereft of the richness I was searching for in my adult life. Searching for determinedly at university.

So what happened? I dallied a bit with *Magic* as university tumbled to its end. I even found a less awful place to play than the Captain's Log and had some good times, squeezed between part-time work, essays and cider-and-substance-fuelled raves. More importantly though, I pulled a good degree out of the bag and perhaps for the first time, felt like I had proved myself. Despite my distaste for the microcosmical British class-system that university was, I side-stepped it by belonging to Bristol proper and, at least in my final year, made it the intellectual meritocracy I hoped it would be. I was motivated, more than I had ever been in my life. I was working 20 to 25 hours a week to scrape by financially, yet energised by my course (at long last) and loving every assignment. I was reading great books. Learning a little about writing. And gladly showing up the carefree squarejaws and blank-eyed preeners in every seminar. I put in a huge amount and got a huge amount out. And I remember with great satisfaction the cheer that went up when I went up to collect my first-class degree at graduation. I had shown that you could land the best marks possible whilst also being a drunken reprobate, dancing down the front every weekend, blowing your whistle and burning your brain cells at an incredible clip. In every way, it was my proudest achievement. And I felt a lot better in the skin that had fit me so badly since life hit the skids a decade or so previously.

Shortly afterwards, I landed my first job in journalism and packed my bags for London. A big, expensive and lonely city, it took some getting used to. At first, I sunk my improved self-worth into a dense period of hedonism. I drank too much beer, ate too much fried chicken and had too many one-night stands. My *Magic* cards, in a box under my bed, blanched at the goings-on above them. At some point though, with my job affording me an impressive amount of time for dossing around, *Magic* websites started to creep back into my bookmarks. I read up on what I had missed over the last few years. Got enthused. And searched out somewhere I could play in London. My futile trawl of London's dating scene was squandering my self-esteem, I realised. Why not do something I liked on a Friday night, instead of someone I didn't? I hoped I could make room for *Magic* now, a simple pleasure that must have stuck with me for a reason.

At London's weekly Games Club, in a seedy hotel on the Euston Road, I began reconnecting with the game. Yes, it remained a conversation topic I eschewed on first dates. Yes, it was still something I couldn't play with closer, non-gaming friends. But increasingly, I felt justified in enjoying it. This, after all, was a game substantial enough to be seducing me afresh after more than a decade in my life. It was something I could perceive as valuable, thought-provoking and plain fun. I could rationalise my involvement with it as a part of a well-rounded adult life, despite my various hang-ups. It was something that wanted me, even if I didn't always realise I wanted it. And as much as I was piecing together an adult identity, in which *Magic* was a puzzling part, the game showed me it still had plenty to teach me about myself.

"… ISN'T THAT RIGHT Eric?"

A chortle broke out among the assembled players. And for whatever reason, the name attached to some pre-tournament quip snapped me out of my reverie. "Who?" I thought, brow furrowed, suddenly recalled to a games store in Reading one Sunday morning in 2009. It was a small affair: 14 players had turned out to play Vintage (formerly Type 1), the game's oldest format and one largely forgotten by today's *Magic* crowd. I had made the painless 40-minute train ride from London, arrived in the unremarkable commuter town in good time, popped across the road from the main station and ducked into the games shop where the tournament was being held. If I had had a coffee, it had been slow to kick in.

Eric. The skinny, angular Chinese chap in glasses. I recognised him almost instantly, but checked the pairings pinned to the wall to be sure, found his surname and confirmed what I thought could only be impossible. A sudden detour down memory lane. The upturning of a stone left undisturbed for many years. An item I had gladly overlooked in my construction of the past, because beneath it lay guilt.

For roughly half an academic year, prior to immigrating to New Zealand, I had shared a class with Eric. I choose those words carefully, as there is plenty to unpack under that stone. But I am being disingenuous. I was not especially friends with Eric. Still; that is not clear enough. Here: I joined in my friends picking on the young, awkward Eric.

I don't remember much about it, but I suspect it must have been horrendous. Because on that Sunday in Reading, the guilt hit me like an icy blast, a spirit-sapping and inescapable chill wind, whipped up by events that played out in a six-month period of the past at most. I hung my head. I would remember nothing about the games of *Magic* I played that day.

At school, Eric had been different to us and we never let him forget it. He was the butt of every joke. The immature (we decided), scrawny, shy, uncool kid with shaggy hair, thick glasses and an ill-fitting uniform. Eric was also from a very traditional Chinese background at odds with our upbringings. Whereas we were eager to start rebelling, he was preoccupied with his parents' academic demands. He was not interested in whether Alice in Chains were better than Nirvana. Or whether Jules would be getting a Super Nintendo for Christmas. Or whether Tom would snog Becky on the bus tomorrow. At least, we assumed he wasn't. I cannot remember us taking much trouble to find out.

Instead, we pounced on him at every occasion, mocking him and his little brother Victor. It was too easy. Too dizzyingly empowering. And, like every kid who wants to fit in – and who is too cowardly to do otherwise – I joined in with Eric's persecutors without much thought. For a cheap laugh, for a rush, and for some degree of perverse kudos among my peers. Never did I stop to think that at a year younger than most of my classmates, half-Chinese, and with my family on the brink of losing everything, I could just have easily been on the receiving end. Or perhaps rather, I knew it even then, on some subconscious level that I never verbalised to myself. I chose to cling to my place among the hunting pack for fear of being taunted myself.

Outwardly, Eric hadn't changed much: he was taller, but still skinny and bespectacled. He seemed a little more at ease though, surrounded by friends from the *Magic* community. I avoided making eye contact, drifted towards different groups of players to talk, and then sat down for my first round, grateful not to have been paired against him. I believed myself to be fairly outgoing, confident and indeed a good person. But cowardice dies hard and I could not bring myself to speak to Eric immediately.

Another round passed, another 50 minutes during which I could lower my gaze and feign absorption in the game. And then an opportunity arose to speak to Eric alone. I said hello. We shook hands. And we acknowledged that we had been at school together. I paused and wondered if I might leave things there. But by offering Eric nothing but small talk, all I would be doing is putting him through the wringer again, leaving an elephant stalking the room and daring him to point it out. By forcing someone I had slighted in the past to be nothing but civil, I would be mocking him anew. No-one deserves that kind of humiliation and thus, I bit the bullet.

"Eric," I said. "I don't think I was very nice to you at school. If I ever was an arsehole to you, I'm sorry." He paused now, caught, I think, by surprise. "Things were bad for a while, but they got better," he replied graciously.

Eric discovered *Magic* as a student at Loughborough University, he told me later. Having stumbled upon fantasy gaming when a Games Workshop store opened near him, he tentatively sought out the university's wargames club in his first year. It was a chance for him to put behind him any travails he had encountered at school and meet a new community, who shared his interests. It was, he says, "a fresh start. At university, you get to wash off the old you and figure out your identity more fully."

That identity soon included *Magic*. Eric had his curiosity piqued when he saw two fellow club members duelling in 1998. Scraping together spare cash from his tight student budget, he began buying a few packs of the current set, *Urza's Saga*, widely regarded as one of the game's most powerful, and began to figure *Magic* out. Hooked by the easy and quick set up of the game compared to table-top wargaming, Eric delved ever deeper into the game. He was helped by the fact that the short-lived UK version of gaming convention Gencon (whose US edition had been so pivotal in *Magic*'s rise) was held for a time at his very university. In 1999, Eric attended and discovered the game's competitive scene. "I didn't do well that year," he says. "But it got me going and eventually I started to venture out on my own, outside of Loughborough to Nottingham, for example, to play in Pre-Release Tournaments and stuff like that." Aided by his first car, Eric started to discover something he was good at. He clocked up the miles to play in nearby Nottingham's bigger, more competitive tournaments and started refining his skills. But with funds still tight, a lack of cards kept him from keeping up with the crowd competing to qualify for the Pro Tour, so one day in his third year at university, he tried his hand at judging. On a personal level, it was a breakthrough for Eric.

JUDGES, LIKE TOURNAMENT organisers, are part of the glue that holds *Magic* together. The role is unglamorous, requires an extensive knowledge of the game's minutiae and, of course, means sitting out tournaments you might rather play in, to enforce the game's rules as well as the official floor rules, which govern players' behaviour (what constitutes cheating, for example). At every *Magic* tournament, every few minutes, a hand is thrust in the air and the call "Judge!" rings out. The demanding role is compensated in cards, including exclusive foiled versions of popular cards which can be kept or sold for a premium on the secondary market – but that is all. Judges receive no cash for the weekends they give up to help others enjoy their hobby. But the role can have its rewards.

"I'm still basically a shy guy," admits Eric. "But judging was good for me. At the start of each tournament, I had to do a little public speaking; I had to be diplomatic, concise, informative. And I had a chance to develop my inter-personal skills." Some of us may take that skill set for granted. But we weren't all picked on at school. For Eric, it was a gateway to a new role – of being an important and respected member of a community. And he made the very most of it. "Judging gave me a real focus," he says. "And even today it still plays that role for me and keeps me going."

Life has by no means been easy for Eric since school. Nor has *Magic* been a solace at all times for him. But judging gave the once maligned kid in the skinny grey flannels and thick glasses a chance to change. It is the bully's modus operandi to deny the possibility of change in his victim. To ruthlessly point out a person's inadequacies and ignore his or her potential to outgrow them or to be defined by anything else. No doubt, it comes from the bully's own deep-seated realisation that he is himself incapable of change, of growth, of anything other than the impoverished outlook of a boor. Eric has changed. I am satisfied that I have changed, too.

And while different players are grateful to *Magic* for different things, I am grateful that, on one Sunday in a game shop in Reading, it gave me an unexpected opportunity to revisit my past and realise it was not as blot-free as I had told myself. Although Facebook friendship is no scientific measure or promise of an ongoing relationship, I can't help noticing when I click on Eric's profile that none of my old school friends, with whom I am also linked, are mutual friends. None play *Magic*. And presumably none have sought to upturn the stone in their past marked 'guilt' either. For that I apologise too, Eric.

(Names have been changed in this chapter. But not Spence's. He died from cancer in 2012. Rest well big man.)

CHAPTER TWENTY

"I started at Wizards, I left Hasbro."

ALTHOUGH CREATING THE Pro Tour proved to be a strategic masterstroke for Wizards of the Coast, it was in many ways the exception that proved the rule. In the late 1990s, there were still plenty of questionable decisions being made at company headquarters. The wild *Magic* ride continued to toss all preconceived business notions up in the air with every new milestone passed, every new balance sheet reviewed and every new bumper payday. Although by 1995 Peter Adkison was completing his MBA and growing into the role of a reformed CEO, there was still plenty of painful spasms for the company to overcome as it transitioned from producing *Magic*: The Fad to *Magic: The Perennial* – the ongoing product the Pro Tour would allow it to become.

That period's most emblematic change would be one many players did not notice play out. Nonetheless, it impacted a key component of the game, which many had grown to love. It was a decision that marked a definitive shift away from the rootsy start-up that had produced *Magic*'s first forays into the market, towards the slick, professional machine it grew into. It was, though, a decision that would end in recrimination, legal scraps and years of bitterness, as some of the figures in the game's early development felt betrayed.

In 1996, in the build up to the forthcoming new *Fifth Edition* of *Magic*, Peter Adkison green-lighted the renegotiation of the terms on which the very first artists had been employed. Originally, those artists had worked for $50 cash and $50 stock up front, in the hope that the radical but completely untried game would become popular enough to yield them royalties. Indeed,

Jesper Myrfors remembers Adkison hoping the same, such was his gratitude for the outstanding contribution the young, unknown artists had made to the game. Says Myrfors: "I remember Peter saying time and time again, 'I want to make sure the artists who were there for us in the beginning get royalties for life'." But by 1996, much had changed.

Magic sales figures were off the chart and some artists had received six-figure payouts for their work. There was a business rationale for scrapping the generous royalty pool and scooping up all rights to the original illustrations so they could continue to be used without incurring a large ongoing cost to the company. While that reasoning made a degree of sense, the manner in which the process was handled would leave wounds that in some cases have still not healed today. "It was a very painful process for all concerned," says Adkison, looking back. "I think that if I would have had then the experience I have now, I could have managed the situation much more diplomatically. But at the time I was in my early 30s and was overwhelmed with my responsibilities." Wizards told the artists that unless they agreed to sign over the rights to their existing work, their artwork would be unceremoniously dropped from future sets and replaced with newly commissioned illustrations. When the artists engaged lawyers to fight the process, bitter wrangling ensued, which at times got personal. The artists felt strong-armed into accepting a diminished financial packet in a move Myrfors says he believes was, "vicious and completely driven by greed." The new breed of middle management flooding into Wizards were focused on the company's bottom line and felt that the artists had been more than compensated for their work. Having had little experience of the fantasy gaming industry, some even felt the artwork had contributed little to the game's success. A seething Anson Maddocks quipped in response: "Try printing rules text on a T-shirt then, and see how many you sell!"

Jesper Myrfors eventually refused to sell all his rights to the company. Others buckled under the pressure. As a sudden loss of income hit many artists – either from the dried-up royalties or because their opposition to the changes damaged their chances of working for the company – many suffered extreme financial woes and some even lost their homes, says Myrfors. Although time, as it is wont to do, has healed some rifts, it was a brutal introduction to the new corporate realities at Wizards for a wide-eyed generation of artists who had given their creative all for the game. "What's done is done," says Myrfors, who himself had left the company in 1995. He returned for a brief stint from 1998 to 2000 and maintains that whatever the business reasons given, the renegotiation of the artists' contracts was propelled by baser instincts. "It was purely greed-driven, primarily by people who came late to the game and wanted a slice, like they deserved it," he says. "I'm a non-believer, but I hope there's a hell reserved just for those people."

Inevitably, the paroxysms in the Wizards' art department were the herald of greater change. The argument made against the royalties system was that it would impede the search for a buyer for the high-flying company. And the hunt for someone to snap up the industry leader was very much on – by 1997, the company had hit revenues of approximately $125 million a year and had even made a hugely symbolic acquisition with the purchase of the ailing company TSR, the publishers of *Dungeons & Dragons*. With the role-playing game that had inspired the generation of gamers behind *Magic* on life-support and rescued by the company whose new gaming form had completely outstripped it, there was simply no bigger brand than Wizards in the market. The time was ripe to cash in on the startling growth, even as *Magic*'s first-to-market advantage began to recede and a new wave of card games prepared to – if not steal – rival, its thunder.

MAGIC WAS A global game by 1997, reaching ever further afield thanks to the internet and Wizards' organised play programme. While 40 per cent of cards were being sold within the US, and another 30 per cent in Europe, an impressive 30 per cent were also being sold in Japan. At the time, that meant that the Japanese were buying more *Magic* cards per capita than any other nation – making them a market the Wizards chiefs paid special attention to.

However, on one visit to the Asian *Magic* hotbed, Peter Adkison and John Jordan, Wizards' head of international, were left flabbergasted by a meeting with their publishing partner Hobby Japan. "*Magic*," warned the company president Mr Sato, "is no longer the number one trading card game in Japan." Adkison was shocked – *Magic* seemed to have cemented its place as the world's primary card game, even at the expense of Wizards' own attempts to create follow-ups like *Jyhad* (later *Vampire: The Eternal Struggle*), *Battletech* and *Netrunner*. What game could possibly be outstripping them in their hungriest market? The answer was a franchise invented the previous year by Satoshi Tajiri for Nintendo – a video game turned paper game called *Pokémon*.

"Oh this is horrible!" thought Adkison upon seeing the game. "We hate this game. It's mass-market. It's dumbed down. It's got ugly anime artwork. And there are cartoons! This is not a serious game like *Magic* is." Ultimately, though, the Wizards CEO was embarrassed to be beaten by the upstart game. A few months later, he was wise enough to swallow his pride: *Pokémon*'s producers contacted Wizards of the Coast and asked if the Seattle company would be their partner in producing a licensed version of the trading card game for the American market. Sensing a stellar business opportunity, Adkison performed a rapid about-face and heartily agreed. Wizards – having worked so hard to elevate *Magic* beyond juvenile status to be a professional intellectual sport – would in December 1998 unleash a card game aimed squarely at kids. And boy did they love it.

John Jackson Miller, who was at the time editing *Comics Retailer* magazine, describes *Pokémon* as, "the second wave of collectible card game hysteria." And, although American audiences initially struggled to get their heads around the all-encompassing property with its idiosyncratic Japanese cartoon, video games and card game, when they did, *Pokémon* hit the playground like cardboard crack-lite: a furiously consumed product and gateway to *Magic*. In fact, it was around this time that any *Magic* player trying to explain his or her hobby to friends would inevitably be asked (much to their chagrin), "Oh – so is it like *Pokémon*?" By the summer of 1999, kids were playing the game on every flat surface available and, says Jackson Miller, "World War Three was breaking out in my magazine's pages between retailers who couldn't get the product and Wizards, who were at the time talking about opening their own stores." Jackson Miller himself would soon be editing *Scrye* magazine, whose pages filled with translations of Japanese *Pokémon* cards yet to be released in America. These were now widely available on a red-hot eBay-fuelled secondary market. It was like 1994 all over again. And, as the joke went in Seattle, Wizards were back in the business of printing money.

*   *   *

On 9 September 1999, toy giant Hasbro announced the news: it had acquired Wizards of the Coast in a deal worth $325 million. Incredibly, some news outlets including the CNN Money webpage didn't even mention *Magic* when covering the story, instead referring to Wizards as the makers of *Pokémon* and *Dungeons & Dragons*. But Hasbro were no fools – and although they saw *Pokémon* as an extremely enticing cherry atop Wizards, they recognised the strength of its most established, core brand. By 1999, *Magic* had been on the market for six years and shown steady performance, now underpinned by the Pro Tour and the organised play pyramid as an evergreen game, rather than a disposable fad. While Hasbro were at the time better known for toy lines like Mr Potato Head, GI Joe, Transformers and My Little Pony, they had dipped their toes in the hobby game market a year previously with the acquisition of famous American war-gaming brand Avalon Hill for $6 million. Hasbro's president Alan Hassenfeld even identified games as "the cornerstone of our growth strategy for the new millennium." In *Magic*, says Peter Adkison, they recognised a game that had the potential to last generations. And thus a deal was thrashed out with Richard Garfield's hugely influential game at the centre of it. "Hasbro ended up paying us a flat fee for the company exclusive of *Pokémon*," says Adkison. "They clearly recognised that *Magic* and *Dungeons & Dragons* were our core business, with plenty of history behind them and based the value of the company on those. *Pokémon* had the potential to be huge but no-one knew how long it would last, as it was being produced as a licensed product. We structured an earn-out for that part of the business and ended up effectively getting royalties for the shareholders on *Pokémon* sales for several years, which amounted to a very healthy amount of money." Garfield meanwhile, whose card game had transformed the lives of gamers everywhere, pocketed a cool $100 million from the deal.

Wizards held a shareholders meeting to approve the Hasbro deal and once it had been rubber-stamped the investors who had rustled up the initial $100,000 it cost to get *Magic* to market celebrated with a well-deserved party. As the champagne flowed, one woman, dressed in an impeccable designer outfit, strode over to Peter Adkison and his former boss at Boeing, Vince Caluori. Caluori, having given Adkison his blessing to leave Boeing after the heady madness of Gencon 1993, had later followed him out of the door to take up the role of chief operating officer at Wizards. But at the shareholders meeting, he was reminded of his previous life at the aerospace giant: "You don't remember me, do you?" asked the neatly turned-out woman. "You do look familiar," said Caluori. "Well," she replied, "I am the woman who used to clean your office every night and, when Boeing banned smoking, empty the ash tray you had hidden in your desk." It was Marilyn, the Boeing janitor who had invested her life savings in *Magic* and the hard-working Peter Adkison she saw staying late every night. With Hasbro buying the company at $2,000 a share, the crazy investment that had infuriated her family, had made her a millionaire. Despite the luxurious clothes she had on, she was, says Adkison fondly, the same old Marilyn. And she delighted in finally admonishing her former boss, the recalcitrant smoker.

WHILE MANY *MAGIC* players greeted news of the Hasbro deal with outright horror, it confirmed in part the tangible effect they had helped have on the society around them. For a company like Hasbro – used to making mainstream toys derided by *Magic* players – to buy up the hobby games giant did not simply mean *Magic* had become a toy. Rather that in its short lifetime, the game's impact had been so great, that even the smartest money-making brains could see that the role of games, their visibility and their acceptability in society was growing. Certainly, the brilliance of Richard Garfield's creation was at the heart of that phenomenon, but both the internet and the Pro Tour had helped to thrust *Magic* players themselves into a new realm and elevate their role in society. Hasbro's purchase – while motivated by profit – was nonetheless a sign that the 21st century was shaping up to be very different indeed. That the smart kids might not simply be left to fend for themselves against the schoolyard bullies, but could make good – like Garfield, like Adkison, like Finkel – in a world of new possibilities. While in the short term, that meant they were seen as a lucrative market to tap, it also meant they had acquired an unforeseen degree of leverage in a society increasingly being shaped by knowledge, technical know-how and the flow of information via internet platforms which themselves had been influenced by *Magic* chatter. There would, in the long-term, be new opportunities for them to seize.

In the short to medium term, there would be casualties at Wizards. Peter Adkison and Lisa Stevens, in particular, felt the company they had created slip gradually out of their hands. Having established *Magic* and set it up for a new millennium, Adkison had rediscovered his thirst for innovation. His goal was to launch a massive multiplayer online game (MMO) using the *Dungeons & Dragons* brand. But the atmosphere at the company had changed. And, say both Stevens and Adkison, Hasbro had no appetite for risk – at least, not on the scale that a group of friends working out of a basement do. Although Adkison's *D&D* MMO would have beaten *World of Warcraft* – today's biggest MMO – to market, Hasbro pulled the plug on the project. "That was the final straw," says Adkison. "I knew that strategically, this was the right thing to do with this brand, but if Hasbro didn't believe me, I didn't know how to help them." Some 18 months after the Hasbro takeover both Stevens and Adkison left the company – Stevens a day before Adkison – and moved on, leaving the business adventure of a lifetime behind them. "I started at Wizards," say Adkison. "But I left Hasbro." He can be vastly proud of the legacy he left behind him.

While the media spotlight tends to shine most brightly on internet start-ups done good, the story of the company started in Adkison's basement is no less remarkable. Adkison's Wizards took risks (not least publishing *Magic* in the first place), made mistakes along the way (particularly in a certain ski lodge after Gencon 1994), but presaged Silicon Valley culture with their early attempts to nurture a thriving, open, creative company. They placed R&D at the heart of the business. They recognised how to turn a possible fad into a game that has gone on to last over 20 years, they created employment, wealth and changed the way a generation of young gamers felt about themselves. Via the Pro Tour, they even helped demonstrate the worth of games to corporate America and the society in its thrall, establishing a model that the booming 'eSports' video-gaming circuit would later borrow. By any measure, Adkison's company was an incredible success – one recognised with a giant cheque from Hasbro. Marketing consultant Seth Matlins, who since helping establish the Pro Tour has worked at some of the world's biggest brands, says the company deserves far greater recognition: "The guys at Wizards were so smart, so strategic and so focused," he says. "I don't know what the odds were for this to not succeed, but they were much higher than it succeeding. A good game comes along rarely. A good game that succeeds and sustains at this level? Even more so. What they achieved is remarkable – and for that, they truly deserve credit." Seattle might be better known for its hotshot companies Microsoft and Amazon, but Wizards earned its place alongside them. The street-smart card-gamers had come very good indeed.

CHAPTER TWENTY-ONE
Buy Low, Sell High

WHILE WIZARDS HAD to carve out their place within America's business culture, their game was positively steeped in it. *Magic* boasts a mercantile core, which, however exportable and however popular, feels like it could only have been born in the nation most in thrall to the free market, the United States. Stanford sociologist and role-playing game expert Gary Fine describes *Magic* as "a manufactured subculture," a leisure world created by an entrepreneur as a capitalist enterprise. While *Magic* is not alone in that sense, part of the game's very rationale is the fastidious accumulation of its playing pieces, rather than, say, the incidental accumulation of new kit to play golf, go fishing or enjoy jogging. "If you get involved in that world, then part of the involvement is a materialist one," says Fine. "For some people, there is certainly a desire to have the best cards." And that desire was created at the University of Pennsylvania, in 1991, as soon as the excited maths crew got their hands on the very first playtest decks. A secondary market for *Magic* cards was an instant and defining offshoot of the game's creation.

While the first playtesters scrambled to trade cards with each other in the frenzied stock market-like environment Barry Reich (Garfield's first-ever opponent) observed, once *Magic* hit the streets for real, simply swapping for the rapidly multiplying cards became impossible. Buying and selling specific singles cracked from Booster Packs was the answer to voracious players' cravings and soon became a huge part of *Magic* culture: from the converted comic shops looking for new revenue streams, to the players auctioning spares on Usenet, to the speculators flipping red-hot boxes of *Legends* in 1994, instilling fear at Wizards HQ of an impending collapse.

A sharp readjustment took place with the release of *Fallen Empires*, *Ice Age* and *Fourth Edition* as Wizards aimed to realign the game for its players, rather than for its hoarders. While the Pro Tour would be the culmination of that process, on the way to that end goal, *Magic* saw its most controversial release ever. *Chronicles* was released in August 1995, featuring white-bordered reprints of cards from *Magic*'s first four (extremely rare) expansions: *Arabian Nights*, *Antiquities*, *Legends* and *The Dark*. While the developers had decided against including some of the most powerful cards in those sets, they did nonetheless include a plethora of highly sought-after cards for casual and tournament players alike, which had rocketed to astronomical prices since they had first seen print. While Wizards wanted to deflate the game's speculative bubble and drive 'locusts' out of the market, this was not just a warning shot across their bows. It was a thumping depth charge that initially decimated secondary market prices for the original black-bordered versions of the 116 cards included in the set. Collectors were up in arms about the hit they believed their collections would take. Many players, who had desperately hoped for even more powerful cards to be reprinted, were disappointed, too. *Chronicles* proved a step too far, or one taken too hastily. And it was nothing short of a PR disaster for Wizards.

As collectors and players decried and defended the set on Usenet, and letters of complaint poured into Wizards of the Coast, the company rushed out a response. In March 1996, they announced the creation of the 'Reserved List', a controversial document that has become a bugbear for a huge number in the game – including many players, but also the game's designers. It would prove a significant and ill-thought-out concession to the slighted collecting fraternity who had fought vociferously to maintain the value of their investment in the game. The Reserved List featured cards that Wizards undertook never to reprint, including the fabled 'Power Nine', certain powerful cards from sets like *Arabian Nights* and *Legends*, plus key rares from each new set. In practice, no new cards have been added to the Reserved List since 2002 when its implications began to be better understood and the collectors it had been designed to appease had become a far smaller part of Wizards' customer base. The initial list was a knee-jerk reaction that has blighted the growth of *Magic*'s older formats and hindered today's designers. But it could have been even more extensive. Skaff Elias was one of the R&D members who recognised the importance of having breathing room for reprints, so Wizards could re-use design capital already invested in neat, functional cards. "I didn't think the Reserved List was necessary and personally, I would not have done it," he says. "It was initially a bigger list and I got some cards taken off it – just useful nice, simple stuff, that could be used in tournament play."

Indeed, Elias (who remained at Wizards until 2004) would help undermine the rationale for the Reserved List's existence at all. His brainchild, the Pro Tour, served to re-position the game to such an extent that it silenced the argument many collectors were making about the worth of their cards. They argued fiercely that whenever Wizards reprinted old cards, the value plummeted. And while that was true in the very short term, if the card was good enough to see tournament play – the game's dominant mode following the Pro Tour's creation – the reverse was actually true. Tournament players actively sought out older versions of the card – often with a different illustration or a more visually appealing black border – as a vanity for their decks. Playability became the main factor behind demand for a card, rather than simple rarity, driving prices for older, re-printed playables *higher* over time. Along with the moment he stood in the excited crowd at the very first Pro Tour, Elias says seeing the results of secondary market research confirming this trend, was his other favourite 'Wow!' moment in the game's history. No more could the game be held to ransom by speculators, as comics and sports cards had been, he thought. "We knew for sure then that competitive tournament play was successful," says Elias. "We had broken the cycle of speculation. Now, we were selling gaming equipment." Appropriately, Wizards subtly re-branded *Magic: The Gathering* from a 'collectible card game' to a 'trading card game', adjusting the parameters of the hobby genre they had created. While an exchange of cards would always be inherent to the game's richness, it was hoped it would never be allowed to dominate it again.

*   *   *

WITH THE ADVENT of the World Wide Web, the secondary market for *Magic* quickly evolved away from the pioneering auctions taking place on Usenet and the bricks-and-mortar retailers with rammed folders full of cards. Instead, platforms such as eBay and specialist online retailers began to cater to the global demand that went hand-in-hand with *Magic*'s rapid worldwide expansion. Although trends in *Magic* retailing have waxed and waned and with them numerous retailers' fortunes, two of the biggest and most interesting players in the market today are StarCityGames.com, based in Roanoke, Virginia and MagicKartenMarkt.eu, based at the other end of the U8 underground line from my home in Berlin. While one is an online retail behemoth and probably the number one brand in the US secondary market (getting exact figures from anyone about market share is impossible), MagicKartenMarkt.eu has taken a very different approach, creating a specialised marketplace for peer-to-peer *Magic* sales within the European Union. Both are wildly popular, both have made waves in the market and both are key components in the daily flow of cash and *Magic* cards around the world; thousands of transactions worth vast sums financially (and emotionally) to the game's devotees.

Pete Hoefling, president of StarCityGames.com, represents in many ways the trajectory of the entire *Magic* secondary market. He discovered the game as proprietor of an 800-square-foot comic shop in Roanoke, when in 1994, a group of kids came in trying to buy cards from the latest *Revised Edition* of *Magic*. Despite Hoefling telling them he had no idea what they were talking about, the kids persisted, coming back day after day. Finally, the comic book store owner relented and one day told his would-be *Magic* customers, "You know what? We did actually get a box in." The four kids proceeded to buy every single pack. Hoefling, who had become resigned to the comic book industry's stuttering fortunes, says, "That absolutely blew my mind."

Cards quickly supplanted comics in his affections and the 800 square feet of his store was rearranged to incorporate more *Magic* cards and ever-fewer comics. Eventually, the comics disappeared completely and Star City Games was born: a *Magic* retailer, game centre and tournament organiser. Hoefling began unloading a lifetime's worth of comics clutter on eBay and tried selling a few cards on the auction site, too. He could spy its potential – and understood that selling cards online was a very powerful proposition.

But only a chance offer from a regular customer persuaded him to take the next step. "The internet was starting to become a 'thing,'" says Hoefling, "But as to online retailing, I kind of got dragged into it." The customer in question had presciently decided to return to school to study web design. One day, he asked Hoefling if he could develop a website for him, so he would have something to put in his portfolio. Up popped StarCityGames.com – loosely based on Frank Kusumoto's Dojo – and a *Magic* behemoth was born. After much trial and error, the site hit upon the right combination of retail offering, tournament organising and content providing that would see it grow and grow. Today, it even stands out in the *Magic* universe, for charging fans for access to a 'Premium' content section – a controversial decision made in 2005 – that has nonetheless proved extremely successful.

In Europe, meanwhile, while online retailers similar to StarCityGames.com do exist, a rising star in the secondary market is MagicKartenMarkt.eu, a site founded in 2007 by Luis Torres. Torres was an itinerant half-Mexican, half-German *Magic* player who had been buying and selling cards in Spain, France and Germany. He had remarked on some of the price differences he was encountering between countries, but also on the frustration of using eBay to sell cards – uploading items one by one, finding a picture, creating an individual description. It was those frustrations and the intriguing nature of the European card market that led him to start programming a marketplace devoted entirely to cards. Soon, the IT engineer had friend Matthias Knelagen on board as a partner and CEO and had moved to Berlin, where the start-up would put down roots. Since then, it has caught *Magic* players' imaginations and irreversibly shaken up the European *Magic* market, far beyond the pair's initial expectations. "We just thought that if we could get the trades that were happening between players on *Magic* forums on to MKM, that would be fine," says Knelangen. In fact, the platform's ease of use (it takes just four clicks to list a card for sale) has seen it capture a far greater audience (100,000 registered users at the time of writing), including StarCityGames.com who struggle to keep up with the demand in the US, despite an insatiable card-buying operation.

But what has really proven revolutionary about the marketplace is the transparency it has created within the secondary market. Instead of buyers and sellers having to scope out recently finished auctions on eBay to determine a card's market value (something even StarCityGames.com does when setting a new card's price for the first time), every card is listed at a fixed price by its seller (with fixed shipping costs determined by the site). That makes the price of a card instantly accessible – and indeed its evolution visible in real time. Much like *Scrye* in the past, savvy traders in Europe now pull out a tablet or smart phone at big events when trading with strangers, to check the latest card prices on MagicKartenMarkt.eu. It might sound like a small change, but its effect has been seismic.

"At the very beginning, professional sellers complained about the degree of transparency on the site," says Knelangen. As private sellers began listing their bulk cards for as low as a few cents, the retailers who had previously had the lion's share of the market demanded MKM set minimum prices to protect their businesses. But, says Knelangen, they eventually saw sense. "They realised after a while, that they don't have to compete with private sellers on price. We also run a shop on the site and we're expensive. But we still sell a lot because we have every card in stock."

While Knelangen believes his service has helped drive down the prices of cards on the secondary market in Germany and much of Europe overall, he also says it has offered a new platform for retailers and professional sellers, too. Having come round to the site's transparency, they are now among MagicKartenMarkt.eu's biggest customers, selling a range of cards that most individuals cannot offer and buying cards on the website to restock their inventories. Together with the steady stream of players joining the site to buy cards at competitive prices, the company has grown far beyond initial expectations. What started as Luis Torres' modest idea is now an established business employing 10 people. Goals have been realigned – and the site expects to grow further in the European market. But Knelangen estimates they are still small fry compared to the biggest US retailers. "Although no-one wants to give out figures so we can estimate what the secondary market is worth," he says, "I imagine that the US market would be bigger than the rest of the world put together."

Indeed, Pete Hoefling has long left his 800-square-foot premises behind. Today, StarCityGames.com employs over 100 people in a 25,000-square-foot headquarters which the company has also "pretty much outgrown", according to its boss. Although he too won't talk specifics, he believes that

StarCityGames.com is the biggest secondary-market dealer today – and while the company's initial foray into the online realm might have been somewhat fortunate, its success since has been predicated on some very savvy decisions. Not only has the site built up a brilliant roster of contributors (which it can pay thanks to pay-wall subscriptions), but it has also used its heft to establish its own lucrative cash-prize tournament series called the SCG Open Series. Stepping into a void created by Wizards of the Coast's decision in 2011 to move all pre-release tournaments in-store and to up the number of Grand Prix, the SCG series has now become the de facto mid-size tournament all over the United States. Hoefling says, "Grand Prix are off the scale now in terms of attendance, but essentially Star City Open events are what Grand Prix were a number of years ago." That means players can come along and compete for a slice of a $20,000 prize pool at weekend-long events, meet and trade with players outside their normal play-groups and, with repeat success, begin building a certain status within the community – perhaps not pro-level celebrity, but enough to earn commissions for articles, attract viewers to a stream or make vital contacts in more rarefied testing groups. In short, the SCG series provides another revenue stream for the aspiring *Magic* pro. It also provides plenty of revenue for the StarCityGames.com coffers, too.

Just as the Wizards-backed Pro Tour championed the Standard format of in-print cards to sustain on-going sales, the SCG Open Series initially made the Legacy format part of its offering. The format uses many old and out-of-print cards, barring the 'Power Nine' and some excessively broken cohorts. Because many of the format's fundamental cards are on the Reserved List, though, it is only occasionally supported by Wizards for fear that limited card availability will create an uneven playing field. By backing the format, StarCityGames.com created a business model, which replicated what Wizards did with their flagship tournament series a decade or so earlier: They created lucrative play opportunities, which stimulated demand for the format's key cards, which they could then sell to their player base. Also, precisely because many of the cards were on the Reserved List, with no hope of being reprinted, they rose in price as buyers gobbled them up as an almost foolproof investment. While that ultimately stymied the format's growth, it helped cement StartCityGames.com as the big daddy of the secondary market. That status sometimes inspires suspicion among Magic players, who rail against the mega-retailer in online forums, accusing them of stockpiling cards to short the market. But Hoefling says, "We're a retailer, not a museum." With key cards often sold out on his website at dizzying price points, he is desperately trying to stock and sell more, as fast as he can.

While Knelangen also scoffs at suggestions StarCityGames.com would stockpile cards, he has previously wondered if Wizards would give the powerful retailer an edge, by supplying them sorted single cards from new sets, rather than making them buy and open thousands of Booster Packs like everyone else. While Knelangen thinks that is impossible – the risk to Wizards' reputation would be huge – it does raise the question of whether a market worth as much as the *Magic* secondary market needs some kind of regulation. Because as the number of players continues to increase (tournament attendance doubled from 350,000 players in 2011 to 700,000 in 2013, for example), the demand for cards is spiralling. That has led to a savvy *Magic* financial community, actively speculating on the value of cards as they would stocks and shares. Worryingly, a new trend has also developed. "I definitely think that the *Magic* finance community has gone from being a community of speculators for the most part to being a community of manipulators," says Hoefling.

Essentially, what that means is that a number of individuals will attempt to 'buy out the internet' of a specific card, depending on current or anticipated importance to the tournament metagame. This might be in light of an interaction with a newly printed card or, more worryingly, a reaction to insider information on a forthcoming printing. One notable recent case saw the under-played card Aluren inexplicably bought up en masse days *before* Wizards announced a reprint of the card Imperial Recruiter. The two cards combine to form the backbone of a powerful deck, which had previously been under-represented due to Imperial Recruiter's scarcity. Whichever individual or group snatched up the global supply of Alurens seems unlikely to have been acting on whim alone.

When would-be manipulators do pounce, cards like Aluren are just what they are looking for. Preferably, the card in question will be an old, obscure card printed in limited numbers compared to modern print runs. Ideally, it will also be a card on the Reserved List, meaning it can never be reprinted to meet demand. When the manipulators strike, they make a concerted effort to buy up as many existing copies of a card as possible, forcing retailers like StarCityGames.com to up their buy price, so they in turn can try and keep the card in stock. Once the buy price has risen to the manipulators' satisfaction, they can unload their stockpiled cards to a major dealer and cash in. "I have no idea how to get them under control," says Hoefling, "And I don't know if it's actually a problem." That business-first response is entirely predictable from a retailer who increases his sale price in accordance with any rise in his buy price – but for the players who just want to go out and enjoy their hobby every weekend, getting shafted by escalating prices can somewhat detract from the fun. A tournament-winning Legacy decklist can now easily cost $3,000 to assemble. "It's just crazy," says Knelangen. "We now see people on MKM almost day-trading in *Magic* cards. While it's fascinating that it works that way, I don't think it's very healthy for the game and I don't think people trying to live off *Magic* card speculation are very healthy."

WHEN DOES A simple hobby tip into the realms of the unhealthy, though? I am not a speculator, not even really a collector, but there have been periods, long stretches in fact, where I have bought *Magic* cards on a daily basis. They are just a click away! A Euro here, a Euro there. They needn't be *that* expensive, if you set yourself a low threshold for satisfaction, shop within your means, and snap up bargains for the simple thrill of interrupting your workday with a tiny but precise hit of retail therapy. That is precisely what *owning Magic* cards has become for me – a deeply therapeutic and nourishing practice that means my attachment to the game is beyond a simply rational one. Beyond a simply healthy one, perhaps.

Yes, there are laser-focused competitive players out there, who borrow cards from friends and sponsors for tournaments. Many of them don't look at the pictures, read the flavour text or indeed give two hoots about possessing Magic cards of their own. In my most lucid moments, I tell myself that I belong firmly in this camp. "Pff goblins... whatever," I mutter to myself, completely indifferent to the nature of *Magic* cards as an object, more interested in what they offer mechanically to the game. I am not a collector. Not like that. I don't assemble sets of cards, chase after misprints and oddities, pay over the odds for mint-condition cards rated by an authenticator and sealed up in hard plastic cases so they may never be sullied by actual play. But I am, I realise, a collector of a different sort. I do have an affinity for certain cards. I do desire them. And each one I capture is a salve, a band-aid on traumas past.

I WAS FIRST coaxed into collecting as a child, hustled even, as if it were an unspoken duty crucial to my development. For some reason, it started with eggcups. I was presented with one as a gift and immediately urged to usher more of them into my life. Soon, I was having them foisted on me at every birthday, pointed out to me at jumble sales and pressed into my hands by diligent parents who seemed very much to want me to care about these poisoned porcelain chalices. Maddeningly, I didn't even like boiled eggs. But soon, I had a shelf on the dresser, cleaning responsibilities and the burden of maintaining a collection I could not honestly give two shits about. How long did this last? A few years at least. And now, a box of dreadful eggcups lurks at home somewhere, waiting to be sprung on me one morning, complete with eggs and toast soldiers. With the same kind of selective memory loss that plagues all parents, mum and dad will wave away my protests with a "But you always liked boiled eggs!" and, in my unwavering politeness, I shall be forced to bite my adult tongue. Grinning meekly, I will spoon the blobby ovum into my gob, accepting as we do the absurd but comforting theatre of being at home, where everyone plays a facsimile of the role they have played since birth, in a performance that lasts until death. Eggs be damned.

I imagine, looking back, that the eggcup collection was a lesson in responsibility for me, much like having a pet. I was supposed to take ownership of these fragile items, sort them, polish them, perhaps prep them for a future appearance on *The Antiques Roadshow*. Never mind that I already had a box of pin badges that I greatly preferred (and which had earned me a Cub Scout collecting proficiency badge, I hasten to add). Nor that my *Stars Wars* toys were quietly piling up into a box-load worthy of collection status. They were appreciating in value all the time – not that back then I ever thought beyond ripping my new Han Solo figure from his blister pack and slamming him against a dull-witted Imperial Storm Trooper, just cruising for a bruising too close to the Rebel base.

Circumstances changed though. That childish insouciance was spirited away, along with my *Star Wars* toys. In a surreal brush with fame, I sold them to Geezer Butler of Black Sabbath for the princely sum of £40. At 13, that was a lot of money – and more than I feared I would see for a while. As my parents' war-gaming company went under, fear crept into our household and steadily chipped away at the comfortable construct of middle-class, rural English life that we had thought ours for perpetuity. The toys had to go. We were leaving home, forced to sell up to settle loans with the bank. Only so much would fit into the container shipping what belongings remained to a ghastly new life in New Zealand. In the upheaval, it was not the only collection lost – my dad sold his thousands of toy soldiers, too. We were in the same miserable boat together.

While I found my solace in *Magic*, I realise now that the game fulfilled (and continues to fulfil) far more than just a social function for me. Beyond playing the game with my Kiwi schoolmates, I developed a need to own cards which I'm sure was inextricably linked with my need to re-establish a place in the world for myself. By accumulating these little treasures, I could reconstruct some of the self-esteem that had been so badly depleted by losing everything and surfacing in a foreign world I didn't know how to fit into. I didn't know how to voice to anyone what had happened to my family, nor how confused and ashamed I felt. With money painfully tight at home, the easy contentment of life as it had been, existed beyond a distant horizon I could never imagine reaching again. My parents tried hard to take steps forward towards a brighter future and at the same time, tempered all expectation in their kids that things would ever quite be the same again. But the teenage environment I was stumbling into was superficial and unforgiving and I felt hideously exposed, my shiny surface cracked beyond repair. I could never hope to have the right trainers, the pocket money to go out, the dollars for junk food at the playground tuck shop. And worse, I felt guilty for wanting them as my parents stretched every buck to breaking point.

IN THE ALTERNATIVE worth of *Magic* cards, though, perhaps I could be rich – even though I had far less money to sink into the hobby than those around me. I would barter for cards, haggle with anyone who might erroneously cede cards for less than the going rate, desperately try and scrape together money for Booster Packs, lunch at Baron of Beef, another trip to Pendragon Games. Sometimes, I would even find myself hysterically talking up the worth of a card I had procured, in an attempt to convince friends I really had landed a humdinger. Thus, I thought, I might earn the kudos I could barely hope to achieve in the social circles beyond the game. I was scrambling for some control on my life, to assert myself, with every precious card accumulated. It is precisely this function of collecting that the late psychologist Werner Muensterberger proposed would offer, "relief of the child's anxiety and frustration that comes with feeling helpless and being alone."

Although things have changed for my family in the intervening years (my dad is once again happily ensconced in an attic surrounded by toy soldiers), *Magic* cards remain something I feel compelled to own. Each one is a balm to bruises buried deep beneath my exterior. Each one has been bought in a moment of need, of sadness, of longing. And there are many thousand of them here – a lifetime of such moments.

However conflicted or troubled the impulse to buy each *Magic* card is, the act of owning them provides resolution. I derive pleasure from seeing them stacked around me or lying around on my table. I fan them out, with no particular purpose in mind, other than to contemplate them and remind myself that these objects do indeed belong to me. I can touch them. I can clothe them in protective sleeves. I can even play with them at some point, should I desire. More often or not though, this is a delusion I feed myself to justify my constant spending on them. Many (most in fact) will never be played with and, really, they don't need to be. Once they have sparked an instant of joy in me, as I stand in the chilly hallway, in front of my open mailbox; once I have wrestled them from their packaging, held them in my hand and soaked up their psychic warmth, that is almost enough. After that, they can go into the cupboard, their place in the mental inventory of my ill-defined collection satisfyingly ticked off. Another anxious moment conquered. Another wound healed.

Still, for all my compulsive hoarding, I have no desire to own every *Magic* card, nor swoop on every pristine promo or showy ultra-rare Korean foil. Instead, I find myself drawn most to old cards, steeped in some indescribable magic of their own. My favourite boast a patina of scratches and finger grease, the kind avoided by most serious collectors. These are humble cards. Every scratch and scuff marks them out as having lived and picked up a little of the damage life is wont to inflict. As I hold them, like tiny mirrors in my palm, I tell myself, they are somehow beautiful, whatever anyone else thinks. These battered and beat-up acquisitions were loved by their original owners and played with, with the same innocence I once did my *Star Wars* toys. And in knowing that, I know what in truth I am trying to collect. Not cards, but the worry-free, pre-pubescent state of permanent summer, of cloudless skies and serene indifference to the real world. Only shadows of it remain.

CHAPTER TWENTY-TWO

Playing a New Hand

WHILE THE WIZARDS bosses had turned their gaming savvy into a remarkable pay-day, a generation of young professional *Magic* players would soon be inspired to do the same. The Pro Tour had given them a thirst for competition, new reserves of self-belief, experience of high-pressure situations and, in many cases, wads of greenbacks burning a hole in their back pockets. When the lights went down at the latest Pro Tour venue on a Sunday night, the celebrations would kick into full swing, with plenty of players' splurging winnings on lavish dinners, wild nights out in exotic destinations and, of course, late-night games of *Magic,* this time with a twist: where once players had anted up cards, the pros would ante up cash won at the main event instead. Little by little, *Magic*'s high-rollers introduced an after-hours gambling culture to the heady Pro Tour scene.

But fleecing friends for their winnings only has so much appeal, and soon a number of *Magic* players began to look elsewhere for a way to monetise their unique skill set. Their inspiration would come from an unlikely source, but it was such a revelation when it did, that there would be no turning back. Jon Finkel in particular recalls its impact well. "I remember thinking, 'I could do that,'" he says, having watched a film that would set the cat among the *Magic*-playing pigeons. That film was the 1998 Matt Damon vehicle *Rounders*.

While the film itself may not have been an unqualified success (today, it scores a 65 per cent 'fresh' rating on review site rottentomatoes.com), what it did brilliantly is expose an impressionable audience to the thrill of high-stakes poker. Damon's character, desperately in need of money to settle debts with a Russian mobster, charges from poker table to poker table racheting up the drama with every hand. As he does, he grows in stature and decisiveness, eventually dropping out of college to try his hand in poker's big leagues at the game's spiritual home of Las Vegas. To say the film struck a chord with *Magic*'s young pros would be an understatement and soon, a breakaway crowd would follow Damon on the path to poker glory and Las Vegas' neon delights.

For Finkel, the film landed at a pivotal time in his *Magic* career. By winning his first Pro Tour in April 1998 and following that up with the Player of the Year award as that season's highest ranking pro, the New Jersey nerd-done-good could not help but feel his appetite for *Magic* wane. Having set out with so much to prove, such a frustrating school-life to leave behind, Finkel had blossomed but left himself few challenges to conquer. "Even without saying as much," he says, "I think I just felt that I didn't have a huge amount left to prove." Poker, though, one of the classic games that *Magic* hoped to emulate in its longevity and reach, suddenly appeared before Finkel like a vast unknown, ripe with promise and potential winnings. For a while, it usurped *Magic* in his affections and set him upon a newly exciting journey. "I got obsessed with having something new to learn, to play, to excel at," he says. "And you know, the money of course was a part of it. But it wasn't just that."

AFTER YEARS OF playing *Magic* at the game's top tables, the Finkel generation brought an impressive card-gaming resumé to poker, one which would have been impossible for them to accumulate playing the classic card game alone. How were, in many cases, teenage kids supposed to learn the game's finer strategic points, let alone the infinitesimal variations in bluffing or reading an opponent in high-pressure situations it entails, without attending casinos or poker clubs? *Magic* became their training ground and, like the youth leagues of any other sport, hardened them for the big leagues when the time came. Instead of learning only physical stamina, though, they could hone mental skills, too, many of which crossed over into poker. Like *Magic*, it was a game combining a delicate balance of both luck and skill.

Also like *Magic,* poker's degree of variance – of randomness – is such that it evens out over time, meaning that just like *Magic,* while anyone can get lucky now and then, optimal play will bring long-term rewards. Finkel asserts that there is only one correct play at any given time in *Magic* – something that highlights how rational one must be in the game. That is a lesson that new poker players can struggle to get to grips with, often becoming flustered ('going on tilt') when hands don't pan out and money wagered at the table disappears down the drain. Separating outcomes from process is the mental discipline required for success at both games – identifying and making the correct play each and every time, no matter whether bad luck scotches your plan and affects your results.

In that sense, Finkel's forte of making quick decisions based on incomplete information was perfect for poker, too. He and the young pros slinging spells at *Magic* tournaments every weekend were essentially developing their ability to stack up probabilities on the fly, judge risk and correctly assess when to commit to a play – or when to hold back. That kind of knowledge is just as invaluable at the Pro Tour as it is at the Texas Hold 'Em tables of Vegas or Atlantic City and, for previous generations of poker players, could be an excruciatingly expensive lesson to learn. But gradually, as *Magic* players reached the legal age for gambling in most US casinos of 21, they began to apply themselves. Spurred on by the *Rounders* buzz and eager to test themselves at a new and more high-profile game, they would shake up the staid poker world in spectacular fashion. Indeed, says Finkel, what they would discover is that, "*Magic* is more complex than poker." It was a fact of life that poker's old guard would learn the hard way.

IN THE LATE 1990s, poker was a sleeping giant, resolutely a game rather than a sport, slumbering as the world around it was undergoing an internet-driven revolution. The game was hugely popular the world over – from teens trying to catch the opposite sex with their pants down (literally) to the hardened gamblers of the Vegas Strip – but it remained a pursuit only casually pursued by the mainstream. *Rounders* suddenly made it look thrilling to a whole new generation of potential players. On top of that, new media created huge opportunities for the game. The fragmentation of monolithic analogue television into digital channels with airtime to fill, the proliferation of the internet – another non-traditional training ground – and the arrival on the scene of brilliant young card-playing minds, conspired to shake up the game beyond all recognition.

The early warning signs were there: Chris Pikula, winner of the 2000 *Magic* invitational and with a string of Grand Prix and Pro Tour Top 8s under his belt, heralded the change. In 2002, he made the final table in one of the events at the blue-riband World Series of Poker, prompting gasps from the game's assembled press pack. In 2003, meanwhile, the game hit the airwaves for the first time as a televised spectator sport, even borrowing techniques gleaned from ESPN2's coverage of the *Magic* Pro Tour, according to Skaff Elias. Then, that same year, an internet player and poker neophyte named Chris Moneymaker made waves with a sensational accomplishment. Having won a free-seat in the $10,000 No Limit Hold 'Em main event of the World Series of Poker in an online competition, he swept aside his rivals to claim the $2.5-million top prize and a coveted World Series championship bracelet. It was his first live tournament ever.

In 2004 then, when the annual World Series of Poker rolled around again, the spotlight was shining on the event brighter than ever before. A total of 2,576 players descended on the main event, many inspired by Moneymaker's fairytale win the previous year. Only 839 players had featured then. Numerous young *Magic* players were among the crowd, totally unfazed by the tournament environment and readying themselves for an assault on the top tables. It was a coming out party for a new poker generation – and Jon Finkel and dozens of his *Magic* friends were included.

While Finkel might have been knocked out after four hours of elite-level poker, the other *Magic* kids stormed onwards. By the end, two of the nine players at the main event's final table were *Magic* players: David Williams, a close friend of Finkel's from the Pro Tour, and the 2001 Swedish national champion Mattias Andersson. Williams had been practising hard for the event alongside another *Magic* player named Eric Froehlich, whose poker speciality was the No Limit game – and it showed. As hand after hand was dealt, and player after player was eliminated, Williams dug in. Although he was eventually beaten to first place, Williams came second to bag total winnings of $3.5 million. It was a remarkable achievement that signalled a breakthrough for the new generation of talent who had cut their teeth on *Magic* and polished their skills in online poker rooms. Says David Kushner, whose book *Jonny Magic and the Card Shark Kids* explores the phenomenon in detail, "It was huge [...] That was the time when the poker establishment woke up – abruptly! – to the power and presence of these young players who were weaned on *Magic* and the Net."

And, while the 2004 young guns stunned the poker establishment, the *Magic* clique took it in its stride. Even Richard Garfield had tuned in on television to watch what felt like a logical extension of his players' triumphs. Used to the Pro Tour's demands, they had already been there and done that. They were veteran card slingers despite their tender years. That included Williams' friend and practice partner, Froehlich. He only became eligible to play in the WSOP the following year – and duly became the youngest player ever at the time to win one of the competition's championship bracelets. He says, "*Magic* was the greatest stepping stone possible for people getting into poker." By putting a bunch of teenage kids under the lights and cameras and having them play an intellectual game for thousands of dollars, the Pro Tour had inadvertently created the perfect set up for success. By the time the Williams, Anderssons and Froehlichs of the world hit the final tables of the WSOP, they had nothing left to fear. "I ended up feeling no pressure," says Froehlich. "To some extent, I felt like I had been there before."

Froehlich had mastered the game online (before he legally should have), watching over his friend Brock Parker's shoulder as he cleaned up in internet poker rooms. Parker himself was another *Magic* player with an impressive pedigree who became a Pro Tour champion in 2003. A year later, while Williams was battling in the main event of the 2004 WSOP, Parker made the final table of the $1,500 Limit Hold 'Em Shoot Out competition. He has gone on to win over $3 million on the pro poker circuit, cashing 41 times at the World Series and winning three of its treasured championship bracelets. Many credit him with turning *Magic*'s pros on to poker, while Parker himself says it was – once again – *Rounders* that sparked his poker habit. Soon after seeing the film, he jumped into the online game and after a year or two, half a dozen or so of his *Magic* friends had joined him, excelling at a game that felt made for them. "If your brain is wired the right way you should be able to be successful at both or either game," says Parker.

The undoubted skill of a new poker generation was not met with universal approval from the poker establishment, however. For every enlightened player, fascinated by the rise of a new generation and a completely alien card-gaming concept, there were also, says Parker, plenty of "condescending jerks" for the *Magic* graduates to deal with. Perhaps that was to be expected. The young players usurping the poker hierarchy were hogging the limelight and further cementing their place in a new social pecking order where gaming was an acceptable trade to ply. As Parker puts it, he wanted to be free of the working week's nine-to-five drudgery and would tread on a few toes to achieve that. For others, poker's new televised, mainstream accessibility and its classic status free of fantasy-genre hang-ups was a motivation to succeed. "A large part is that people know more about what poker is, at a high level," says Finkel. "They know it's a difficult game testing something meaningful. A lot of people just have no idea what *Magic* is or that it's really that big a deal to be really good at it." Winning titles and piles of chips in front of the cameras at Vegas is a step up in legitimacy – even from the Pro Tour's edifying heights. It was natural then, that having tasted success and garnered self-esteem playing *Magic*, the game's very best players would seek to spread their wings and test just what they might be capable of in the wider world. Poker, as it turned out, was the perfect port of call for some of those players and a neat adjunct to the *Magic* lifestyle. The effect has been a powerful and productive crossover that ultimately boosts both games' standing. Says Froehlich: "The existence of *Magic* has brought together a lot of the brightest people on this planet to help them conquer both games simultaneously." That can be no bad thing.

Still, for Froehlich, there is no forgetting where he came from, no escaping his first love. While poker has been the lucrative end point of a formative and empowering journey, the journey – as always – is what counts. "I enjoy playing *Magic* more and the community is composed of all my closest friends in life," he says. "In the end that's because *Magic* is my hobby and poker is my job." His is a career built in cards, the thinking man's sport. It is also one which may never have been possible without Richard Garfield's creation, the Pro Tour or the nurturing environment it helped create. Says Froehlich, "I owe *Magic* everything."

CHAPTER TWENTY-THREE
Lords of the Pit

As SOON AS the idea for *Magic* had slipped Richard Garfield's lips and lit up Peter Adkison's brain like a shiny ball bearing blasted into the luminous depths of a shuddering pinball machine, doubt – however fleetingly – set in. Would a game so radically different, so maddeningly modular, even be possible to design? While Garfield's own brilliance put those doubts to rest, there were legitimate question marks over how to keep the design process going, once the game had been released. Garfield, despite throwing together the game's first expansion *Arabian Nights* single-handedly, was quick to acknowledge that he would be unable to design every single *Magic* card himself. Instead, he delegated the next expansions to different teams: his loyal friend Barry Reich would work on a set codenamed *Spectral Chaos*, Skaff Elias and a number of other Philadelphia playtesters would set to work on *Ice Age*, another group began work on a set dubbed *Menagerie* – and on top of that, a pair of enterprising Canadian playtesters cooked up the backbone of the set that would become *Legends*. It was a frantic race to produce cards for the clamouring player-base, but not a sustainable one. Once Richard Garfield left his teaching job at Walla Walla's Whitman College to join Wizards full-time, his first major task was to set up a functioning R&D department, which could guarantee a steady supply of cards as the game's production settled into a less frenetic rhythm.

While initially, that meant hiring many of the game's first playtesters to fill seats and generate ideas, Garfield could see that a division of labour would also be vital to ensure quality control. With key figures like Skaff Elias juggling several roles, working 100-hour weeks and sleeping under his desk, there was a need to provide structure in *Magic* card production. Otherwise, there was a risk the process would bottleneck at one over-worked individual or become sloppy and nix the game's surging popularity. In order to do that, Garfield split R&D into two halves. On the one hand, a design team would originate new card ideas. On the other, development would check and tweak their designs to make sure they were up to scratch. The developers would be the rigorous engineers to design's fanciful architects.

The search for capable developers led to a new influx of faces into *Magic* R&D. Perhaps the most important of those recruits would be Mark Rosewater, who had been proving his worth at *The Duelist* magazine, where he devised fiendishly complex *Magic* puzzles for each issue. Rosewater's background was as a writer (he penned scripts for the sitcom *Roseanne* before joining Wizards). His affinity for words and concepts, rather than numbers like the University of Pennsylvania alumni, would have a profound influence on R&D's approach to making *Magic*.

EVERY DAY AFTER rising early to pack off his kids to school, human dynamo Mark Rosewater springs into action. First, *Magic*'s head designer publishes his online comic strip called *Tales from the Pit* (the 'pit' being R&D's chunk of the Wizards office), a single-frame of unadulterated geek humour. Then, steeling himself for the onslaught, he takes to Twitter (where he has almost 50,000 followers) to wade through some of the many questions he gets bombarded with. *Magic*'s design supremo is quick to hear from players, whether they love or loathe his work. After that, the loquacious designer records a rapid-fire podcast on his drive to the Wizards office, before rocking up to his desk, with more already done than many achieve in their entire working day. The morning disappears in a flurry of meetings, phone calls and interviews; then at lunchtime, Rosewater works out. In the afternoon, he might find time to work on a few card designs, before finally waving his colleagues in the pit goodbye, journeying home, putting his kids to bed, spending time with his wife, then squeezing in some writing before eventually, gratefully, passing out.

Despite his incredible workload, Rosewater has regularly professed to having his dream job – one he is wont to describe in psychological terms. *Here in* Magic *R&D*, he once wrote, *our job is to create a game that makes players happy.* That remains his focus – and has shaped his vision of the game, ever since he walked through R&D's doors in 1995. Then, he was the lone words guy amongst numbers guys. Now he is the design overlord – and his knack for verbalising what the *Magic* design process should be has helped create a template for the game's evolution. From an eager chancer who approached Wizards for work at Gencon '94, the effervescent Ohioan has become one of the game's most important custodians. Drawing on design theory from across the spectrum (one of his influences is Dieter Rams, the modernist behind Braun's most popular designs and proponent of the *Ten Principles for Good Design*), Rosewater has elevated his work from cranking out 600-odd playing pieces a year to being a holistic and highly conceptual designer, irrespective of field. It is an impressive development and one which has been aided by Timmy, Johnny and Spike, three chaps who joined R&D quickly after Rosewater. Spike came first, ushered through the door with the Pro Tour's creation in early 1996.

JUST AS THE big-money Pro Tour transformed players' lives, it also had a knock-on effect on the game itself: as its fans raised their standards, its producers had to, too. One key area in need of attention was the game's rules. They had functioned – more or less – for kitchen-table gaming when the game came out in 1993, but needed to be better codified for the Pro Tour's heightened stakes. While the over-arching rules were tightened up, with major revisions taking place in 1999 at the release of *Sixth Edition*, there was also a drive under Joel Mick, lead designer from 1995 to 1997, to improve the quality of the rules text on each printed card, too. One of early *Magic* design's characteristics was that cards were dreamt up in a vacuum and little thought was given to consistency. Mick aimed to template key functions in the game so that cards the designers felt *should* do the same thing actually did perform that way in the context of the rules. Although it would be an ongoing process that lasted many years, the evolution kick-started by Mick was part of *Magic* design maturing and trying to put an end to the endless rules headaches, ad hoc judge rulings and reams of errata issued to clarify how cards were supposed to work. The guts of the game had to stand up to scrutiny by a new breed of customer: 'the tournament player'. The tournament player wasn't simply someone jamming a couple of Starter Decks together in the hope of squishing his pals with Craw Wurm and Lord of the Pit; the tournament player was in the game for one reason only: to win. Not only would he or she be reading up on the latest deck 'tech' on the Dojo, but he or she would be collaborating with friends trying to 'break' cards for a decisive advantage at the nearest PTQ, Grand Prix or Pro Tour – to eke out overpowered interactions made possible by an R&D oversight, an unforeseen combo or ambiguous card wording. "The Pro Tour really saw the start of rules lawyering," remembers 'Schools of Magic' author Rob Hahn. Understanding the game on an atomic level could now be worth thousands of dollars.

What would cause huge ructions at Wizards was the emergence of players who understood the game better than those making it. While *Magic* production had settled into a steady rhythm of one core set (derived from *Alpha* and featuring a rotating number of reprints) and three expansion sets (which together formed one 'block') every 12 months, R&D had become isolated from the Pro Tour arms race and hot-house collaborative innovation it had inspired. Whilst the designers were coming up with ever-more outlandish ideas, the development team had not yet figured out how to tweak those cards' power levels. The engineers were struggling to reign in the architects, or at least fully understand the implications of their creations.

This dysfunction was highlighted by a run of three fateful blocks in *Magic* history – *Tempest* block in 1997-98, *Urza's Saga* block in 1998-1999 and *Mercadian Masques* block in 1999-2000 – which peaked with the so-called 'combo winter' of 1998-99. *Tempest* block was the first to properly feature Richard Garfield on the design team since *Arabian Nights* and caused great excitement among players at its release. What they discovered when ripping open their Booster Packs were a host of powerful cards, including environment-defining staples such as the red creature Jackal Pup and artifact finisher Cursed Scroll. Both were aggressively costed at a single mana and greatly sped up the game.

While that visceral upping of the game's power level may have thrilled many players in the short term, it presented a problem for R&D: namely, what to do next? The result was the block of three sets focused on the character Urza, an artificer whose story had been hinted at in *Antiquities*, the game's second expansion. *Urza's Saga* was released in October 1998 and was followed by *Urza's Legacy* (February 1999) and *Urza's Destiny* (May 1999). As players quickly perceived, R&D's response to *Tempest* had been simple – in a panic almost, they had attempted to out-do the preceding block with yet more powerful cards. What R&D failed to spot, however, was just how 'broken' some of their new cards were – and how ruthlessly tournament players would exploit them. Cards such as Tolarian Academy (a land which produces multiple blue mana), Time Spiral (a blue card-drawing spell which refills both players' hands) and Stroke of Genius (an instant which can make either player draw as many cards as its caster pays in mana) were all released in *Urza's Saga*. All were sussed out in record quick time by the Pro Tour players and had an immediate impact on the tournament metagame.

What these cards did was provide the heart of a combo deck – one that generated huge amounts of mana (much like Mike Long's Pros-Bloom deck had in 1997), which could then be used to fuel a Stroke of Genius big enough to make an opponent draw all the remaining cards in his or her library. Dubbed 'decking', running an opponent out of cards is an alternative way of winning the game. While the design of the Tolarian Academy deck cooked up by *Magic*'s keenest minds was in itself slick, smart and brutal, it was a PR disaster. Combo decks generally seek to win as quickly as possible, with as little interaction as can be managed with their opponent. Rather than summon creatures that chip away at an opponent's life total – leaving opportunities to riposte – a combo deck is focused on one plan and will try to execute it in as streamlined a fashion as possible. This normally culminates in one inevitable turn where the pilot 'goes off', finding all the necessary pieces in his deck, casting them with enough protection to fend off opposing counterspells and finally destroying a helpless opponent who has been forced to sit watching for long stretches as their game loss is played out in front of them. While combo decks have a place in a balanced metagame where control, aggro and combo archetypes boast the same power and can keep each other in check, the *Urza's Saga* metagame was anything but balanced. Combo ruled supreme – and if you didn't want to play such a deck yourself, you had two options: one – lose as your showboating opponent stomped you into the ground, or two – stop showing up to your local tournament altogether. As players in their droves chose the second option, Wizards freaked out. Cards had to be banned in the company's flagship format, Type II, the worst possible fate for Wizards' business plan. Type II had been created to level the playing field for tournament players who did not have access to old and expensive cards – the notion was that with those cards kicked out of the format, players could use any of the cards they opened from current Booster Packs. But banning cards meant hitting sales – who would want to buy a Booster Pack knowing the cards inside might not be permissible in their decks? As Mark Rosewater would later write, the whole *Urza's* block mess was, *the one and only time Magic R&D has ever been brought to the CEO's office and yelled at in my entire time at the company.*

To avoid another tournament fiasco, sales collapse and humiliating dressing down, R&D swung completely in the opposite direction for *Mercadian Masques* block. Having been made so rudely aware that the power level of their cards was faulty, they played things as safe as they could – ultimately producing one of the most watered-down blocks in *Magic*'s history. *Mercadian Masques* served up a turgid play experience that did little to entice players back after the combo winter's degeneracy. It was a duff block, at the opposite extreme to *Urza's Saga*, which made it clear that *Magic* R&D was floundering. What they needed was someone who could help them understand exactly how cards were being used in the real world, an archetypal tournament player. Luckily, in the Pro Tour, Wizards had created the perfect recruiting ground for *Magic* experts.

In 2002, Mark Rosewater wrote an article that 'Who's the Beatdown' author Mike Flores describes as the most influential in *Magic* history. The article in question is called 'Timmy, Johnny and Spike' – and while it might sound like the start of a sketch from Rosewater's sitcom days, it is something very different indeed. It is so significant, says Flores, "because it actually defines who all of us are."

Rather than real-life R&D staff, the titular trio of Rosewater's article are nicknames given to three psychographic profiles that emerged during the late 1990s in R&D – the archetypal players who the guys making *Magic* realised they were trying to make happy. The first to emerge was the 'tournament player' – a loose description that was fleshed out as tournaments became integral to *Magic* culture. He (or she, though it is mostly he) derives his pleasure from winning games, in whatever way that can be most effectively accomplished. The tournament player is competitive, plays to win, plays the best deck out there (net-decking without scruple) and enjoys triumphing over his opponent via superior play skill. He, in particular, had feasted on *Urza's Saga* block and, after some initial head scratching, earned the moniker Spike.

While the quantity of wins is Spike's motivator, it is the quality of wins that interests both Timmy and Johnny. Heck, sometimes they're not even that bothered about winning. Timmy, whose profile Rosewater hit upon during the design of *Tempest* block, is what R&D dub the 'power gamer'. As Rosewater wrote in his article, *Timmy likes to win big. He doesn't want to eke out a last-minute victory. Timmy wants to smash his opponents. He likes his cards to be impressive and he enjoys playing big creatures and big spells.* Timmy can often be a young, inexperienced player – but lurks in a lot of grown-up *Magic* players, too; those for whom the game is first and foremost a social experience, occasionally augmented by a big, splashy play.

Johnny, meanwhile, was christened during the development of *Urza's Saga* – and represents in many ways Rosewater himself, still the arch-puzzler from his *Duelist* days. Johnny is creative, innovative and loves to build his own decks around overlooked cards, often ones screaming out to be turned into a powerful combo. Johnny was well-served by *Urza's Saga*, a set packed with cards that dovetailed to produce powerful plays. Unfortunately, the cards designed to make him happy were over the mark in terms of raw power and degenerate combo potential. Rosewater argues that while the psychographic profiles are extremely important, most players in real life are a hybrid. Little did R&D realise just how many Johnny-Spikes there were out there, happy to tune their combo decks into lean *Magic* machines, that would break the back of the tournament metagame.

When R&D did then turn to the Pro Tour to recruit, they were after a Spike with enough self-awareness to explain his thought process; a *Magic* turncoat who could break cards in-house (so they could be fixed), rather than at the Pro Tour. While a few names were bandied around (Brian Weissman was one of them, but failed to show up for his interview), it would be a university student named Randy Buehler who would land the coveted gig. His task on the development team was repairing the damage done by the three troublesome blocks that had provoked Wizards' biggest wobble to date. Champion of Pro Tour Chicago 1997, Buehler arrived at his desk at Wizards in October 1999. "It was," he says, "like switching teams."

Development had malfunctioned. But Buehler credits Richard Garfield for perceiving how important the department would be in shaping a desirable metagame at source. "He recognised that no-one can call their own kids ugly," says Buehler. "He could have been the man who dictated how *Magic* was going to be. But he was the one who felt that a fundamental distinction had to be made between the designers, whose job it is to make it is as cool as it can be. And developers, whose job it is to sort the balance out." Buehler's mission would be to buttress development's competency, while educating design about the problems they were causing further up the chain. As Buehler set about his task with relish, working firstly on *Invasion* block, the players to really benefit from his expertise were those with an inner Timmy. Buehler – the former Spike par excellence – could see that there was a huge imbalance in the game between the power level of its spells (its sorceries and instants – cast for a one-time effect) and its creatures (in theory at least, the main way to kill an opponent). That disparity had been highlighted by the combo winter, but was built into the game at a far more basic level.

"When I showed up, Serra Angel [the finisher in Brian Weissman's The Deck] was a card that was considered maybe too good to reprint by R&D," says Buehler. "I was like, 'what are you guys talking about? Big creatures are terrible right now! I don't care what you *think* your power curve is, this is what's actually good. This is what is true about the game.'" Counterspell, at a cost of two blue mana, could stop any opposing spell before it came into play. Lightning Bolt, for one red mana, could deal three damage to any target – enough to pick off most commonly played creatures. Swords to Plowshares, for a single white mana, could remove any creature entirely from the game. These spells, says Buehler, were so efficient compared to creatures that they had become completely stifling. It was time to redress the balance. "It was me betraying the Spike that I was, everything I knew about how to win in the game," says Buehler, "I was saying to R&D, 'You guys gave me spells that were too good.'"

On Buehler's watch then, two key trends emerged: big creatures were ratcheted up in power and playability. Concurrently, the answers to them were made more awkward than the triumvirate of Counterspell, Lightning Bolt and Swords to Plowshares. For many experienced players, this was tantamount to reducing the game's skill level – particularly, when a 'cycle' (a thematically linked group of cards, often with one example per colour) of powerful creatures was printed in the *Onslaught* block. In Draft and Sealed Deck in particular, each 'pit fighter' from the cycle essentially won the game when it came in to play. Some players felt that this was a deliberate attempt to up the game's variance – the random element to winning. Whoever drew the killer creature first, just won. Kai Budde, the 'German Juggernaut', complained to Buehler that he was now prone to losing to worse players. But Buehler was unrepentant: Wizards wanted – every now and then – the worse player to be able to win. *Magic*'s element of imperfect knowledge (its hidden hand and cards yet to be drawn from each player's deck) and the variance that entailed, could become an exciting, dramatic part of the game if managed correctly. While Buehler accepts that in the case of those *Onslaught* creatures, R&D were very consciously pushing the envelope, a happier balance has been struck since. Current top professional Luis Scott-Vargas says that it is ultimately to the game's benefit, "A lot of what grows *Magic* is somewhat higher variance designs and even designs which are simply friendlier to new players." Whereas back in the day, top players loved to wrestle their powerful control decks against each other, with the most skilled player emerging victorious, Scott-Vargas says that is not how to grow the game. "If you want a game like that, play chess – where the better player always wins. *Magic* has experienced its biggest successes when it has moved away from that." While that means replicating Budde's seven Pro Tour wins will be nigh-on impossible for today's generation of pros, it does feed the game's aspirational model: if you face Scott-Vargas at a Grand Prix, you *do* have a chance of beating him, fuelling your desire to keep playing the game.

BUEHLER QUICKLY CLIMBED the ladder at Wizards, becoming a lead developer, then head of *Magic* design and development, with Mark Rosewater becoming *Magic*'s head designer in 2003, reporting up to Buehler. Thereafter, Buehler would move to the company's digital division and *Magic* design would be spearheaded by the ebullient and ambitious Rosewater, with Aaron Forsythe (director of R&D, *Magic: The Gathering*) his foil. Forsythe says he is the 'bad cop' of the two, the straight man, who tends to announce sensitive issues such as card bannings. Like Buehler, he joined Wizards from the Pro Tour and says the relationship between design and development is fundamental to *Magic's* success today. "The tension is necessary and wonderful, a similar checks-and-balances system to a well-functioning government." That said, passions run high on both sides of the divide, with creative energies being poured into the product by both teams. "We have a lot of arguments in R&D," says Forsythe. "But they're often settled amicably and everyone goes home happy."

Ultimately, fostering that delicate balance between the two R&D functions is down to Buehler and the expertise he brought to the pit when it was down on its luck. "I feel like getting development up to the point that it could do enough with the card sets so the world wouldn't break every time a new mechanic came out did a lot to stabilise the game and build the foundation from which it has been able to keep growing," he says. Fixing the yin and yang between design and development quietened fears about the game's longevity, smoothing out the peaks and troughs of the *Tempest, Urza's Saga* and *Mercadian Masques* blocks. Today, cards are rigorously tested in the famed 'Future future league', an in-house tournament environment that mimics the way Standard (formerly Type II) will look years down the line. Here, the former pros in the pit dust off their deck-building skills and flesh out the main archetypes they expect newly designed cards to fit into upon their release. While they might not be tuning decks down to the last sideboard card, they are trying to make sure the environment is balanced – and that another combo winter can never happen again. Knowing how badly *Urza's Saga* block affected the game means that striking the right balance remains 'nerve-wracking' for Forsythe and co as they play out *Magic's* future. Development's dozen or so testers are pitted against the entire *Magic* brains trust. So far, they have kept another winter largely at bay.

* * *

ROSEWATER, MEANWHILE, IS steering the game's design via a carefully thought out roadmap. Ever the verbal reasoner, Rosewater has studied the game's past and delineated what he calls *Magic*'s different "stages of design" in an attempt to plot out its evolution. The first stage of *Magic* design was characterised by the very individual nature of designs – cards sculpted one-by-one as they had been in the playtest days at the University of Philadelphia. That changed in the second stage of design, lasting from 1996's *Mirage* to the conclusion of the lacklustre *Mercadian Masques* block in 2000. And while that period featured some notable disasters – including the dreaded combo winter – it nonetheless established the notion of the 'block'; of multiple sets, linked by setting and game mechanics. The third stage consolidated that concept. From *Invasion* up until *Kamigawa* block's conclusion in 2005, each block was given a crystal-clear theme, was tuned for Limited play (Draft and Sealed Deck, where players build decks from sealed product) and featured cards aimed at all player types: Timmy, Johnny and Spike. It was the last before Rosewater began his reign as head designer (don't be confused by the dates – he began his stint in 2003, but new sets begin their journey through design and development two years in advance). Rosewater ushered in design's fourth stage, featuring integrated block planning, inter-block compatibility (so that the different blocks in Standard had plenty of interactions) and finally, better integration between the design and creative teams to create rich, compelling settings from both a gameplay and flavour point of view. This was not simply design, but design thinking – the sculpting of the process towards achieving certain goals, rather than the designing of cards that fixed individual needs or problems. As industrial designer Charles Eames said, "Design is a plan for arranging elements in such a way as best to accomplish a particular purpose" – and that goes for the entire process, too, not just the finished product. Rosewater, with his peculiar skill set, helped pull back the camera and look at the wider picture. It was a huge step forward in the conception of R&D's work.

While the fourth stage had its hits, notably the wildly popular *Ravnica* block and the *Scars of Mirrodin* block which drew the period to a close in 2010, it did also feature a period of dangerous 'complexity creep'. Rosewater strongly believes that the one factor which could hamstring the game in future is if the barrier to entry becomes too high – if the amount of knowledge required by a player encountering *Magic* for the first time is simply too huge to grasp. Thus a trend dubbed 'New World Order' has gripped R&D, aimed at simplifying the game wherever possible. Superfluous rules have been nipped and tucked and on-card text has been scrutinised for anything headache-inducing. It is an approach entirely in-keeping with Rosewater's perception of *Magic* as a product that, when it comes down to it, should make people happy. Inevitably, this has led to accusations of dumbing down from sections of the player base. Rosewater, though, is adamant that the *Magic* experience has been improved for most players and, all importantly, for new players. "I think a lot of our recent success has come from us spending more time thinking about how to make it easier to learn and play *Magic* for the beginner," he says. Booming tournament participation and steadily growing sales would seem to back him up. By 2013, *Magic's* annual revenue had grown to an estimated $250 million, after growing 182 per cent in the previous five years. The game now makes up five percent of Hasbro's total revenue. Making the game accessible safeguards its future.

Meanwhile, *Magic* design has now entered its fifth stage under Rosewater. "Its key tenet is that making cards is about finding a way to interweave all the components together," he says. "Mechanics aren't separate from flavour but rather part of the flavour. The gameplay itself is key to making the game feel the right way." Notable examples of that philosophy were presaged in the *Scars of Mirrodin* block, which represented the gradual victory of the poisonous 'Phyrexians' with changes to the game's mana symbols on certain spells – packing the message into the medium in a wholly post-modern way. Similarly, the *Innistrad* block was conceived from the top down, designed to translate gothic horror tropes into the *Magic* gameplay experience. It was an indisputable hit, despite initial controversy over another innovation: double-sided cards. These played up the notion of transformation in horror – from experiments gone wrong that turned scientists into monsters, to werewolves shifting shape at full-moon. Players were up in arms when the cards were announced, but loved them once they got their hands on them. Why? Because the marriage of flavour and the mechanism used to translate that into gameplay was seamless. Rosewater says, "I'm a big believer that games are emotional far more than they are intellectual and that *Magic's* success has a lot to do with how we're able to make things that 'feel right.'"

Indeed for Rosewater, that harks rights back to the game's origins. Garfield's key strength was understanding how important that feel was, and this is precisely the reason *Magic* took off as quickly as it did.

The breaking of new ground like *Innistrad*'s double-faced cards also hints at *Magic* design's future. "What's the sixth stage of design going to be? That one I'm not sure of yet, but I think it will have to do with us taking things we think of as being unchangeable and changing them," says Rosewater. That might send a shudder down the spine of many *Magic* players – especially Spike, whose focus on winning nudges him towards conservatism. The more the game stays the same, after all, the easier it is to rely on past lessons to keep winning. But *Magic* design is not staying still and new ground continues to be broken. For many fans, this process entails peril and the risk of 'power creep' is one that has to be wrestled. Whatever R&D do, they must be careful not to make increasingly powerful cards that at once obsolete previous designs and strangle the scope for innovation down the line. Currently, it is a line some feel they overstep too often. The game has been noticeably sped up by a vast improvement in cheap-to-cast creatures for example. "I feel like on my watch, spells got worse and big creatures got better," says Randy Buehler. "But since I left, the smaller creatures have gotten better, too. The game is a little faster now than I like." It is a concern echoed by numerous other players, but may simply be a necessary evil, as generational change hits the player-base. Those who have played the game for the best part of its two-decade lifespan are perhaps getting long in the tooth or at the very least nostalgic. "I often look back fondly on formats past," says *Magic* columnist Mike Flores. "I think the game is too fast at the moment – you can't play these long, cerebral games that I enjoyed playing in my younger years – but I think that's a function of many things. Maybe Wizards are going for an audience with a shorter attention span for instance. And, if it's better for the game if they cultivate that audience, then you know what? Maybe people like me have to suck it up and change, which I find to be an acceptable outcome."

Either way, *Magic* R&D will continue to do its best to satisfy Timmy, Johnny and Spike, playing a delicate balancing game with a product that has become the cornerstone of a community and an integral part of people's lives. Rosewater makes no apologies, though – that will involve pushing at barriers, just as the game's designers have tried to do for over 20 years, while being kept in check by the souped-up development department that is Buehler's legacy to R&D. "That's the big lesson," says Rosewater. "*Magic*'s evolution is about us constantly re-examining what's possible. There are things I do today that I never could have dreamed I'd do 10 years ago, which means who knows what I'll get to do 10 years from now." It is in part what makes him able to state with conviction what many *Magic* players only cautiously dream: that there are – at least from a creative standpoint – plenty of *Magic* cards still to come. "I have no doubt in my mind," says Rosewater, "that *Magic* will outlive me. The game system is so robust that it can be extrapolated for centuries." Whatever his initial fears, Garfield got his design more than right. *Magic* is not just modular, but almost endlessly expandable. It is, in that respect, a marvel of modern design.

CHAPTER TWENTY-FOUR
It's a Small World

MAGIC'S EVER-EXPANDING universe took it worldwide in record time. While America was the game's epicentre, the international market soon picked up on the shockwaves after its seismic breakthrough. As early as November 1994, *Magic: The Gathering* became *Magic: L'Adunanza*, an Italian translation of the game. Despite the meagre supply of English-language product making demand almost impossible to gauge, it proved a runaway hit. *Magic* seemed a game capable of striking a chord with very different cultures and in Italy it slotted into a long tradition of playing card games like bridge and briscola on sunny terraces, as much as it did into a *Dungeons & Dragons* heritage. It was not only a globalising game, but one that offered the same response to globalisation that savvy marketers would also hit upon later: mass personalisation. *Magic* was the paper precursor to the Nike ID store – an adaptable product, that could be tuned to personal whims in the face of the cultural homogenisation augured by each new world trade agreement, each new conquest by the market economy.

More translations followed and today the game is available in 11 languages, with many foreign cards prized for their exotic chic. *Magic*'s rapid proliferation has been aided by the ease with which it can be played against opponents speaking different languages. Compared to more narrative role-playing games, *Magic* is structured and mechanistic, many cards are iconic and recognisable from their art, and a handful of key words from the game's rules are usually enough to get through a match with anyone. As Wizards' organised play programme kicked in, that meant a brilliant smashing together of gamers from very different backgrounds and a broadening of horizons for often previously shy players. Peter Adkison explains games as a structured way for people to interact, when perhaps they lack the confidence to do so spontaneously. *Magic* would prove capable of doing that across cultures, even if I personally sometimes stumbled on hang-ups that stopped me clicking with opponents in new lands in the way the focused tournament set did. Brian Weissman, creator of The Deck, remembers what a buzz it was meeting players from across the globe in hotel lobbies, bars and bedrooms as professional play attracted a cosmopolitan crowd. "*Magic* was like a universal language," he says. "I can remember back in the early days of the Pro Tour just sitting round on hotel room floors in various parts of the world, playing game after game against people who could barely speak English at all and we still had this social bond around the game. That was pretty amazing."

As Pro Tours started to be staged abroad, starting with Pro Tour Paris in 1997 and the schedule of Grand Prix swelled, *Magic* encircled the globe. The emergence of low-cost airlines (such as easyJet in 1995), as well as the rise of an online *Magic* culture helped knit players into a closer community. First, they came together to play at international tournaments, then they stayed in touch online. And, as the rest of the world caught the *Magic* bug, it was perhaps no surprise to see America's primacy at the top of the *Magic* tree challenged, nor that the nation to do so would be the one buying all the cards in the late 1990s, the most per capita in the world: Japan.

In 1999, the World Championships made their way to Tokyo, in recognition of the Japanese market's importance. It was hoped the event would consolidate the buzzing *Magic* scene there and inspire the best local players to new heights. While there might not have been a local champion to crown at the event, it did ratchet up the enthusiasm of Japan's player base. The first generation of Japanese pros began to work diligently on their skills, particularly at two key shops in the local *Magic* scene: Tokyo's DCI Tournament Centre and Osaka's Adept. Adept was opened by a legendary figure in Japanese *Magic*, the now-deceased Muneo Shibata, a dedicated *Magic* judge who took the shop's young players under his wing and schooled them in the finer workings of tournament play.

It would be one of Shibata's fledglings who would strike a blow for

Japanese *Magic* by racking up the country's first Pro Tour Top 8 at Pro Tour Tokyo 2001. Tsuyoshi Fujita, a brilliant deckbuilder, lost in the final to the iconoclastic New Yorker Zvi Mowschowitz, but his performance helped crack a glass ceiling the Japanese had been butting up against in their efforts to mix it with the world's best. It was a watershed moment, which the nation's pros still credit as a huge inspiration today. That would be followed in 2003 by Mashahiro Kuroda smashing the same glass ceiling for good. He become the nation's first-ever Pro Tour victor at Pro Tour Kobe in February 2004 and would later credit his mentor Shibata as the most important figure in the history of Japanese *Magic*.

Notably though, both Fujita and Kuroda made their breakthroughs on home soil. Travel from Japan to tournaments in Europe or North America could be prohibitively expensive. But Japanese players also had significant cultural barriers to contend with. Japan's location and history (for example, its collectivism in the wake of World War II), have often led to its culture being described as insular. It would take a gradual broadening of horizons before pioneering pros from the South-East Asian archipelago would feel comfortable enough to smash their opponents in far-flung lands.

The player who embodied that journey best was Kenji Tsumura, from Hiroshima. Tsumura, a gangly and painfully shy boy, grew up as a rabid fan of the Manga series *Yu-Gi-Oh!* which featured a fictional card game based on *Magic*. One day in 1998 the 11-year-old Tsumura was devouring an interview with the series' creator Kazuki Takahashi, which explained his fictional card game's origins. Curious, Tsumura asked his best friend if he had heard of *Magic* and, as it turned out, he had. His older brother was a *Magic* player and, as is often the way amongst siblings, he soon had the two younger players hooked. Tsumura remembers gleefully opening the then sought-after Paladin En-Vec in his first Booster Pack. Not long after, he was cycling to tournaments every weekend, obsessing over the game and most of all, basking in the distraction it offered him from school. Academically, he felt like a failure for not netting the grades his parents expected and socially, he felt shut out of his school's popular clique. By the time he was in his late teens, he had dropped out entirely in favour of another goal: making it on the *Magic* Pro Tour.

Tsumura's first-ever professional event was also his maiden voyage beyond

Japan's shores. Pro Tour Chicago 2003, when it came, was a huge challenge to the boy who feared big crowds and was lugging a lifetime's preconceptions with him. "Because they are taller and bigger than Japanese, I was scared of foreigners," he says. "But getting to travel abroad for the first time showed me they are very kind and that made me far more comfortable." Not only that, but the trip to Chicago, though unsuccessful for Tsumura, opened his eyes to just how good the best players out there were. Whenever his matches finished he would rush off to watch his heroes Jon Finkel and Kai Budde from behind his dyed and floppy fringe, soaking up everything he could from their excellent technical play. Budde in particular was an inspiration and when Tsumura returned home he attempted to replicate the German's play style when practicing with his best friend Masashi Oiso. Soon, as their quest for Pro Tour glory intensified, they were joining other Japanese players practicing feverishly in a rented house in Tokyo. Itaru Ishida, Katsuhiro Mori, Tsuyoshi Fujita, Osamu Fujita, and Masahiko Morita were a formidable brains trust and all had a part in influencing the young Tsumura.

Surrounded by such high-quality players and with his phobia of *gaijin* kicked to the kerb, Tsumura was primed to make his breakthrough. It duly came in 2005, with not one, not two, but a staggering three Pro Tour Top 8s in one incendiary season. On top of that, he added four Grand Prix Top 8s to his list of achievements in that single season and, beating Frenchman Oliver Ruel by a single Pro Point, ended up claiming the coveted Player of the Year award for 2005.

Humility dies hard and Tsumura claims his success owed much to generational change (the game's two heavyweights Finkel and Budde were both stepping away from it at that point). While that may be true to an extent, nobody would have predicted just how decisively a new generation of Japanese players would step into the breach. For five years in a row, the Player of the Year was Japanese, beginning with Tsumura, then followed by Shouta Yasooka in 2006, Tomoharu Saitou in 2007, Shuhei Nakamura in 2008 and Yuuya Watanabe in 2009. It was an unprecedented era of dominance by a single nation and one that transformed the face of global *Magic*. It even had significant ramifications at home in Japan, says Tsumura, as the legitimising effect the Pro Tour's creators had dreamed of proved capable of transcending cultures. "The perception of gaming has changed a lot in the last decade," he says. "When I was a child, card games were considered *otaku* [obsessional] and people would hide playing them. But now, lots of people have experienced them and an older generation has seen their children playing them. We can discuss them far more casually now." On a personal level too, the Pro Tour affected its Japanese participants: Tsumura became fascinated by foreign cultures and religions and finally found his motivation to be a more diligent student. He recently put the finishing touches to an English degree.

Japan remains a key territory for *Magic* and receives special marketing attention from Wizards, including unique promotional cards as well as its own tailored coverage from the Pro Tour in Japanese. Nonetheless, while Japan's Pro Tour hot streak was a brilliant rattling of the game's established order and a marvellous performance by a coherent and communal *Magic* scene, in years to come it may also be considered the high watermark of nationhood in *Magic*. While the US can today legitimately claim to be the world's top dog again, it is such a huge and diverse nation with hot spots of *Magic* productivity so dispersed that it arguably still fits into a post-national landscape for the game. Rich Hagon, Pro Tour statistician and commentator, says team composition is evolving away from nationality. "There was certainly a point when you could have said, without fear of racism, 'What will the Japanese bring to Pro Tour Montreal?'" he says. "Ten years ago I could have said that, because there really were the Japanese, the Dutch, the French, some weirdoes in Britain, the West Coasters and the East Coasters. Even five years ago, there were a dozen Japanese players practicing in one room for a fortnight [...] But that's not true now." Instead, says Hagon, an increase in the number of Grand Prix worldwide – and the need of professional players to rake up Pro Points at them to boost their ranking – has driven an ever-increasing amount of international travel, cemented new friendships and forged new team links. Shuhei Nakamura now tests with an American team, there are British players testing with Norwegians and Belgians, French and Germans working together and so on. In many ways, it highlights the almost anachronistic incongruity at the heart of Richard Garfield's game – that as a paper product intertwined with the digital age, it has remained not simply fuel for online chatter, but a physical social network. One aided by the ease of digital communication, but one rooted in coming together to share a social experience.

That said, the ways for *Magic* players to communicate when not together in the same room have been greatly enhanced since the days of Usenet and the Dojo. While content websites, forums, and social media play a huge role in the online *Magic* conversation, it is perhaps the creation of *Magic: The Gathering Online* which has had a decisive effect on the ability of players to interact with far-flung friends and opponents. The game was developed on Randy Buehler's watch as head of R&D and is in essence a direct digital adaptation of the paper game of *Magic* – complete with the crucial collectible aspect intact. That means, in order to play the game, players must purchase virtual cards either in Booster Pack form from Wizards of the Coast or from friends or bots (automated buyers and sellers of virtual cards) inside the game economy. And while the currency used to make those purchases is called 'Event Tickets', often abbreviated to 'Tix', it is roughly equivalent in value to the real-world dollar.

Magic Online has proven a huge source of revenue for Wizards since it went live in 2002 and is worth anything up to $100 million a year, according to some sources. In keeping with the game's symbiosis with the internet, it has also helped prove the validity of an increasingly attractive online business model. "In a lot of ways, I feel like *Magic Online* is the first real American success story of the item sales business model," says Randy Buehler. "The game itself is given away, but you know that you are trying to get your customers to pay for stuff. Obviously, charging the same price for a digital Booster as we were for a physical Booster was controversial, but it worked. The game has been making money since 2002 and it's in its second decade." By 2015, the global market for virtual items, characters and other goods was estimated to be worth $49.7 billion by researchers.

Magic Online has had a sometimes-troubled life, though, suffering numerous technical setbacks that started with Wizards' decision in 2003 to ditch their initial development partner Leaping Lizard. Bringing the game in-house was a decision many of the service's 300,000 or so registered users found hubristic – and was followed by server woes, games crashes and stalled development (there is still no Mac version, for example, let alone one for smartphones and tablets) that blighted the experience of playing *Magic Online* for many users. Although new iterations of the client and a gradual rebuild of the game's codebase have addressed some problems, even Chris Kiritz, *Magic Online*'s business manager, has said it is neither the "prettiest or the easiest to use." As further improvements to the client continue to meet with delays, some users believe too little of the revenue the game generates is re-invested in its development. Says one regular user Jan van der Vegt, "This is a false economy for Wizards."

Van der Vegt, better known by his online handle Dzyl, should know. He spends countless hours on *Magic Online* and represents the new breed of aspiring professional player that the digital version of *Magic* has given birth to. The 26-year-old from Amsterdam is a lapsed student and part-time tutor. He rises late most days and gears up for a nocturnal practice session on *Magic Online*, where players can now find an opponent, irrespective of their proximity to a local shop or scene, at any time of day or night. What is more, the game's engine has the rules built into it, too. Whereas previous unofficial ways of playing online simply allowed players to represent their decks and cards and play as they would in person, *Magic Online* actively enforces the games rules, meaning players cannot perform anything illegal or incorrect in-game. Combined with the convenience of playing for long hours from the comfort of their homes, this has driven the skill level of the average PTQ grinder ever upwards and contributed to the erosion of geographic importance within the game. As Japan's star was fading in the mid-2000s, a player like Terry Soh was able to blaze a trail with GP and Pro Tour Top 8s, without a local scene to speak of. Soh lives in Petaling Jaya, Malaysia.

Dzyl is the next generation of a player like Soh: not simply using *Magic Online* to practise for his own pleasure or advancement, but also as a platform for social interaction, self-promotion and even earning. Because, when Dzyl plays *Magic Online*, he is not simply alone in his flat in Amsterdam. He is being watched, live, by thousands of fans who tune in to his performances streamed over the net, via the specialist platform Twitch. Twitch allows gamers of all stripes to broadcast their sessions direct from their computers and has turned people like Dzyl into entertainers. In the summer of 2014, Amazon snapped up the platform in a headline-grabbing purchase worth $970 million. Jeff Bezos' online behemoth could spot the value in providing content tailored to an audience increasingly turning off linear TV. And *Magic* is the site's most searched-for game.

Dzyl stumbled across Twitch when the service was still relatively new, shortly after its launch in 2011. While aimed originally at video gamers, it had become a channel for *Magic* tournament organisers to film paper games and broadcast them out to fans. Dzyl noticed that a few people were also using it to stream their regular *Magic Online* games and decided to have a crack at it himself. And, through a mixture of timing, play skill and personality, he rapidly built an impressive following, with some 2.3 million views of his stream to date. Already, after a week on the platform, he had the highest viewer count of any *Magic* streamer on Twitch, and then two weeks later, he won the *Magic Online* Championship Series that qualified him for a big-money tournament in Boston. It made him an instant online celebrity and attracted a flock of new users to his stream.

But while Dzyl is undoubtedly a decent player – and one who through dint of practising dozens of hours a week is rapidly improving – he was no big-name pro when he began his nocturnal hobby. Keeping his legion of fans happy has been a process of trial and error; a recipe still very much in the experimental phase in the emerging medium. "I've been trying to figure this out for a while," says Dzyl. "What do I have that other streamers don't? I'm definitely a better player than most of the other streamers; certainly I'm up there with the better players in the Netherlands. But in my opinion, that is less relevant than being entertaining. People want to see good *Magic*, but I think people actually like me for having a bit of an abnormal personality! You have to keep talking, which is hard – but I try and interact a lot with viewers who are talking to me on chat and make the stream fun to watch." Dyzl's trademark is a hotel lobby-style bell, which he 'dings' with every exciting or funny play. It is a small touch – but one which has won him a devoted following, who rush over to say hello when they spot him at Grand Prix. Dyzl has manufactured his own celebrity within the community, one savvy mouse click at a time.

That in turn has monetary consequences for a player who has reached the Pro Tour a handful of times, but has yet to cement his place on the 'gravy train', where through consistent performances he would be permanently qualified and paid an appearance fee – essentially the threshold for being a 'professional' *Magic* player. Twitch shares its ad revenues 50:50 with streamers, meaning that popular players like Dzyl can earn a modest amount of cash from their stream; currently around $200 a month in Dyzl's case. Although that is quickly spent on virtual cards, travel to tournaments or a takeaway while broadcasting, Dzyl believes there is plenty of room for growth in the streaming space. "The more you know about the game, the more you can get out of watching a stream," he says. "There are lots of new players taking up *Magic* at the moment and they are an audience still to discover streaming."

Magic Online, meanwhile, is having a considerable impact on the player base at the opposite end of the scale; the game's grizzled veterans. The same flexibility it offers to ambitious players like Dzyl has allowed many older players to stay in the game far longer than ever before. Thirty-something *Magic* players with kids can now squeeze in a few games, once the children have gone to bed. Or can fit *Magic* in around a busy work schedule without having to factor in travel to a tournament or hanging out in the kind of grimy shop they might have outgrown. Similarly, a bulging collection of paper cards that can start to take over an apartment need not fuel domestic discord: playing online eliminates the fiddly and time-consuming annoyance that managing an enormous stack of paper *Magic* cards can be. It has become a grown-up way to keep *Magic* in one's life.

Of course, this does beg the question why or whether Wizards would continue printing paper *Magic* cards at all, when the game mechanics translate well online, the virtual business model in place is even more profitable than 'printing money' and indeed, when the game's social aspect is increasingly, arguably, replicable via streaming. In March 2014 for example, Blizzard Entertainment, released an online-only card game called *Hearthstone: Heroes of Warcraft*, which with its slick, tablet-friendly interface, free client and big brand, attracted 20 million users within its first six months. For *Magic*, a game whose very fabric is tied to the internet's, going virtual seems like a seductively logical future step. But looking forwards, Helene Bergeot, Wizards' director of organised play and trade marketing, says, "In 20 years from now, *Magic* will still be a game that brings communities together to share the same passion and the excitement of competing against each other. I strongly believe the community is what makes *Magic* the game it is today and what it will be tomorrow." While frustrated *Magic Online* users might argue that Wizards' software is simply too bug-ridden for the game to go virtual-only, anyone who has ever made an unexpected friend, face-to-face, at a *Magic* tournament will hope that no-one among Wizards' – or Hasbro's – top brass is contemplating ditching paper just yet. Long may that continue.

CHAPTER TWENTY-FIVE
He Works Hard for the Money

YOU CAN'T FAULT mountains for their ambition. Towering limestone peaks, stretching for the sky, even as gravity aligns against them. "I must be more like those mountains," I tell myself, one chill spring morning in 2013, on Lake Annecy's shores on the French-Swiss border. The breathtaking Bauges Mountains encircle the region and, each May, provide the awe-inspiring setting for Europe's most epic independent *Magic* event. Bazaar of Moxen is an annual gathering that brings together around a thousand players for four days of card-playing, most notably in two of the games most storied formats, Legacy and Vintage (formerly Type I). Between them, these two 'Eternal' formats allow players to build their decks with cards from the entire 20-plus years of the game's history. Many are worth hundreds, even thousands, of Euros and, inside the utilitarian *Salle Polyvalente* housing 'BOM' (as the tournament weekend is nicknamed), the accumulation of decades-old cards on the tightly packed tables is as breathtaking to the game's aficionados as the landscape outside. This is a truly special event.

It is, though, my first BOM: a rare chance to play my favourite format, Vintage, surrounded by peers who also froth nostalgically at the sight of Moxen and Black Lotuses. It is also, I realise, a chance to build on the friendships with *Magic* players I left behind when I moved from London to Berlin in 2010. Since then, I have popped back for events like Grand Prix London in February 2013 (at 1,970 players then the biggest British *Magic* event ever) and been grateful to rekindle and recalibrate relationships with old opponents. Now, I am staying in the same hotel as the London contingent, a grand dive called the Hotel Riant Port. For the first time, I think, I feel completely comfortable with the idea that these are real friends – not simply friends of convenience with whom I share a limited, overlapping area of interest. Friends versus *Magic* friends. That uncomfortable dichotomy that exists quietly for many players in the community – perhaps players of a certain age, for whom *Magic* is not the only concern in life, and who wish it could be enjoyed in concert with those other concerns; broken out after a dinner party like a board game, for example; shared with colleagues and companions, with whom relationships already exist on another foundation.

Ever since leaving university on a high, the community I found in Bristol and the sheer indulgence of intellectual specialism, I have been worried about being a dilettante; too insecure to belong to anything with abandon. I don't know if that feeling pre-disposed me to journalism or if tumbling into the trade reinforced the trait. I do know that part of my motivation for writing about *Magic* was to allow myself to express how much I do care about something – and to share what it feels like to make a minority pursuit a badge of honour, worn proudly in the outside world. Going on holiday with fellow hobbyists is one way to do that – combining social incongruity with the normal conspicuousness of being a tourist. The trick is learning how to fold completely into a collective indifference to it all.

Being distant from my former London *Magic* friends has also helped transform them into normal friends. Not only, per the cliché, does distance make the heart grow fonder, but also in these days of online friendships, there are opportunities to see more of someone with every single status update. Yes, we tend to present a caricature of ourselves on our social feeds, but they can still give a more general impression of someone outside the hours of regular gaming meetings. There, our identities were often confined to the boundaries of the shared interest we were meeting to indulge. Even the banalities of someone's life become fascinating when you see them for the first time.

Part of what makes BOM so enriching, though, is that the event's picturesque destination and extended nature, lend it to actual holidaying. Numerous players bring their partners to Annecy. Before and after sessions testing decks or playing competitively in the main hall, they can explore the local area together. An onus is put on getting together to eat, drink and make merry after the day's gaming. While talk does drift to *Magic* – what tweaks to make to a deck, what glorious plays or horrendous misplays one has made – there is also ample room for non-*Magic* conversation. That might sound like the most obvious thing in the world. But having been stuck on the periphery of most communities I have ever sidled up to, I have not always been able to recognise the unique individuals amongst them. I feared the only way to get to know them was to lose myself in their midst. Perhaps I am a particularly distrustful and cynical person, but it feels like a leap of faith to assume you might have more in common with someone than just the interest you most obviously share. Taking that leap and discovering the full breadth of common ground is a reward. Over raclette and Leffe, I am not simply talking to *Magic* players – but making friends with a trumpet-playing musicologist who also plays *Magic*, a mining-engineer-turned-stand-up-comedian who also plays *Magic*, a screen-print artist and English teacher who also plays *Magic*, and so on. Hopefully, I am introducing them to an itinerant journalist who alongside *Magic* also quite likes football, prog rock and bicycles.

For four days, we share everything. Not just breakfast, lunch and dinner – but every decision, every giddy triumph, every crushing defeat. We *are* the *Magic* community – and in the practice time we have each morning before our tournament rounds begin, we share exactly the kind of heated strategic debate that formed the basis of *Magic*'s culture. The idea is simple – cram in game after game against your friends, to fine-tune not only your deck and sideboard, but also your play against different styles of deck. Each game of *Magic* involves not only playing against the cards you can see, but a constant attempt to perceive and evaluate the plethora of decision trees open to you at any given moment. To understand in a given format, what strategies and specific cards your opponent may be playing, to anticipate not only what is in his or her hand waiting to be deployed or to answer your threats, but what may be added to that hand with each nerve-jangling draw. Similarly, you are not only reliant on the cards in your hand, but on the cards you will draw from your deck. And having built it, you should have an idea of the probability of what is coming next – and how that impacts the use of the resources currently at your disposal. It is a process that, round after round, makes you clench your jaw as the adrenalin pumps through your body, makes your palms sweat, the fingers holding your cards twitch nervously and your tired eyes strain to see everything laid out before you. *Magic* is not just a game, it is an ordeal. A test of concentration, calculation and decision-making. It leaves you elated when you overcome it, dejected when you stumble and always, always exhausted.

By the end of BOM, I have played 21 50-minute rounds of Vintage across two trials for the main event on Sunday and finally, the main event itself – the largest Vintage tournament in Europe with just under 300 players taking part. That might sound like a small number compared to an event like a 2,000-person Grand Prix, but with most decks involved costing about as much as a small car, it is an impressive showing. Although I do not come anywhere near winning anything, I do emerge from the punishing few days with a respectable record of wins, draws and losses, plus a host of stories to trade during the boisterous and bleary-eyed final dinner we share. Gleefully, we cram fajitas into our maws, slosh them down with cold beer and restore ourselves after an intense but wholesome gaming getaway. Bazaar of Moxen proves to be the kind of shared experience, short in duration but rich in feeling, which cements friendships. I am sad to say goodbye in the dim and lugubrious lobby of the Hotel Riant Port and promise myself to see these people again soon. For *Magic*. And for the things beside *Magic*, that make life good. First though, I have a plane to catch.

DOWNTOWN SAN DIEGO is an urban centre undergoing a constant process of merciless manicure; somewhere so pristine, so glitteringly superficial, I want to claw at it in search of its blackened entrails. It is a city in a state of blissful insouciance, seemingly devoid of self-awareness, because there is so little untoward in the blinding Californian sunshine to prompt internal questioning. The only graffiti I see is one hastily sprayed tag as it is removed from the back door of a Starbucks. A woman hidden from the neck down in shrubbery leads her dog off to crap in private. When I do see one small concrete ledge scuffed by grinding skateboarders, I utter quiet words of gratitude for their enlightened gift to the citizens of these parts. Old Europe it ain't. And little more than 24 hours on from Annecy, it is, in its overwhelming pleasantness, too much to take in.

Thank god then for the sea, San Diego's saving grace. Still alive, still unpredictable, still pungent, unalterable, evasive and wild. It is the morning of Tuesday, 14 May 2013 and I am up early, too early, as my body crashes into another time zone, disorientated and on skittering feet that threaten to slip out from under it at any time. Still, my early start has permitted me the chance to eat a bulging Californian apple and stare at the salty green water lapping at the yachts in the Embarcadero, suddenly alone again after an extended weekend of camaraderie, before I head off for my next appointment.

A few streets away, on Sixth Avenue, an elite group of *Magic* players are at work in the conference room of the Hotel Solamar, a plush residence in the thronging and touristy Gaslamp Quarter. They are not playing for fun, but are preparing for the *Magic* season's final professional event, Pro Tour *Dragon's Maze*, which begins just days later on Friday. They are the standard-bearers of today's generation of professional players, a group revered for their performances at the biggest tournaments, as well as the stream of ideas and opinions they provide via the website and online store that lends them their name. They are Team Channel Fireball and their head honcho is the much-loved Luis Scott-Vargas, a player who hails from Oakland where he grew up testing himself against the likes of Brian Weissman. More commonly, Scott-Vargas is known by his nickname LSV. It is a moniker that nearly everyone in *Magic* knows and uses, expressing something of the desire they share to call him a pal. To count him among their *Magic* gang. To hear the familiar, avuncular voice from his many instructional videos at their side, in their shop, at the Draft table on a Friday evening. In short, LSV is pure A-list *Magic* celebrity.

This being *Magic*, though, he does not quite conform to the image of a normal A-list celebrity. He is self-effacing, modest, quiet even. Bespectacled and clad in flip-flops, he wears his hair in an unreconstructed side-parting that makes him look endearingly Rockwellian, as if, instead of dispensing *Magic* wisdom, he could be leaning over a diner counter dispensing milkshakes and wise cracks in some golden pastiche of inter-war America. He is Team Channel Fireball's captain, not because of a domineering personality, but because of his sagacity – and the respect his peers have for his exceptional record in the game. Since dedicating himself fully to professional *Magic* in

2007 (after a handful of earlier Pro Tour appearances), LSV has accumulated five Pro Tour Top 8s, won Pro Tour Berlin in 2008, been crowned US national champion in 2007, triumphed at four different Grand Prix *and* established a blistering record with a 16-0 winning streak at a previous Pro Tour in San Diego in 2010.

These are not achievements that have been stumbled upon through luck, intuition or skulduggery. Being a top *Magic* player, competing at the Pro Tour's upper echelons, is work. Hard work. There is something appropriate, then, about the scene behind the black double doors of the Hotel Solamar's Commodore Conference Room. The air-conditioned command centre is decked out in ochre and black, with a distinctly West Coast carpet, all maritime motifs and Hispanic influence. The room's centrepiece is a boardroom table – oval, truncated at both ends, also black – around which high-powered businessmen usually do their thing. Here, though, are a rotating cast of the world's best *Magic* players, no less serious about their work, no less determined in their pursuit of a slice of the pie – the $250,000 purse on offer at Pro Tour *Dragon's Maze*. They might be wearing shorts and T-shirts instead of pinstripe. They might be using the black leather place mats as play mats. They might work strange hours (from a leisurely lunchtime start to the early hours of the morning), but they are no less sharp-witted, focused or cutthroat than this room's normal inhabitants.

The core group of Channel Fireball testers represents a who's who of *Magic* in 2013. Alongside LSV are Eric Froehlich – the old-school *Magic* pro who made a splash in professional poker, too; Paulo Vitor Damo da Rosa – a Brazilian star, who at the age of 25 has already been inducted into the Pro Tour Hall of Fame and has nine Pro Tour Top 8s under his belt; Conley Woods – a vocal pundit, respected deck-builder and now professional game designer; Ben Stark – Pro Tour Paris 2011 champion and a Limited (Sealed Deck and Draft) mastermind; David Ochoa – a quietly brilliant young player and bon vivant; Martin Juza – a Czech pro and relentless traveller with four Grand Prix titles to his name; Shuhei Nakamura – a gnomic Japanese legend, Pro Player of the Year in 2008 and Hall of Famer; Shahar Shenhar – the team's newest member and at 19, one of the game's brightest young stars; Brian Kibler – A Hall of Famer and one of the game's most authoritative voices; Matt Nass – an up-and-comer with a predilection for combo decks;

and last but not least Josh Utter-Leyton – a diligent Pro best known by his online handle 'Wrapter', who has three Pro Tour Top 8s on his CV going into this latest tournament. Always alongside them is Honey – Eric Froehlich's playful Pomeranian who, as her name suggests, matches the room's ochre walls and adds a note of levity to proceedings with her undeniable cuteness.

By the time I meet the team, I have been playing *Magic* solidly for four days and feel like my modest chops are the strongest they have ever been. In those four days I have, I believe, got a solid handle on the Vintage format – one that includes the bulk of the game's 13,000 cards. In contrast, Team Channel Fireball assembled 10 days previously to spend a week testing at Eric Froehlich's palatial Las Vegas pad. Since then, they have been testing for around 12 hours a day to prepare for the Pro Tour's format, *Return to Ravnica* block, featuring both Draft and Constructed rounds using cards from the sets *Return to Ravnica*, *Gatecrash* and the newly released concluding set in the block, *Dragon's Maze*. It is a format boasting a grand total of 679 possible cards. And still, Team Channel Fireball are not done yet. "In the book *Outliers,* Malcolm Gladwell says you need to do something for 10,000 hours to master it," says Luis Scott-Vargas. "Everyone in that conference room has spent far more than 10,000 hours thinking about and playing *Magic.*"

Scott-Vargas' journey to mastering the game began when he was 11. He and a friend bought two *Revised Edition* Starter Decks and taught themselves the game, or at least something approximating the game. After losing interest for a while at high school, Scott-Vargas was lured back to *Magic* by its strategic complexities while an international relations student at UC Davis. By his third year he was starting to take the game more seriously and nurturing a competitive streak that had previously surfaced at inter-school *Street Fighter* meets. "I was looking for an outlet," he says and he found it by attending the many *Magic* tournaments in the region. Soon, he was attending Pro Tour Qualifiers at the behest of friends determined to reach the game's top tables. It was a distant dream that for Scott-Vargas initially held little appeal: at his second-ever PTQ, he reached the Top 8, but conceded to an opponent who was desperate to travel to the following Pro Tour. Says Scott-Vargas, "I wasn't interested in flying to a *Magic* tournament. It just sounded like an alien concept."

All that changed in 2004, with the announcement that that year's Pro Tour would include a stop in San Diego. Suddenly, with an elite tournament within driving distance, the proposition seemed an attractive one. Scott-Vargas duly won a PTQ feeding the tournament and embarked on a life-changing trip to America's self-styled 'finest city'. The Pro-Tour debutant made the cut to reach day two – but wasn't hooked simply by his success. Instead, he found himself surrounded by more like-minded individuals than he had ever met before, from all corners of the country and even further afield. The seeds of friendships were sown and Scott-Vargas felt motivated to raise his game. "The social aspect is really what kept me in the game," he says. "Now, whenever anyone asks me what they need to do to get better, one of the first things I say is: find a group of friends who likes playing the game as much as you do. You can cheer for each other when you do well – and commiserate with each other when you do poorly."

Slowly but surely, Scott-Vargas found his friends cheering for him rather more than they were commiserating with him and his climb up the professional ranks gathered pace. Professional players earn Pro Points each season through high-place finishes at Grand Prix, Pro Tours and the World Championship. The more points you accrue, the more benefits – including Pro Tour qualification, travel costs, accommodation and appearance fees – you can earn. Although the exact brackets used to separate the professional echelons have changed over time, with enough time, skill and dedication a pro can eventually reach 'the gravy train', where he is qualified by ranking for all the Pro Tours in a year (currently four), rather than by having to win Pro Tour Qualifier tournaments. For Scott-Vargas, that achievement occurred in 2007 and he began to earn something like a living wage from the game. That said, Scott-Vargas was realistic about what joining the *Magic* Pro Tour meant: "The 'Pro' in 'Pro Tour' really should stand for 'promotional' rather than 'professional'," he says.

TESTING CONTINUES APACE in the hotel conference room amid the fluttering sounds of frantic card-play: the riffle shuffles, the rapid switching of cards in hand like rosary beads (Kibler is renowned for this) and the satisfying slap cards make as they are laid on to a tabletop, the tension in the flexible stock causing them to hit the surface with a percussive note as the final corner is released from the fingers. At any one time, four or five games of paper *Magic* are going on, to test decks for the Constructed portion of the tournament. Paulo Vitor explains that there are, broadly speaking, three macro archetypes viable in the format: aggressive red or red-based decks, green-based mid-range decks (which, as the name suggests, aim to win in the mid-game) and blue-based control decks (the latest descendent of Brian Weissman's Deck). That breaks down further into around 10 identifiably different decks, which must all be solidly tested for strengths and weaknesses. Ideally, Team Channel Fireball would turn up with a deck that beats all three of the main archetypes – but it is very rare for one deck to be able to achieve that, while also passing under the radar of the rest of the players. Instead, what the players are looking for is the deck they feel has the strongest match-up against the two archetypes they expect to dominate the metagame, while having a worse, but acceptable, chance against the final archetype. Each game throws up new lessons as to what cards and plays are key in a certain match-up – but the players also keep an eye on the emerging online metagame, too. Decklists outputted by the thousands of players also exploring the format following the release of the final set in the block, *Dragon's Maze*, may just throw up a new approach to one of the decks being put through its paces by the pros.

While half the team are testing for Constructed, the other half is practising drafting the format on *Magic Online* via any one of the three or four laptops open and glowing in the room. Draft strategies – what order to pick cards in, what bearing that has on the archetype you can expect to build and what signals that sends the other players in the draft – are the source of much heated debate, and several pairs of eyes scrutinise each pick in order to try and optimise the team's plans for the Pro Tour.

There is an intensity in the room. With the forthcoming Pro Tour the last of the season, there is much at stake beyond either glory or prize money for a number of the players gathered. This is the final chance to earn Pro Points at the conclusion of a gruelling season, meaning many will find their status in the Pro Player's Club for the following season defined by their performance here. That, in effect, will go a long way to deciding how viable their existence as professional *Magic* players remains, following an extended period of tumult in the way Wizards' organised play programme has been structured.

While it is true that the Pro Tour cemented *Magic's* status as a perennial game, rather than a collectible fad, it has not come cheap. In straitened economic times, with Wizards' owner Hasbro embroiled in a costly restructuring process, growing the base of the *Magic*-playing (and -consuming) pyramid rather than its peak, has proved a more desirable goal. While Wizards would certainly agree with Luis Scott-Vargas that the Pro Tour is a vital promotional tool, it has been forced to juggle the competing needs of slimming down the Pro Tour, without destroying the livelihood of its stars, whose exploits have created massive investment in the game from adoring fans. From a high of six Pro Tours that included the World Championships in 2007, Premier Play was by the end of 2012 in a very different place. While the number of open Grand Prix had doubled to over 40, the Pro Tour had been forcibly slimmed down to three plus the heavily overhauled World Championship, featuring only 16 players.

Living or dying by the flip of a card is not the basis for a sustainable career – and while players such as Scott-Vargas promised themselves never to go into a tournament needing to win money to pay the rent, they do need to know that the time and effort they pour into the game will at least be a break-even prospect. Under the system in place for the 2011-2012 and 2012-2013 seasons, even this was starting to look a bleak proposition.

The problem was, that in cutting the number of Pro Tours (where the highest number of Pro Points can be won), doubling the number of Grand Prix and compressing the Pro Players' Club from nine to three levels, the job of getting on and, more importantly, staying on the Pro Tour became much harder. With less Pro Tours and less incremental thresholds available to get on the 'train', a huge amount of significance became focused on Grand Prix, with their fields of several thousand, rather than the exclusive 300- to 400-person fields of the Pro Tour. The result was a punishing travel schedule – often at a monetary loss – for some of the world's biggest players, even as they tried to hold down Monday-to-Friday jobs.

Along with Scott-Vargas, the most vocal pro in protesting the system was Brian Kibler. While he accepts the need for top players to have other revenue streams outside of *Magic* ("You need to be a pro/writer – or in fact, a writer/pro"), he found himself on a painful trek around the world in 2012, desperately trying to accumulate points to make his continued involvement at the top level worth it. Founder of the company behind the popular games *Ascension* and *Sol Forge*, Kibler works full-time during the week. Yet in 2012, he found himself on the road to play *Magic* for over 20 weekends of the year – catching a late flight from America's West Coast on Friday nights and hauling himself out of bed at 4 or 5 o'clock the following Monday morning to make it home in time for work. His girlfriend began accompanying him to tournaments, simply to see him at the weekend. His performances began to slip as fatigue took hold. And, he says, both he and Scott-Vargas reached the point where they decided that the following season, they would simply give up on Grand Prix and radically scale back their involvement in the game. That would have been a PR disaster for Wizards and could have hit interest levels in their flagship game hard. Punters want to cheer on heroes like the genius-next-door LSV and chiselled charmer Kibler – not a rotating cast of faces who qualify for a Pro Tour once and then disappear again, unable to keep up with the demands of staying qualified. A huge re-think was necessary; one that tacitly acknowledges *Magic*'s maturity as a game that can be socially compatible with adult life and, after over 20 years, one with players old enough to want to lead that adult life, with its aspirations both professional and personal.

Thankfully, although Hasbro has now reigned over Wizards of the Coast longer than Peter Adkison did, the customer-centric ethos that Adkison established lives on, facilitated greatly by the communication channels opened up by social media. Aaron Forsythe, director of *Magic* R&D, says he wants players to know he can see things from their perspective. The former Pro Tour player understood the issues facing today's crowd. "I'm not some of kind of corporate shill," he says. "I was out there spending time and money on *Magic* just like they are now." Organised play boss Helene Bergeot, is also one of the company's most outward-facing employees and was quick to take on board the message coming from the professional community. In the weeks leading up to Pro Tour *Dragon's Maze*, Wizards announced a host of changes in an attempt to stop its celebrity players burning out and walking away from the game's most fanatically followed tables. As of the 2013-2014 season, a fourth Pro Tour would return to the calendar, whilst only a player's top-five Grand Prix finishes would count towards his or her annual Pro Points tally. The relief in the Hotel Solamar's conference room is palpable.

"The first wave of pros simply had to walk away from the game at a given point," says Scott-Vargas. And while a number of them have been able to return since 2005, thanks to earning lifetime invites via induction into the Hall of Fame, an all-or-nothing relationship to *Magic* is not what today's players want. Proving themselves on the Pro Tour has opened doorways for them into the professions that have flourished in the game's lifetime – be it in game design, in website production or *Magic* retail – and made the game an integral part of their lives. "For this generation like Brian, Paulo and myself, that have been playing for five or six years, we want to try and balance our day-to-day lives with being a *Magic* pro," says Scott-Vargas. Only time will tell how successful they can be – but as the game endures, it is a conundrum that will not easily disappear. "I might slow down a little bit at some point," he says. For now though, he has a Pro Tour to play...

CHAPTER TWENTY-SIX
Good Afternoon Sports Fans!

"WELCOME COMPETITORS!" SAYS the sign above the door. This must be the place.

It's 5pm on the dot on Thursday evening. The 1964 San Diego Concourse, a refreshingly patinaed concrete complex in the heart of the downtown, opens its doors for business. As soon as its two slightly baffled security guards unlock the entrance, the 388 players invited to Pro Tour *Dragon's Maze* begin to pour in, all eager to register for the start of competition the following day. They have schlepped to San Diego from every corner of the world. From as far afield as Armenia, Brazil, New Zealand and Taiwan, all have come with backpacks full of cards and dreams. As they begin to arrive, in small gaggles – with their countrymen, with impromptu testing teams, with girlfriends or new acquaintances encountered at their hotels – the excitement in the Concourse's faded lobby builds. Instead of nerves, there is release. After a tense build up, kicking heels in an unfamiliar city, finally, the Pro Tour is a reality.

Two official card dealers flog their wares to the growing crowd and are quickly swamped. Not only by those desperate to make last-minute additions to their decks for the weekend's Constructed rounds, but also by those hoping to get a read on the metagame, by seeing which cards laid out in the flat glass cabinets are spiking in price or out of stock. Any clue could just give someone the edge – but they must beware of subterfuge. Experienced players and teams often disguise what they are buying when it gets to the wire, padding their orders with decoys in front of prying competitors.

The electricity in the air fizzes and pops as the game's big names roll in, in their star-studded teams, and join the queue to register. Suddenly, players at their first ever Pro Tour (the vast majority of the crowd) are rubbing shoulders with legends like Jon Finkel and Kai Budde and the aspiration that has fuelled their desire to play the game finds itself fulfilled. The game's celebrities for their part are most at ease with their team-mates. They do not go unnoticed and plenty of fans will want to meet them over the course of the weekend. Plenty will want to beat them, too, which only adds to the quiet aloofness of some of the pros: they are being eyed up at once as heroes, but also as the subject of future pub anecdotes, future gaming Goliaths taken down by plucky Davids. They are here to win, to play and promote the game they love – but also, unwittingly, to feed the dreams of newbies as high-profile whipping boys.

The team sponsored by StarCityGames.com are the first stellar constellation to arrive. Featuring Jon Finkel and fellow Neutral Ground graduate Zvi Mowshowitz, as well as players like Patrick Chapin and Bob Maher, the team is a Harlem Globetrotters of *Magic*, packed with players who for the most part made names for themselves in the Pro Tour's early years. As such, there is an ever-so-slight nerd edge to them, the faintest trace of a different gaming generation. One a little more unreconstructed in its otherness to the mainstream. A little more unkempt. A little less fashionable. A little more accustomed to being the odd one out.

It is barely perceptible – but thrown into relief as Team Channel Fireball saunter in, in good humour, at ease and well scrubbed up. Gone are the shorts and flips-flops. LSV has even donned a button-down shirt for the outing. They might not have settled on what deck to play, but they look comfortable in themselves. As if they could be in the queue for any activity in mainstream San Diego – a cinema to watch something other than the new *Star Trek* film, a thronging bar in the Gaslamp Quarter, SeaWorld, the Zoo or a gallery in Balboa Park. They are a generation of pro players not only keen to ensure that *Magic* is compatible with their day-to-day lives, but also a generation who have benefited from *Magic*'s role in a more visible gaming overground. The internet's unique ability to unite fragmented sub-cultures and gift them the weight of numbers to be visible to the mainstream has helped normalise previously marginal pursuits and the young players in Team Channel Fireball are the beneficiaries: post-internet *Magic* players (post-*Magic Magic* players, even) who have grown up in a society where their hobby is not seen as an entrée to Satanism, where geeks are billionaires and where hobby gamers are no longer viewed as oddballs, loafers or weirdoes. "It's been very gratifying to see how the player base has evolved," says the game's creator Richard Garfield. "At the very beginning, I told people to look out for that. That our champion, our player, was going to look less and less like a backwards nerd and more and more like an intellectual athlete. If you're smart enough to be good at games, you can be smart enough to be good at other areas of your life, too." Kibler for example – sponsored by StarCityGames.com but tellingly more at home testing with Channel Fireball – is buff enough to make the most conventional woman swoon. Cool as a cucumber, he wanders over to one of the card traders who has put aside an order for him, collects it discreetly without having to reveal its contents and foils anyone's attempt to guess what he plans to play.

AFTER THE THRONG of huge tournaments like Grand Prix and even Bazaar of Moxen, the most remarkable thing about the Pro Tour is just how small it is. In years past, Pro Tours were open to the public, who could spectate and play in side events run concurrently with the main tournament. But, in expanding the number of open Grand Prix tournaments, Wizards decided to make the Pro Tours private, with less distraction for the participants. "All things considered, it was the right decision," says organised play boss Helene Bergeot. What it does mean, though, is that apart from the lucky few attending as guests of players, the vast majority of *Magic* fans will have to find another way to follow the drama as it unfolds in the San Diego Concourse's Golden Hall, a windowless ballroom decked out in black, burgundy and gold.

Where once Wizards were buying up time on ESPN2 to showcase their game, the proliferation of high-speed broadband means that coverage of premier *Magic* tournaments has taken on a whole new dimension. Today, Wizards can side-step sceptical television audiences to reach fans more efficiently and effectively than ever before – on their laptops, on their phones and on their tablets. After two decades, *Magic* is closer than ever to being the 'intellectual sport' its creator Richard Garfield had hoped for – and it is, to boot, a passionately followed spectator sport.

While even footage of the very first Pro Tour in New York in 1996 was made available for download by forward-thinking Wizards, online *Magic* coverage has really come into its own over the past decade. First, former pro and Wizards R&D member Randy Buehler took the helm as an affable host and excitable commentator. Today, an increasingly slick and professional broadcast team run the show. The turning point came in 2006, when a British *Magic* fan by the name of Richard Hagon began offering his skills to the coverage of European Grand Prix. Hagon had at the time been producing a *Magic* podcast, but his colourful past had seemingly pre-destined him for a role in the *Magic* world's limelight. On stage since he could toddle, Hagon has sung, danced, acted and joked his way through life, taking in about every facet of the entertainment industry in the process. And while he might never have landed a BAFTA or Oscar in his time, the loquacious 41-year-old did hone one very valuable skill: how to tell a good story.

"*Magic* is such a technical, scientific game, that there aren't many entertainers in terms of their background in there," says Hagon. What the professional game was crying out for – like all the best sports – was a narrative. Viewers needed to understand not just who was winning or losing a particular match, but why it mattered – in the battle for Pro Tour victory, or a landmark record, or in the race for the coveted Pro Player of the Year title. With a love of American sports – and the heavily statistic-oriented analysis it prompts – to match his love of gaming, Hagon embarked on a quest to bring professional storytelling to *Magic* coverage. Spurred on by the untimely death of his father in 2005 – six weeks after Hagon had himself played in the Pro Tour for the first time – the lifelong entertainer began podcasting and then working on official coverage of the European Grand Prix circuit. It was not long before he came to the attention of Wizards' newly appointed global coverage boss Greg Collins. "What is your vision for coverage?" Collins asked Hagon – and Hagon identified exactly the structures put in place by Rick Arons, Skaff Elias and Seth Matlins a decade previously. "*Magic* has so many parallels with tennis," Hagon told him. "There is so much structurally that is the same: the one-on-one, the choosing of a path through that season's tournaments, the rating points, the invitation-only 'slam' events, the different surfaces – like different formats…" It was a story that *Magic* was failing to tell as well as it might. And, as a former producer at ESPN, it was exactly what Collins wanted to hear. Seven years on from that conversation, Hagon has become the 'voice of the Pro Tour' – its dapper, ginger-curled, teddy-bear-like host. He also directs and produces coverage of all the European Grand Prix. While his very jovial, very British delivery is sometimes at odds with a global audience's expectations, they perhaps take for granted the level of professionalism and broadcasting know-how Hagon has brought with him in his tenure in front of – and significantly, behind – the cameras. It is, says Hagon, "The best job in the world." And with his generosity of spirit and showbiz chutzpah, Hagon is doing it very well indeed.

"EVEN MY MUM watches the coverage," says Josh Utter-Leyton. The Team Channel Fireball star has taught his mother the game's basics, so that she can follow the action should her son make it to the Pro Tour's feature match area – where four matches taking place simultaneously can be filmed depending on how exciting they are or how quickly they progress. Given his impressive string of performances during this season, it is likely he will make it there at some stage during the weekend. But the first Channel Fireball member under the spotlight is none other than Luis Scott-Vargas. The first three rounds of day one will be *Return to Ravnica* block Draft – where each player in an eight-man 'pod' opens three successive Booster Packs, takes a card, then passes it on, until all the cards in the pod are drafted. Each player then constructs a 40-card deck from the pool they have drafted to face off against opponents within his or her pod.

Drafting is one of *Magic*'s most fascinating and perfectible skills – and at the heart of each pod lies a tension: between picking what you most need for your deck and picking off key spells that could benefit an opponent. At its highest level, drafting is not only about choosing powerful cards in a vacuum, but also signalling and influencing others in the pod. If you choose the only red card in a pack and pass it on, the player next to you should realise that red is a bad option for his or her deck, because the pair of you will be competing for cards. Thus 'hate-drafting' a card which may benefit an opponent can come back and bite the drafter if it sends the wrong signal, and a card which could otherwise make it into his deck is interpreted as available and cut by another player. It is a process laden with pitfalls and compelling in its complexity. And, as the producer of numerous videos on how to draft better – as well as a player with a penchant for some unusual picks – LSV is the pro that fans watching at home most want to see. Accordingly, a camera hovers over his shoulder and sneaks a glance at every card he selects. A judge sets a metronomic rhythm from the Tannoy. 388 players set their minds on winning Pro Tour *Dragon's Maze*. "Open pack one," says the judge. "You have 40 seconds." The clock ticks down. "Draft," says the judge. "Pass the cards to the left. There should be 14 of them." The time allotted decreases with each pass, as the number of cards left to select from also decreases. "You have 35 seconds." The players focus, concentrating on the strategies they have developed in testing, scouring each pack for hidden strengths or cards they might successfully 'wheel' around the table in case they must pick something more valuable to their deck this time round. Trying to juggle colours, archetypes, mana costs and ratio of spells to creatures on the fly, they force themselves to remain calm even as the adrenaline surges in their systems. "Draft," says the judge, like a mantra. "Pass the cards to your left…"

As LSV DRAFTS his deck, each pick is analysed by experts in the commentary booth for the eager viewers at home. Their numbers will climb as time zones around the world align and *Magic* fans race to a screen to watch the latest developments. Crucially, Hagon has driven up production values and made sure there is no dead air between rounds to spoil their enjoyment. Instead, alongside former Neutral Ground boss Brian David-Marshall, he will tell the story of the tournament – how each match has impacted the standings, which new players are giving the veterans a run for their money, how the chase for vital Pro Points is progressing and so on and so on. It is music to the ears of Pro Tour fans – and it is no wonder then, that the audience is growing with every broadcast. Although Wizards will not give out specific numbers, Twitch, the website Wizards use to co-host coverage of the Pro Tour alongside their official site, shows the scale of *Magic* viewership: the official *Magic* channel was viewed 17,308,404 times in its first 18 months.

Hagon's reference point is the UK subscription channel Sky Atlantic, which broadcasts HBO's hugely popular series like *Game of Thrones* and *Boardwalk*

Empire. "Although I am not allowed to give out specific numbers, I can say that Sky Atlantic is immeasurably dwarfed by the viewing numbers we get for Grand Prix and Pro Tours – by a distant order of magnitude," he says. On a good night, Sky Atlantic attracts tens of thousands of viewers, which gives some indication of just how popular watching *Magic* has become. This is despite it lacking the action of a traditional sport – or the frenzied pace of something like *League of Legends*, one of the foremost video games streamed online for its own legion of fans to watch. Instead, *Magic*'s strength is its connection with its audience. "The game might not be visually arresting," says Hagon, "but it is very thought-provoking." Every player watching at home has an idea of how to play and can empathise with the pros as they play out their games, with the very same cards they have at home. Sometimes, that can lead to screaming at the screen in desperation, when a player is about to make a misplay that will cost him the match. Other times, it involves sitting back in awe at just how brilliantly a pro is able to play a complex control deck or marvel at how a big-name star can extract improbable victories with a mediocre Draft deck. It is a learning experience for a hugely invested viewership. Ultimately, says Hagon, the goal of the coverage is simple, "We want people to be better at *Magic*. Because when you get better at *Magic*, you want to play more of it."

BACK IN 2009, Luis Scott-Vargas teamed up with friends to launch the website Channelfireball.com. Picking up on a model made successful by websites like StarCityGames.com, it would be at once a card shop and content provider, offering its users strategic advice from the very best. Scott-Vargas' task as editor-in-chief was to provide plenty of content himself – both written and in video form – as well as to recruit the original writing roster. Most of those players can now be seen wearing the site's distinctive logo on their shirts at the Pro Tour and other big tournaments. The website is something Scott-Vargas is proud of. It gave him ownership of a project having previously only contributed to other websites. It was also a role that allowed him to play *Magic* for a whopping 20 to 30 hours a week, the kind of practice that can only bring impressive results.

In early 2012, though, Scott-Vargas took on a new challenge, moving to

Denver to work as a full-time game designer. He handed over Channelfireball. com's editorial reins, but still remained the face of the website, part owner and one of its principal contributors. With a regular job to juggle though, the amount of time he could spend practising *Magic* per week plummeted to around 5 to 10 hours. To the uninitiated, indeed to most casual players, that might sound a lot. But the effect on Scott-Vargas' performances was huge. As Grand Prix after Grand Prix piled up – with all the attendant travelling – he went to tournaments under-prepared and could not replicate his earlier successes. The negative spiral of results had a knock-on effect on his Pro Tour play, too. For four in a row, he finished outside the money (which extends down to 75th place) and found himself increasingly jaded. His enthusiasm was on the wane. And the cheerful demeanour and self-assuredness he normally displayed at tournaments was cracking under the strain. He would a need a huge finish – a place in the Top 16 – at the final Pro Tour of the season, if he wanted to continue as a Platinum-level pro the following year: the highest professional status and one which would qualify him for all Pro Tours, reimburse his travel and accommodation costs and earn him a $3,000 appearance fee for each of the marquee events. "Platinum is where it goes from a hobby you pay for to a hobby that pays you," says Scott-Vargas. "It's what truly distinguishes you as professional player."

But in San Diego, at the season's crunch event, things do not start well. Despite drafting a solid-looking 'RUG' (red-blue-green) deck in front of the cameras, LSV ends the first three rounds a disappointing 1-2 (with one win and two losses). If he is to finish in the Top 16, he can afford a record no worse than 12-4, meaning with 13 rounds still to play, he is already under immense pressure. Lose more than two further matches and his future in the elite of professional *Magic* will be thrown into question. The lifestyle, the profile, the earnings, financial assistance, the authority as a pundit, his social life... quite simply, Scott-Vargas' ability to pursue his passion at all.

The constructed rounds cannot start soon enough. Scott-Vargas, along with the majority of Team Channel Fireball, has chosen to play the team's 'Esper' deck (a nickname derived from an earlier set for blue-black-white decks), one they have fine-tuned throughout the week in San Diego. A controlling deck – which traditionally leverages the pilot's play skill – it also packs objectively the most powerful cards in the format and should have a decent match-up against the rest of the metagame. Traditionally, Scott-Vargas has fared better in the Constructed portions of Pro Tours. He is also a skilled control player. And, he can tell himself, the team did not cut corners with their playtesting, working late into the night for the past 10 days. With a deep breath, he steels himself and heads back to the playing area for round four.

The match, against fellow American Paul Ewenstein playing a green-white midrange deck, does not even go to three games. Drawing badly in both games, Scott-Vargas can do nothing to stop the steady flow of creatures from across the table and crashes out, losing the match in helpless, horrendous fashion. Both players sign the results slip, Scott-Vargas as swiftly as possible, before excusing himself and getting the hell out of the playing area. On tilt, emotional and suddenly full of questions and self-doubt, he cannot help thinking, "that round of Constructed felt like it summed up my entire year." If things continue this way, he might be out of the reckoning before he has even had a chance to make a play for Platinum status. I bump into him as he exits the hall. When I ask how he is getting on, he tells me his record ('1-3') politely, but is clearly in no mood to talk to a stranger. Instead, he needs fresh air and his team-mates around him.

The Californian sunlight can be a good tonic. And more importantly, the friends that Scott-Vargas has around him in his close-knit team – the very reason he fell in love with professional *Magic* in the first place – are good to him. The sporty Ben Stark has helped him not only with his drafting skills but his fitness, too – hauling him to the gym at regular intervals during testing. Eric Froehlich, with discipline and focus honed at Vegas' poker tables, is a confidant and mental coach to his friend. Even the enigmatic Shuhei Nakamura offers words of advice in his second language. Just as Scott-Vargas had hoped, the team he has assembled cheer each other on – and commiserate with each other when things don't go well.

Starting with the following round, Scott-Vargas starts to play. His opponent is a wildcard entry to the tournament, famous video game streamer Sean Plott, better known by his *Starcraft* and Twitter handle Day9tv. While Plott is one of the weaker players in the room, he is one of its most engaging personalities. Invited by Wizards in the hope some of his legion of fans would tune into the Pro Tour, he is also just the opponent Scott-Vargas needs. Their games are close, played out in a friendly spirit and most importantly fun.

The Team Channel Fireball chief finds himself enjoying the tournament again – and crucially, emerges victorious. Buoyed by success and the kind of social encounter he has always loved at these events, LSV is back.

The next three rounds are a blur, as he topples one opponent after the next – including team-mate Shahar Shenhar – to recover something of his swagger. By the end of day one, after much soul-searching and a huge mental effort, Scott-Vargas has battled back to a healthier 5-3 and, along with everyone else in the team, made the cut for day two. Although some have only scraped in with disappointing 4-4 records, other members are building momentum nicely, including Josh Utter-Leyton, who is 6-2 after day one, having crushed all-comers with his aggressive red-white deck. It is a focused performance from a player who shut out distractions during drafting with a pair of expensive-looking headphones and souped himself up for the day's play with the largest frappuccino I have ever seen. Clearly, it is a recipe for success.

THERE IS AN old German saying that goes, "*Im Bett ist alles wett*" – "Bed makes up for everything." A good night's sleep, cocooned away from the world and its woes, can work wonders. And, after a curative kip back at the Hotel Solamar, Scott-Vargas emerges refreshed and confident ahead of what will almost certainly be a dramatic, season-defining Saturday for him. Starting the day in 132nd place, he settles down to draft again – this time away from the cameras – and proceeds to assemble a tightly focused black-white deck, as the cards he needs seem to reveal themselves perfectly on cue in each pack he is passed. Built on the back of some of the same powerful cards Scott-Vargas is also playing in his Constructed deck (notably the controlling black-white creatures Sin Collector and Blood Baron of Vizkopa), the expertly compiled deck stands him in good stead for day two's Draft rounds. As a fan of Scott-Vargas' regular Channelfireball.com Draft videos once observed, "LSV could win a horse race on a pig." Thankfully, this is a thoroughbred of a deck – and Scott-Vargas canters to three vital wins in a row to put the previous day's harrowing Draft behind him. His record stands at 8-3. He has moved up to 42nd in the standings. And it's not even lunchtime yet. No wonder this guy has 40,000 Twitter followers…

A number of those followers gather round to watch his clash in the first Constructed round of the day, the tournament's 12th in total. It turns out to be one defined by the powerful and very hard-to-remove creature Aetherling, deployed on both sides of the table. As the match goes long, more and more players, having finished their matches, gather behind the railing nearest Scott-Vargas' table to see if he can scrape the victory. But in front of the growing throng – including a number of his team-mates – he once again comes off second best, against form, against expectation, against hope. The final loss he could afford has come – and with it, huge pressure to win the four concluding rounds of Swiss play (before the cut to the tournament's Top 8), if he is to seal Platinum.

In the following round, the improbable dream looks already to be shattered. After both players snatch an easy win each in the opening games, an epic game three evolves to a precipitous point for Scott-Vargas. His opponent Jérémy Dezani, on 14 life, has an army of 1/1 tokens ready to deal lethal damage on the next turn. He also has an uncounterable counterspell in hand – called Counterflux – meaning that whatever Scott-Vargas tries to play to save himself (he is on one lonely life point and has a single Aetherling in play), can be countered without response. Knowing all this, knowing that his opponent will kill him next turn and effectively end his season right there and then, he draws dejectedly from the top of his deck and sees the one card that under normal circumstances could save him. Jace, Architect of Thought is a blue planeswalker card which can give opposing creatures -1/-0, enough to prevent the damage from Dezani's 1/1 tokens. If only he did not have Counterflux in hand!

Going through the motions, Scott-Vargas half-heartedly taps his mana and throws out his Jace, waiting for the inevitable counter and already calculating all the ways – big and small – that losing Platinum status will impact his life.

"OK," says Dezani.

And with those two syllables, the match turns on a sixpence. It is a horrific mistake from the French player, who is so focused on sandbagging his Counterflux for the answers Scott-Vargas could draw once Jace is in play, that he misses the fact that he must counter Jace itself in order to kill his opponent when the turn passes to him. Once he has verbally agreed that the card comes into play, though, the rules enforcement at this level of play means there is no going back. The one card that could save Scott-Vargas if he could somehow get it into play lands on the table with far more weight than a thin piece of cardstock has any right to. In the blink of an eye, it reignites Scott-Vargas' entire season. From being 'dead on board' (staring down a lethal, losing position), an error, a miscalculation (the kind of mistake that is completely normal after playing a draining and demanding game all weekend, but which highlights precisely the level of concentration required to be a professional *Magic* player) hands Scott-Vargas the breathing space he needs to win an unwinnable game. He does just that – sealing victory in the most intense and emotional match he will play all weekend. It is an incredible turnaround – and after a demoralising year, a sign that whatever pig Scott-Vargas' fortune is saddled to is changing course and heading once again towards the head of the pack.

From there, from being dead and buried, it is all now a comparative breeze for Scott-Vargas. Peaceful, contemplative, Zen, as anyone who has just sidestepped disaster must be, he squares the shoulders beneath his black Channel Fireball shirt and simply does what he does best. As the 388 individual stories of Pro Tour *Dragon's Maze* reach their crescendos around him, as ever-more fevered coverage is broadcast by Rich Hagon, Brian David-Marshall and co, and as the other members of Team Channel Fireball alternatively surge forward and fall by the wayside, LSV strides on. One by one, his remaining opponents fall, until he faces Ari Lax up on stage in a match both must win to make Platinum next season. It is an 'Esper' control deck mirror match, which should take an age. Instead, it is over in a dozen or so turns, as LSV serenely stomps his opponent in two one-sided, rapid-fire games. And just like that, a goal which all season had seemed so distant, which all weekend has teetered on the edge of the abyss, is captured in a whirlwind game of cards. LSV bounds off stage – having sealed an 11th place finish – to embrace his team-mates. *$5,000, Platinum, relief, excitement, happiness,* he writes later in his tournament report. More than that, though, a rekindled love for the game. A reminder that skills seemingly blunted over the course of a discouraging season are still there, stored in one of *Magic*'s finest brains. And, that with practice, support and encouragement, one of the most-admired members of the game's community will still be with us, at the top of his game, whatever he chooses to do with his 'real' life.

Team Channel Fireball also have another phenomenal achievement to celebrate. By reaching the Top 8, Josh Utter-Leyton has Hoovered up enough Pro Points at the end of a season of mind-blowing consistency to come from behind and win the hotly contested Player of the Year race. Although he is finally eliminated during the semi-finals on Sunday (as Luis Scott-Vargas watches on as an expert summariser from the commentary booth), his acceptance speech sums up exactly what makes Team Channel Fireball so remarkable and yet so utterly familiar to players around the world, at every level, watching online. "We are a group of friends who also love playing *Magic*," says Utter-Leyton. "And that's awesome."

CHAPTER TWENTY-SEVEN
Magic's Missing Tribe

WHILE PRO TOUR *Dragon's Maze* may have been a triumph for Josh Utter-Leyton, Luis Scott-Vargas and its eventual champion Craig Wescoe, it was not a triumph for diversity: out of the field of 388 players in San Diego, only two were women. Wizards of the Coast are reluctant to give out information on the demographics of their player base, but this was not a fluke. While in many ways, the demographic playing *Magic* has evolved to feel a little more self-confident, a little more mainstream, a little more mature, the miniscule showing of women at the Pro Tour is a sight that hints at the limits of the game's gradual normalisation. The gaping gender gap might not be quite so bad at less competitive levels (Wizards does say 38 per cent of the game's 'fans' are female – people who have played in the last six months or who have heard of the game), where wives, girlfriends and sisters (mine included) have often been cajoled into playing. But the lack of women in the game overall is a stark imbalance that persists in the *Magic* community, contrary to trends in other sectors. In June 2013, for example, the Entertainment Software Association released a report putting the proportion of female computer and video gamers at a whopping 45 per cent. Clearly, a decent number of women like playing games, but *Magic*'s progress in attracting them remains at best stuttering and at worst glacial. For a game in otherwise rude health, that is a crying shame.

Considering the game itself is one of mental dexterity rather than physical strength, *Magic* should at least, in theory, be able to provide a level playing field for men and women. But the hardcore strategy gamers the game was first aimed at – those who might be lingering between sessions of *Dungeons & Dragons* at conventions – were an overwhelmingly male-dominated audience. Despite *Magic*'s eruption into something like mainstream consciousness during its most heady and fad-like moments in the early to mid-1990s, it failed to pull in a new wave of female gamers, much to creator Richard Garfield's dismay. "I had a lot of ideas about getting women to play games and I naively thought that perhaps what we did with *Magic*, making it less festooned with bikini babes, would bring them in," he says. "I thought it was a good first step but it proved to not have much impact at all." For a product so radical in every other way, it is a notable and frustrating blot on its copybook.

There were, however, women involved in the game early on: Wizards' vice president Lisa Stevens, Kathryn Haines, the editor of *The Duelist*, or a figure like Joanne White who founded the magazine *Scrye*. But as the game became tournament-focused with the Pro Tour's creation, casual and competitive strands of the game split and seem to have left most of the small number of women players stranded on one side of the divide. Beth Moursund, one of the most recognisable female names in the game's history, says she is not surprised. She got into *Magic* having discovered a free Booster Pack in her goody bag at a convention called Dragonflight in 1993, a few weeks after *Magic* had gone on public sale at Gencon. She got hooked on the game, playing it casually, before becoming involved at Wizards initially as a 'net rep' – one of the numerous enthusiasts the company fielded on Usenet to help new players with rules questions. Moursund went on to write extensively for *The Duelist*, and became heavily involved in judging, eventually developing the game's Comprehensive Rules alongside Bill Rose and Paul Barclay. And while she was immediately attracted to the complex interactions the game produced, she says in her experience, "Women seem on average to be more into the social type of games rather than the hardcore strategic games."

That much was also immediately evident to Sabina Browne, a tournament organiser from Richmond, London, when, having picked up the game around the time of *Ice Age* in 1995, she ventured to her first big event. "I nearly turned round and walked out the door," she says. "I thought, 'there's no-one like me here' and only a friend convinced me to stay." Still, she sat down and played and remembers her opponent trembling like a leaf as they dealt out their cards. "He was absolutely perturbed to be playing against a woman," she says. "I think I won just on that basis."

While such anecdotes should have been consigned to the game's past, the reception for women at the 500,000 *Magic* tournaments that take place each year has been slow to change. In that sense, the few women who have graced the game's top tables should be lauded for their perseverance and the performances they have turned in (even as inane, misogynistic comments fly around chat rooms filled with, so it seems, almost uniquely adolescent boys or bigoted men). Melissa DeTora is the Pro Tour's most impressive and consistent female player, one who has continually broken new ground for women with her performances. Having played on the Pro Tour on 11 previous occasions, cashed several times but never cracked the Top 64, in February 2013, DeTora stormed her way to the Top 8 of Pro Tour *Gatecrash* in Montreal. She became the first woman ever to reach the knockout-round benchmark and finally scotched any notion that women were inferior players. Still, as I watched and cheered her progress in front of the coverage, I saw posters on online platforms queuing up to denigrate her. "The first woman to reach the Top 8 and she has to be ugly," wrote one wit. It was thoroughly deflating stuff, which brought to mind Joseph Conrad's quip, "Being a woman is a terribly difficult task, since it consists principally in dealing with men." *Magic*'s men in particular have struggled to temper their attitudes and welcome women into the community with courtesy and respect. Nonetheless, DeTora believes her sistren are following her example and taking up the game. "It's not as rare as you think," she says. "A lot of women play, just not competitively. If you go to gaming groups on college campuses, for example, you will find women playing *Magic*. If you go to a Pro Tour Qualifier though, then that is when there are few women."

THE QUEST FOR the Pro Tour remains as exciting and thrilling a motivator for a swathe of *Magic*'s player base as it did when it was first conceived and galvanised would-be champions everywhere. Certainly, that has brought with it a cut-throat atmosphere to the qualifying circuit, as many players give their all for a shot at the game's big-money circuit. While many players are courteous opponents, there are those who will take any advantage they can, showing off their gamesmanship, testing the limits of the acceptable, probing for a psychological edge. While that might not appeal to everyone – male or female – there is evidence to suggest that is does appeal to more men than women. A 2007 Stanford University study for example determined that, when given a choice to compete, over 70 per cent of men will seize the opportunity to do so, compared to around 35 per cent of women.

What is unclear, though, is whether this is a genetic factor or a consequence of socialisation; whether this is nature or nurture at work. However, in creating the Pro Tour at all, Wizards rejected the idea that a generation of brainy young men were innately pre-destined to be lonely flag-wavers for their high-school athletes. For Wizards (and the *Magic* community itself) to now nonchalantly chalk up women's supposedly lesser desire to compete to nature would be a travesty: the Pro Tour's legitimising effect changed the lives of young men who might have felt on a hiding to nothing by transforming their socialisation. Now, it must attempt to break barriers in what may be a question of opportunity and education for women, too.

There is, though, almost an embarrassment within the game to suggest ways of helping women who may want to step up from the casual level to playing competitively. *Magic*'s great levelling effect (as a mental not physical game or sport) should make gender irrelevant, after all. Practically though, after 20 years, that has proved insufficient to capture a sizeable portion of female players – nowhere near the number of video gamers, for example. However level the playing field in theory, it has not proven the case for most women taking their first steps into a real-world *Magic* environment, where being the only female in the room at a tournament can be an isolating emotional experience. When a sexist remark is an easy way to ruin someone's performance. When a cheap shot at someone's gender (or any other distinguishing trait) can win a game or discourage a potentially skilled opponent from ever returning. That is an uncomfortable facet of competition that has been recognised far more successfully in other similar games.

Carrie Oliver is a British player who Top 32ed at Pro Tour Nagoya 2011, then the best finish by a woman at the Pro Tour ever. It was the culmination of a ride that had seen her go from bullied school kid, to computer gamer, on to accidental *Magic* player, before she honed her skills to the impressive level she reached on the Pro Tour. What is also noteworthy in her ascent to

Magic's upper echelons is her experience of competitive bridge – a 'mental sport' as much as *Magic* is – that she argues provides far better structures for supporting women that *do* want to raise their game to a tournament level.

During her time at university, Oliver practised regularly with the England Under-25 women's bridge team, whose name reveals the approach that card game has taken to involving both sexes at its competitions. Bridge, says Oliver, has both mixed open tournaments and separate women's tournaments. The result is, by her estimation, a field that is split roughly 70-30 in men's favour at open, mixed tournaments, already an unthinkable number compared to *Magic* tournaments. To put that into perspective, the proportion of women in the Pro Tour *Dragon's Maze* field was a little over half a percentage point. The proportion at an open event like Grand Prix London 2013, which I attended with almost 2,000 other players, was even less. At a most optimistic count, including ambiguous first names such as Sam and Alex, the figure for that tournament was 3.76 per cent. Clearly that is a tiny amount – and while it is perfectly possible that it does accurately represent a competitive 35 per cent of the total, female *Magic*-playing population, it is a number that does not present a well-balanced, diverse community. That should be a goal in itself because, quite apart from anything else, broadening the game's player base will allow it to continue to grow in future and ensure its survival. Therefore, upping the amount of women playing at all levels – with the knock-on effect of increasing the share of women at the highest level – is something *Magic* should be trying far harder to do, given two decades of relative failure to address the issue.

"When I did well at the Pro Tour, I had a lot of girls contact me and say they had been really inspired. That they wanted to get better, compete and do what I've done," says Oliver. But what needs to exist for those women is a pathway to join Oliver and her Pro Tour peers. For that, Wizards' current hands-off approach may simply not be enough. Indeed, says Oliver, "I get the feeling that Wizards of the Coast are very reluctant to single out women as a community. And, actually, I think they need to." Although no-one wants to see women patronised with products or events catering to any kind of lower perceived skill level, a once-yearly women's tournament with a decent prize pool, for example, (including byes for a future Grand Prix or a seat at the Pro Tour), comprehensive coverage and a positive, celebratory atmosphere could go a long way in creating new heroes for aspiring female players to cheer. It would also create a stepping stone into the highest levels of organised play for the female *Magic* community. While it is possible the average skill level at the tournament might be lower than some current events (precisely because it would operate as an initial way into competitive play for many women), it should be no less competitive within itself – after all, not only bridge, but women's sports exist across the board. There is a hunger among every woman on the Women's Tennis Association Tour or Ladies Professional Golf Association Tour to be the best in their field. And like their male counterparts, sportswomen compete with steely determination for status and spoils. Given the success of such a model elsewhere, Wizards reluctance to try it out seems intransigent as the community itself continues to prove stubbornly slow at changing its own composition.

IF THE SLENDER ranks of women tournament players are in fact representative of the numbers playing the game at a more casual level, an effort to bring more female players in at the bottom of the *Magic* pyramid is clearly needed, too. For a start, that might include leveraging the marketing value of players like Melissa DeTora, Carrie Oliver and their fellow regular Pro Tour colleague Jackie Lee. In the time since Oliver broke through at the Pro Tour, it is something that, if Wizards have not overtly exploited, a plethora of other *Magic* websites have. Oliver began writing strategy articles for a major website – and very soon afterwards, every site worth its salt had some kind of female voice on its writing roster. "In some ways we took the initial abuse for the community," says Oliver, referring to the acerbic comments she and other female authors have faced below the line. "But now it's accepted: we do write for the *Magic* websites, too. And that's a good thing."

The level of nastiness and casual sexism flung around in the online *Magic* space is sometimes written off as the disproportionately loud outpourings of a brash and toxic minority, but unfortunately goes hand-in-hand with similar behaviour at all levels of what remains a primarily in-real-life game. The computer games industry recognises what a problem online abuse is, as Michael Patcher, an analyst for Wedbush Morgan, told Forbes in 2009, "The biggest obstacle to growing the female gaming community is the trash talk that goes on in the online area." With face-to-face still the main mode for *Magic*-card slinging, the effect can only be more intimidating to women trying to pick up the hobby. It is perhaps worth noting that even Wizards of the Coast's director of organised play Helene Bergeot was threatened with rape – 'jokingly' – by one player on a public forum. He received a lifetime ban from sanctioned DCI events.

While Oliver, meanwhile, has rarely been insulted to her face, friends she attends tournaments with have reluctantly had to mention to her the occasions when men have bad-mouthed her behind her back. She says the prevailing attitude at events remains juvenile and prejudiced: bragging players will tell their friends between rounds, "I played a girl, so obviously I won!" or be mocked if they didn't for "losing to a girl." The same mutterings at games stores, clubs and events the world over add up to an intimidating atmosphere for any woman wanting to get into a new hobby that is, above all, supposed to be fun.

Tournament organiser Browne, who runs a weekly *Magic* club, says players in her experience are often even stunned to discover their event is not an exclusively male affair. "They expect a male organiser," she says. "They get strangely confused half the time when I appear. I think they do expect it to be fully male." That might explain the bizarre situation acclaimed *Magic* artist Terese Nielsen found herself in at San Diego Comic Con a few years ago. As she stood at her booth, her artwork laid out before her, a young man stopped to peruse her prints. "Wow, these are really good," he said to Nielsen. "When's he going to be back?" Clearly, there is an education issue here, an experiential one, too. Not only does a mixed and diverse crowd need to become the norm to change attitudes, but also the community needs to police itself and hold its members to higher standards.

But were it that easy, were *Magic* simply the level playing field it should be, this would be a non-issue 20 plus years into the game's lifetime. And therefore, it is encouraging to see initiatives taking place at a grassroots level. One of them is the Lady Planeswalkers Society, which meets regularly at Card Kingdom, a Seattle game store which itself sets a new standard for a welcoming, clean, bright and social space. It even has a café attached where diners can play almost any game available in the store over a plate of nachos and a toothsome craft beer.

The Lady Planeswalkers Society is the brainchild of Jennifer Meyen, a relative newcomer to the game who has also worked at Wizards of the Coast as an assistant brand manager for *Magic*. When Meyen discovered the game in 2010, she threw herself into it with vigour – attending store-held events like Friday Night Magic and even a Grand Prix and Pro Tour Qualifier in her first six months. Despite taking a brave and headstrong approach, she quickly found herself being made to feel like a bad player – rather than an inexperienced one on a steep learning curve. Though it should not have, her being a woman exacerbated the feeling. Meyen felt she was letting female gamers down, fulfilling the easy stereotype the guys around her had of the quality of women players.

Meyen recognised that while, through sheer bloody-mindedness, she was able to raise her game and not wilt in the face of the mostly male competition she was facing, it was not an approach that would suit most women curious about the game. Thus was born the Lady Planeswalkers Society (planeswalker being a type of character within the game and the loose role each player is supposed to assume) as an attempt to remove some of the barriers to women getting into *Magic*.

A few years on, Meyen's play-group meets weekly to play different formats and to teach new women how to play the game in a welcoming and friendly environment. There is no obligation for women to play the game this way – if they are already battle-hardened with a strong and supportive group of friends, they can of course jump feet-first into any tournament the store runs – but for those who would rather learn the game with more nurturing peers, this is the place for them. Crucially, when Meyen runs small tournaments for her members, she allows any men to play who have accompanied a woman to the meet-up, the idea being to forge the links necessary for her players to become part of the larger, male-dominated community, too. "Including men helps us to be accepted by the *Magic* community as a whole," she has explained on the Wizards website. "We are not an exclusive group outside of the community, but a subset within [it]." Now, the model is being taken up by similar play-groups around the world, as a positive way to empower female gamers and get them playing a game that so glaringly needs their contribution. While Meyen stressed her initiative was strictly unofficial, it spoke volumes that a Wizards employee identified the need to recognise and support women as a distinctive part of the community – while further up the food chain, inertia seemed to prevent the company from trying the same fresh approach at a competitive level.

WHAT WIZARDS DO recognise, though, is the paramount importance of bringing new players into the game at all. Just as R&D have implemented a 'New World Order' to keep the game as accessible as possible, so on the digital front have they forged new ways for would-be players to encounter *Magic*. When Randy Buehler moved upstairs and out of the daily cut and thrust of R&D's 'pit', he petitioned Hasbro for funds to get Wizards into digital publishing. Buehler's plans were persuasive and saw him take up the role of vice president of digital gaming in early 2007. And while challenges both internally and in the wider economy would eventually see Buehler leave the company in 2008, one very important product did issue from his tenure: the arcade-game style *Duels of the Planeswalkers*. The game gave players a chance to play a stripped-down version of *Magic* against their machine – battling bosses with pre-constructed decks to unlock new, more powerful cards or entirely new decks altogether. The attractive graphical interface presented real-life *Magic* cards, but simplified some of the game's actions (for example, choosing what mana to tap to cast spells), while also introducing players to some of the game's harder-to-grasp concepts, like the abstract notion of the 'stack', used for resolving in what order multiple spells cast at the same time take effect. "While I am honestly surprised it took me as long to get funded and made as it did," says Buehler, "I sort of knew that it was absolutely the right thing to do for *Magic*. We had to do it. And I think it's certainly contributed to the continued growth of *Magic*."

Crucially, *Duels of the Planeswalkers* has also helped create the first bridge between primarily digital gamers (and that enviable 45 per cent female audience) and *Magic*. It was, in fact, precisely how Carrie Oliver first discovered the game, as a student who saw friends playing *Duels of the Planeswalkers* at their digs. Soon, it had invaded her shared house, too, and became a staple on the console beneath the living room TV, fiercely contested by her and one of her flatmates. He was more aware of the link between the digital game and the paper game and started purchasing a few cards that he showed to Oliver. Soon, the pair were making their first trip to a tournament, a large, regional Pre-release event (before they were moved in-store) for the expansion *Worldwake* in January 2010. Oliver emerged with a creditable 2-2 (two wins, two losses) record and was bitten by the *Magic* bug. *Duels of the Planeswalkers* had not just helped convert her from a video gamer, but also offered a pathway into the game that proved the perfect learning experience for her. Instead of ever feeling like a bad player, as Meyen did, she was playing against the game's artificial intelligence – one that never smirked at her when she made a mistake, high-fived its buddies when it beat her or called her 'lucky' if she won. On top of that, it gave her a chance to learn some of the game's intricacies before ever having to set foot in a specialist game store, most of which, though havens for the young men in them, are dingy, close-knit and elitist. "I think if I had had to go to games shops to learn the game cold, that would have been very intimidating," says Oliver. "I remember even after playing in that first Pre-release, I wanted to play more and discovered there was a local shop where they had weekly Draft events. But it took me a few weeks to work up the courage to go. I had never been a role-player or table-top gamer, so walking into the midst of that group for the first time and saying, 'I want to play *Magic*' was quite scary."

In that respect, *Duels of the Planeswalkers* may well be the perfect first step for women into the *Magic* community. With that in place, though, it should be incumbent on players and Wizards to support their next steps – be it with play-groups like the Lady Planeswalkers Society, a high-level women's tournament or simply the respect, acknowledgement and courtesy that human beings regardless of gender, race, creed, orientation, ability or any other trait, deserve. Currently, *Magic* is missing out on too much richness – and failing to offer the same empowerment it offered a once maligned group of nerds and geeks to other minorities in its midst. There are now small victories – like DeTora's Top 8 or transsexual women who play the game winning tournaments and writing about their experiences. But there are also lows, like the incessant misogyny slung around online, chipping away at the community's fibre. While there is naturally confusion about how to proceed, and a reluctance from Wizards to single out a portion of an audience playing a game that should present equal opportunities to all, the harsh reality is that, empirically, it does not. There have been some encouraging signs from the Wizards marketing department, like a tie-in with new-media celebrity Felicia Day's *Geek and Sundry* website, as well as the introduction of female commentators to the Grand Prix coverage roster. These moves can be a boon to all fans of the game. But as long as the DeToras and Olivers remain rare, Wizards must consider implementing a stepping-stone for women into competitive *Magic* – while the community itself needs to speak up about prejudice in its ranks and shed some of the defensive, insecure behaviour that can translate into intimidating aloofness at grubby game stores all over the planet. The long-term goal for all involved in *Magic* needs to be growing the game – and that means making it accessible to new audiences. Via video games like *Duels of the Planeswalkers*, by creating welcoming physical environments like Card Kingdom and nurturing play groups like the Lady Planeswalkers Society and by being advocates of a positive, enriching experience. Anyone who has played *Magic* should know what it has brought them in their lives. Why let others miss out? After over 20 years of glorious isolation, it is time to share it with others, rather than guard it jealously out of misplaced tribalism.

CHAPTER TWENTY-EIGHT
Meeting the Maker

I'M CUTTING IT fine. Lost in a sprawling upscale mall in the affluent Seattle suburb of Bellevue, I am hunting for a branch of Starbucks that seems to have disappeared in a distant corner of the TARDIS-like shopping pantheon. By the time I realise my mistake – the Starbucks is in a separate annex, where coffee goes to percolate in peace – I have to pace it there frantically, with my nerves already a-jangle. This is the moment of truth. Meeting the man who started it all; meeting Richard Garfield.

When I do find the Starbucks, *Magic*'s creator is already there with his long-time friend and collaborator Skaff Elias. I grab a tea, absorb the tasteful, subdued décor that finds its way into every Starbucks on the planet and attempt to break the ice. My first question concerns Garfield's socks, which have famously always been odd. As the words escape my mouth, I realise that it is entirely possible that every interview with him over the last 20 years has begun with this question. Certainly, as I later discover, an interview with him in the very first issue of *The Duelist* goes into great detail on the subject. In it, Garfield describes the time-saving qualities of his sock-box – a collection of odd socks he can pluck from blindly every day, without wasting precious brain power on matching things up. An apocryphal tale says that Albert Einstein did something similar. The physicist supposedly owned only identical sets of clothes so he wouldn't have to waste attention selecting what to wear. And while that might not be wholly true (Einstein was a sucker for a plain grey sweatshirt in later life, though), it does hint at the kind of lineage Garfield descends from – a proud tradition of gently 'mad' geniuses, consumed by concerns more scientific than sartorial. Indeed, Garfield is the great-great-grandson of President James A. Garfield (the United States' 20th President, for 200 days in 1881), while his great-uncle invented the folding milk carton and held patents for another 200-or-so devices. A certain kind of unbridled smarts runs in the family. But just as Einstein's second wife Elsa instilled a level of practicality into her husband, styling him for his public sorties, so Garfield today says he has someone in his life who makes sure he has matching socks. "My original intent was to save the amount of time I spent on socks," he says. "But it has actually meant I spend a lot of time talking about them." As ice-breakers go, I could have chosen a different question.

Garfield is – complete with matching socks – dressed casually. His outfit is just the kind of garb Seattle and its surrounding landscape calls for: practical with a hint of outdoorsyness, suggesting the wearer could go from office to light ramble in a flash. In fact, Garfield has always enjoyed the outdoors and has a penchant for cross-country skiing and crayfish hunting. When in search of inspiration, he has also been known to head outside, just as he did in 1991 after meeting Peter Adkison for the first time. Back then, Garfield was the distracted games designer in mismatched charity shop clobber, who made an instantly positive impression on the Wizards' boss, despite his anarchic outfit. "My first impression was that he was either a genius or a complete misfit," says Adkison. "Either way, I was happy to work with him."

As Garfield pondered the brief Adkison had given him for a quick-to-play, convention-friendly product, a card game he had had in his closet since the early 1980s, sprung to mind. He called it *Five Magics*. The game boasted five colours of magic power, each with their own distinct feel and relied on land cards to generate the resources a player needed to use their spells. The gameplay itself was constantly in flux, as Garfield intermittently pulled it off the shelf, incorporated a new idea, tinkered with the rules, gave it a quick play, then, never completely satisfied, shelved it again. It was at the time just one of 50 or so other half-completed games he had on the go. The framework of a decent game was there. But it needed something else, a spark, to take it to the next level.

To this day, Garfield does not understand quite how the inspiration hit him. But he does remember where he was when it did. Having returned to his parents' house after meeting Adkison, he sought out the verdant Oregon countryside, hoping to fill his lungs with fresh air and oxygenate his deft and dextrous brain. A hike took him up to the nearby Multnomah Falls; 600 feet of cascading icy water that tumble into the Columbia River Gorge in two spectacular stages. It was here, perhaps touched by the sublime, that Garfield had his eureka moment. A vision for a different type of card game. Instead of having one deck for all the players, why couldn't each player have their own? It was the moment of sudden insight that sparked the eventual transformation of *Five Magics* into the game we know today, even if the implications of that breakthrough, tumbling through Garfield's mind like the torrent in front of him, at first left him overwhelmed. "I was all at sea," he says. Thankfully, over the coming months he would steady himself and, with pen, paper, glue and assorted other gaming gubbins, begin the process of fashioning the world's very first pile of *Magic* cards.

GARFIELD'S FLASH OF inspiration may have hit him like a zap of cosmic wisdom, beamed to him via the rebellious hair which sticks up antennae-like atop his now thinning pate. But it was almost certainly made possible by the cultivation of gaming knowledge that has been his stock in trade since he was a child. Growing up in an itinerant family, the young Garfield was introduced to games by his parents as a way to entertain himself and make friends in new and unfamiliar surroundings. Before that, though, they had slipped into family life as a surreptitious protective measure. During a stint in Bangladesh, where Garfield's architect father was working, a game of "hit the ground!" regularly took place in the household. Whenever the Garfield parents yelled the phrase, Garfield and his two little sisters would throw themselves down, ostensibly out of fun. But, outside the confines of the Garfield home, dangerous times were unfolding. The game's real aim was to drill the children in what to do should the house get hit by gunfire. Thankfully, it was never used in earnest and after a few weeks in violent, revolutionary Bangladesh, the Garfields were evacuated to safer environs.

They pitched up in Nepal next, and it was here that Garfield got to grips with gaming proper. At the US aid centre, he found a copy of the military boardgame *Stratego*, in which battling opponents control armies fighting over a flag. The seven-year-old Garfield loved the game so much that he painstakingly made his own detailed copy of it. In the evenings, meanwhile, he would play boardgames and cards with his parents, discovering not only games' social function but also, increasingly, their inner workings, too. The young Garfield was hooked and never turned down a chance to play. Games became a cornerstone of his life that he would lean on again after another move – this time to somewhere a little less exotic.

When he was 11, Garfield's family settled in Eugene, Oregon. Having grown up in far-flung realms, surrounded by the kind of fabulous flora and fauna most kids only experience in books or at the zoo, he could not help feeling like an outsider. The excitement and adventure (however dangerous at times) of his travels had left him brimming with experiences beyond his age. That meant, that instead of slotting easily into a new social group, the worldly Garfield was left looking for one that shared something in common with him. It was on this quest that he stumbled upon a copy of *Dungeons & Dragons* in his local game store. It was the perfect antidote to his incongruity – a fantasy world he could plunge himself into, to rediscover the visceral excitement of his peripatetic upbringing. From that point on, gaming became Garfield's number one hobby and he spent all his time scouring game stores looking for new ways to play. Inside every box, he found a gateway to a wider world. "Games are a great way for people to get to know one another and to learn to deal with one another, particularly if they are introverted or less socially capable," says Garfield. Armed with fistfuls of dice, a rulebook's guiding lines and a reason to get together with people, Garfield found a connection to new friends.

However much Garfield loved his games though, he realised early on that, in 1980s Oregon, the career path to becoming a games designer was an obscure one. It was certainly not the kind of job he could ask his careers adviser about or circle with a red pen in the back of the newspaper. Instead, Garfield sunk his academic energies into maths, which presented the same sort of mental challenge as games, while also offering a path towards a tangible career. By 1987, he had started his PhD at the University of Pennsylvania, which, he hoped, would leave him plenty of time to indulge his passion on the side.

Garfield's curiosity for games never abated. He investigated them with the same rigour he did his chosen field of combinatorics, not just playing them anymore, but looking under the hood, poking around and getting his hands thoroughly greasy. "I was academically interested in games," he says. "I would research games that I had heard of and try and figure out what made them tick, including games from different cultures." What amazed Garfield, though, was that no-one in the academy seemed to share his excitement. Games were still, it seemed, poo-pooed or deemed unworthy of serious study. Instead of the vast shelffuls of books on film or literature Garfield could find in the library or bookstore, the games section invariably stocked a couple of books on gambling and something on parlour games. And that was it. "It was a huge intellectual area that was completely raw," says Garfield. "It was pathetic."

Thankfully though, times have changed. Despite the difficulty of developing a critical language for a field as diverse as games, there is at least an acceptance that they exist and are made by clever, dedicated and creative people – just as *Magic* was by Garfield. Indeed, his book *The Characteristics of Games* would at least be a first port of call for anyone digging through the library shelves today looking to become a game designer. Combined, of course, with a colossal video-gaming industry edging Hollywood into the shade, *Magic*'s success has helped make games more legitimate and the career path that seemed non-existent to the young Garfield, a realistic ambition. It is perhaps no wonder then, that Garfield is revered by a legion of fans. Their childhoods – and increasingly after 20-odd years, their adulthoods – are bound up with the game he created. The adulation is something Garfield describes as 'daunting'. He admits to feeling a keen sense of responsibility for the impact he has had on the lives of everyone who has shuffled up a deck of *Magic* cards. That is why, despite his fame, he tries to remain accessible to his fans, to conduct interviews like this one and to stay humble – even if the hobby-gamer he once was has long since become a multi-millionaire; the sire of a generation's fevered cardboard dreams.

While Garfield remains solidly down-to-earth, he is still prone to the odd bout of what Skaff Elias calls his "spaciness". "You can immediately tell he's a very deep thinker – or a former drug addict!" jokes Elias. "Sometimes, he looks like he's thinking about something else at the same time," he adds. "Because he probably is." But that is all part of what makes Garfield so engaging and endearing. There is no hint of ostentation about him, no trace of aloofness. He is utterly obliging and in many ways the same Garfield that invented *Magic* two decades ago – "just with less hair", says his friend. He is also someone so wholly identified with *Magic* that at times, it must have proved challenging to step away from it.

Almost instantly, though, once Garfield had designed the first *Magic* expansion *Arabian Nights*, the need to pull back from the game arose. Garfield knew he could not respond to the huge demand for new cards single-handedly and was soon surrounded by Elias and the other East Coast playtesters in a new office at Wizards HQ. He handed over his baby to the newly founded R&D department and in turn, they raised it, nurtured it, and helped turn it into a phenomenally successful game that continues to go from strength to strength. How hard was it, though, for Garfield to pass *Magic* on to new custodians? "From the stories I've heard, I think it sounds like other people have had far more difficulty passing on their creations than I did," says Garfield. "There were a couple of things that helped me with it: one was, just as I wanted there to be real variety in the card art, I really wanted to get a broader palette of designers involved. The only way to do that was to get them creatively invested in the game – so not a situation where they design and I okay it. It had to be, 'you guys make your decisions, I'll advise you and you really feel like you've got the autonomy to go where you feel you ought to.' That helped everyone improve.

"The other thing which allowed me to hand it over was that I really wanted to design other trading card games and I knew I couldn't if *Magic* was going to be my full-time job. So, I went on afterwards to *Vampyr: The Eternal Struggle*, *Netrunner* and *Battletech* and different card and board games, to explore that territory."

It would be fair to say, though, that no other game designed by Garfield has had – nor probably could have had – the same success as *Magic*. Although there have been popular titles, like his recent dice-based monster game *King of Tokyo*, they are evolutionary additions to the gaming realm, rather than revolutionary new gaming forms in the way that *Magic* was. But Garfield has had the pragmatism to accept that such paradigm shifts occur only rarely. Pinning his hopes on instigating another would be futile. "Pretty early on, I realised that trying to make the next *Magic* was going to make me unhappy," he says. Instead, he has resigned himself to being forever in his creation's shadow, while resolving to never stop doing what he loves most: making great games. Today, the number of unpublished creations in his closet is even bigger, as he continues to research, experiment, tinker and tweak.

Garfield left his full-time role at Wizards in 2002 and initially invested his energies into the online gaming world. He has since become disenchanted with the medium, having become frustrated at the huge investment of time and energy required for relatively little payoff. Instead, he describes himself today as a "game designer and game academic," trying to further the understanding of gaming, trying to add to its canon and critical language. With each new insight he gleans from diving into new games with the same relish he did as an out-of-place teenager, he feels he is, in some modest way, contributing to the future of games. But what should not be underestimated is the impact he has had on the future of games, simply by creating a new generation of designers. They have been inspired by *Magic* to apply their intellects to serious and smart play, in just the way *Dungeons & Dragons* inspired Garfield's generation. Some have struck out on their own, like The Deck's creator Brian Weissman (*Path of Exile*) or Hall of Famer Brian Kibler (*Ascension* and *Sol Forge*). Others, like Randy Buehler or Mark Rosewater, made their way to Wizards of the Coast and deployed their talents there to elevate the craft of making games to new heights, perpetuating *Magic* as an archetypal model for a perennial and professional mental sport.

It is perhaps no wonder then, that the lure of R&D's pit can prove hard to turn down. Garfield is all too happy to spend his time hanging out with his protégés and making great *Magic* cards. Although no formal relationship exists between R&D and Garfield, he still chats regularly with Bill Rose (vice president, Wizards of the Coast R&D). He also, as he puts it, "comes in now and again to work on an expansion," which he did most recently with the extremely popular gothic horror-themed set *Innistrad*. It is, says Garfield, a blast returning to *Magic* even after 20 years. "It's so much more rewarding working on *Magic* than my other games," he says. "New games are a lot of work, with an uncertain outcome. I enjoy doing them, but they may never be published or may never find an audience. With *Magic*, though, you know there are so many people out there who appreciate it. Plus, it's so easy, because I'm so good at it by now and there are so many people who are good at it that I can correspond with. The only limitation is that if I let myself slip into it, I could do that for the rest of my life – and I want to do something else."

That means continuing to put his trust in the game's current designers, just as he did when he handed off the game the first time around. Is he satisfied with R&D's work? "By and large," he says. Garfield is someone who has always been willing to recognise when he is wrong – just as he did when he backed down over *Arabian Nights*' putative pink cardbacks. Therefore, although he sometimes argues against developments coming out of Wizards HQ, he does accept that he is not always correct. "For example," he says, "I don't like the planeswalker cards," referring to a new card type added to the game in 2007, a sort of hybrid design. Each planeswalker represents a powerful wizard character, has several abilities, but can be attacked like a player and killed like a creature. Garfield admits that were he in charge, they would never have been made, as he finds them both too complicated and too restricting in their design. "On the other hand," says Garfield, "I do acknowledge that they create a focal point to the game and an identification to the world and its characters, that I've always been weak at. I also acknowledge that, while they are much more complicated than I would choose to do, if you spend a 'dollar' from your 'complexity budget', you want to make sure you get at least that much back in gameplay. These cards are very expensive complexity-wise, but they do pay off a lot. Are they worth it? I wouldn't have done it. But I acknowledge the other side, that they're pretty fun to play with and a lot of players love them."

Planeswalkers aside, Garfield is confident that after over 20 years, *Magic* is in a robust state, which should see it endure for at least as long again. The environment the game finds itself in today has been hugely changed and gaming, be it *Magic*, poker or on consoles, tablets or smartphones, is an increasingly mainstream pursuit. Two decades into *Magic*'s lifetime, the conditions are in place for it to cement its place in a public psyche ever more in tune with intellectual fun and the face-to-face interaction it can provide. "Games as a genre can have credible longevity," says Garfield, pointing out a milestone more important perhaps than *Magic*'s recent 20-year anniversary. "If there are people now playing *Magic* who weren't born when it was designed, there's no reason why the next generation won't play as well, just like *Scrabble* or poker. There are no guarantees, but for the first time I might actually bet on it!"

Certainly, he is not alone in hoping that the game continues on its stable footing, surviving changing tastes, economic uncertainties or any potentially bad business decisions. Life without *Magic* would be unthinkable for the millions of players it has touched – perhaps for its creator, too. "As most people, I'm sure, I wish I had many lives to live," says Garfield. "I did enjoy mathematics, for example. I'm sure this is the life I would have chosen, but if you're intellectually engaged in a lot of life, you just don't have enough time to do it all. *Magic* has opened up many, many doors, but we only have so much time and I couldn't go through all of them."

With that, Garfield does find one door to go through, rushing out of Starbucks with a caffeine-fuelled spring in his step. Parental duty calls and he must collect his kids (who also now play *Magic*) from school. Garfield being Garfield, though, it is hard not to imagine his racing mind exploring new ideas for cunning gaming mechanisms as he dashes to the school gates. As he disappears rapidly into the distance, I realise with sudden certainty that I have just met a hero. Not a celebrity, not a star necessarily, but someone who has had a huge impact on my life in a way he might not even believe. Someone, who after a childhood on the move, fashioned the antidote to another child's upheaval. Right then, right there, in that identikit coffee shop corner, I want to burst into tears. Seeing that figure walk away – all illusion of intimacy and friendship that establishes itself during an interview blown away – creates an instant void in me, a realisation that I have just lived the emotional peak of this story and might be left contemplating a steep downhill gradient. It is impossible not to feel deflated in that instant, not to feel like it all went too quickly, that the questions I asked were somehow insufficient, that I failed to internalise the experience as fully as I should have, or even impress upon the man just how grateful I am to him. Garfield inadvertently gave me something I badly needed in my life and his game continues to sustain me to this day.

Of course, according to the cliché, you should never meet your heroes. But it is something I have always shrugged at. I have interviewed plenty of sports stars in my day job as a football journalist, though perhaps never realised how limited my actual affection for them was. Here though was a hero, not just to me, but to a whole community who would have had no reason to call themselves such if this one particular man hadn't been so passionately possessed by the idea of making great games. If this one man hadn't cared quite so much about other people's fun. Or hadn't sensed quite so keenly from his own upbringing what it meant to be an outsider. *Magic* is steeped in Garfield's generosity of spirit. And it is for this reason that it has opened life's doors for everyone who has played it.

CHAPTER TWENTY-NINE
The Best Game in the World

I ONCE HAD the pleasure of interviewing *Fever Pitch* author Nick Hornby for a German football magazine. Hornby, whose brain chews over football games and pop culture inside a shaven head with pointy *Pinky and the Brain* ears, is a man who understands obsession. He has lived it, as a long-suffering Arsenal fan. And he has chronicled it, in his memoirs, novels and essays. Intrinsically, he seems to get why people lie awake at night, incapable of switching off their desire to explore every nook and cranny of their particular all-consuming interest, sometimes to their own detriment, often to the bewilderment of others. I told Hornby about my obsession, *Magic: The Gathering,* and although he had never heard of it, his dark eyes flashed with fascination for the first time in our interview. He had done a long, exhausting day of press, but could suddenly feel the talk veering towards a topic dear to him. Turning the tables on his interviewer, he asked me, "Have you thought about it since you came into this room?"

"No," I lied politely.

Obsession goes to the heart of the nerd tag so prevalent in the decades between *Dungeons & Dragons'* creation and *Magic's* birth. It is a term burdened with a semantic baggage connoting a mind under siege, which it acquired in the 16th century. Later, obsession would even be equated to the hostile action of an evil spirit, like 'possession', but without the helpful excuse of an uninvited demon pulling the strings. Nerds were considered to be obsessed with their interests and, what is more, those interests were deemed too throwaway to be of importance to the well-rounded, God-fearing, Volvo-driving folk of the decent majority. Games, TV shows, popular music – the cultural crud that fascinates Hornby's characters, too – were often seen as incompatible with the full richness of life's tapestry. This was stuff to be digested and excreted quickly by the mind. "Get a life!" William Shatner famously told *Star Trek* fans in a 1986 *Saturday Night Live* sketch. Yet no-one seems to say that to the suited and booted staying late at work. Or to the legions of golfers feverishly working on their swing. Or to art critics. Society has set up its values and would rather we conform to them, thank you very much. Investing time into the disposable facets of pop culture is bad. Move along please, there is nothing to see here.

There is an assumption that obsession is strictly zero-sum: that it shuts out everything and brings in nothing. This is partly true: if I play *Magic* for five hours on a Saturday, I cannot spend those five hours reading poetry or raising orchids or making sushi. But that view greatly underestimates the value of what can be learned through one's obsession. How it can open gateways in understanding. How it can facilitate social interaction. Or how it can provide a framework for self-expression, inspiring the writing of a book, for example. Obsession can certainly frustrate and it is in that sense a double-edged sword, but it is not so distant from its virtuous cousin, 'passion' whose praises are so gleefully and routinely sung. In one of the schoolbooks still sat on my bookshelf, a quote from Georg Wilhelm Friedrich Hegel is circled in pink highlighter, *Nothing great in the world has ever been accomplished without passion*, it says. It is perhaps this link which has allowed nerdism to shrug off its sad connotations and, with the relentless thrust of post-modernism, to give way to self-identifying 'geeks' – a group whose 'obsessions' have aligned with the new millennium's 'passions' in a moment of celestial serendipity and karmic come-uppance.

Geeks have power and influence in the 21st century and it is now generously accepted that you can invest time and energy into pop cultural pursuits, while also having sexual intercourse, enjoying physical exercise or owning a house. There is still a distrust of obsession, though, a fear that it leads to blind spots in a person's make up. That obsessives might be puzzlingly unmotivated by the high-fiving capitalistic race to make more money (hence the importance of the Pro Tour in 'legitimising' *Magic*). Or blind to the delights of 'high' culture – as defined by the tastemakers in a largely, white, male, middle-class media. Or, indeed, incapable of doing anything genuinely 'creative' – the ultimate goal of over-educated, under-employed hipsters everywhere.

More often than not though, my obsession is a great comfort to me. Richard Garfield once described *Magic* as a "game bigger than the box" and he was absolutely right. It has become my 'screensaver': the default setting my brain switches to when it can no longer compute or create or construct. The permutations of everything about the game of *Magic* – in its widest possible sense – flood my mind with a level of mental activity which can be gently ratcheted up or down to whatever level is compatible with the background noise of real life. Mulling over combinations of cards for a deck, mulling over how that deck would play out against another deck, mulling over where and against whom I might play that deck... and so on and so forth. It is like toying with a Rubik's Cube of endless complexity. I shift pieces of a puzzle back and forth in my brain, sometimes combining them in pleasingly fluid and familiar patterns, and at other times becoming exasperated at their stubborn refusal to click into place. It is an experience that I suspect instinctively I share with other *Magic* players, although it is one we rarely discuss. The tangibles of gameplay tend to dominate players' conversations and why not? From a rational, intellectual point of view, there is no doubt in their minds: *Magic* is not just a game, but *the* game. The best game in the world in fact.

Brian Weissman, who as The Deck's creator proved his understanding of *Magic*'s inner workings early on, is convinced that there is nothing better. During regular gaming chats with fellow Seattle locals Richard Garfield and Mark Rosewater, he says it has become clear to him what defines *Magic*'s brilliance. "From chess to tic-tac-toe, if you look at the curve of all the people who play a game and their skill level, the longer that curve is – so, the bigger the gap between the best and worst – the better that game is. And I think of all the games that exist, *Magic* probably has the biggest curve." Because the game's modular design has made it almost infinitely expandable (providing head designer Rosewater's brain doesn't explode one day in the pit), it has continued to add a degree of variety that makes it accessible at a plethora of different levels, yet never completely decipherable. "Super computers have effectively solved chess," says Weissman. "*Magic* is a totally unsolvable game. It is effectively infinite and because it has infinite permutations, it has an infinite curve of skill, which makes it in my assessment by far the best game ever made."

It is a view echoed by the Pro Tour commentator Rich Hagon. From his chair in the booth at every elite event, he sees the game's best unpick its secrets and the number of viewers logging on to watch *Magic* climb. He compares *Magic* to a video game that can never be beaten. "*Magic*," he says, "will never disappoint you by going, 'The end. Game over.' It can't. It's too complex. If you like exploring, if you like knowledge, if you like cool stuff; it's heaven." Just as the game has an arching skill curve, it has a myriad of modes in which players can enjoy the game. They can be as creative as they like, they can be as casual as they like. Or, they can emulate the pros, and seek out the planet's most testing competition at the Pro Tour. "It is a voyage of discovery that lets you be competitive along the way," says Hagon. There is, at every point along *Magic*'s rising curve, a way for its players to find vast satisfaction.

While that unrivalled breadth might sound intimidating to potential players, the game has been explicitly broken down into more manageable chunks. *Magic*'s different formats, created at the birth of the Pro Tour, have allowed players to engage with it at a level commensurate with their knowledge, desire or budget. Standard, at the heart of Wizards' business model, is the key. "Now when someone joins the game, it doesn't matter if there were 10,000 or a billion cards printed previously," says Richard Garfield. "They only need to worry about the previous year's 1,000 cards. And that clearly works." Digital technology, too, like *Duels of the Planeswalkers*, has helped the game reach a host of new players. And a series of blockbuster movies planned by 20th Century Fox should be the next stride into terra incognita – a decisive crossover for a well-marshalled brand into a mainstream more attuned to gaming than ever before.

Hopefully, that should make the next intake of *Magic* players more diverse than the first who took up the game. Not just another generation of teenage boys hankering for a way to meet new friends and prove themselves, but adults with careers to juggle, looking for a stimulating hobby they can squeeze in online, too. Or women, who are flocking to video gaming, but who might also thrive on the opportunities *Magic* provides to compete and socialise. Even if the latter's recruitment may be happening slowly, it is clear from rocketing tournament attendances and revenues that, each year, more and more players are discovering just how exceptional the game is. At just over 20 years old, *Magic* has categorically not peaked.

Those coming to the game afresh will not just discover the very rational, intellectual reasons for its success: its cunning design, its deceptive simplicity and almost endless complexity. I am almost certain, the first thing that will hit them when they sit down and play, is the same irrational feeling that hit me – that hit every player their first time around: a visceral "wow!" An inescapable, incomprehensible sense that they are discovering something awesome. Strangely though, the emotional response to the game is something players rarely verbalise. We talk far more readily about what we have done, rather than how we feel, as if discussing our reaction to an experience designed deliberately to make us *feel* good, is somehow the breaking point of the ties that bind us. As if we want to pretend we have distanced ourselves from the very reason we started playing in the first place – an overwhelming emotional reaction to the game almost as certainly as an intellectual one. We wear stiff upper lips as social armour. We guard against embarrassment. We are afraid of saying, "You know what? I bloody love this game."

I cannot deny that my feelings about *Magic* needed much scrutiny as I set out on the mission of writing this book. Was I a '*Magic* player' or just 'someone who liked playing *Magic*'? Did I want to belong to a group sometimes stigmatised by old nerd behaviour – painful awkwardness, defensive aloofness, sometimes even misogyny best left in a 1970s role-playing dungeon? I wanted to write about something that I cared about and kept returning to the idea of *Magic*. But I wondered if my obsession with it was one I regretted. If I could not be anything more than sheepish about it. If I, too, could not proudly proclaim that I love this game.

Setting out, part of me felt that many of *Magic*'s players were too close to the game, too focused on its minutiae to explain it to norms who scoffed at gaming, fantasy and anything even vaguely geeky. The one-foot-in, one-foot-out dance I had been doing since leaving New Zealand meant at least I might be able to describe the game's appeal in a broader context and highlight its importance to the wider world. Throughout my life in the game, I had found myself trying to justify my own involvement in it – to see if it meant anything to me beyond its irrational, almost therapeutic role. By stacking up all the sensible reasons for *Magic*'s popularity I thought I could at once do my bit to help legitimise the game and feel less marginal playing it myself.

With every new player I met on my travels, every interview I conducted, every chapter I sweated over though, I felt my scepticism recede. In its place, I felt excitement. I felt enthusiasm. I felt belief, not only in what I was doing, but in every member of the community, sinking their energies into the game. Why? Because I was ditching my dilettantism and finally joining in. As Greg Leeds, then president and chief executive officer of Wizards of the Coast, told Buzzfeed.com in July 2013, "*Magic* is the ultimate strategy game, but the reality is our fans aren't playing a game; we say they joined a community." While that might sound like woolly nonsense in the mouth of any other company, Wizards is not just any other company. It is one built on foundations laid by Peter Adkison, an iconoclast, an idealist, an innovator, who wanted above all to teach the world to sing. Or at least to get its geeks to game together. Without him and the connection he strove to forge between customers and company, *Magic* might be just any other product – or worse, a fad gone bad. Instead, it is far more than that – a game, yes, but as its full name *Magic: The Gathering* implies, also that very real community.

After over 20 years, it is a community of genuine cultural significance. Look at its impact on the nascent internet, its influence on phenomena such as poker and German-style board games, or at the emboldened strides its players and creators have made into a new, tech-savvy business world. What began as an inspired twist on classic card games and a riff on the rule-breaking *Cosmic Encounters*, has grown into far more than just a game in the traditional sense. In an age where the idea of a 'social network' applies primarily to virtual friends, *Magic* has been the analogue bridle harnessed to the digital foal, in control of the web's technology as it has bolted from under other riders. *Magic*'s incredible symbiosis with the internet has meant that new channels of communication have always been in the service of the game; in the service of what remains a powerful premise left over from analogue days: meeting people face-to-face; getting to know them warts and all; using a shared hobby to build meaningful relationships. *Magic* can be a real, supportive 'social network' in an ever-more apparently social age; one in which time online has become an ersatz for time spent with cherished friends.

Thankfully, that realisation made me understand that meeting Richard Garfield was not this story's emotional high point at all. Instead, the ensuing journey of writing it was, knowing that at the end of it, I would have something to share with a community to which I wholeheartedly wanted to belong. As much as I want to belong to *Magic* though, I want *Magic* to belong to as wide an audience as possible. For that to happen, the game needs to reach out and meet the rest of society halfway; to demonstrate that the skill, talent and energy it pours into every deck or duel is something it can share. If the *Magic* community can do that, then I believe those traits will meet with the recognition they are due and the same acknowledgement I have tried to give them in these pages. Aaron Forsythe, the game's director of R&D says, "The more people that play, the more new people they draw in and the less prevalent the stigma associated with playing a fantasy trading card game becomes." That gradual socialisation requires a new openness and a new willingness to reach out to non-traditional gamers, to show them precisely how enriching *Magic* can be.

Because, despite its occasional sins, *Magic* is enriching. For me, it has become a supranational home; something that helps soothe the deracination I feel after a lifetime on the move. It is the best game in the world because its cunning ruse of being 'just a game' has allowed it to slip into the lives of those who needed it most: an awkward generation still caught on the cusp of the internet-connected, knowledge-based world we take for granted today. It gave them not only a reason to hang out together, but via the aspiration created by the Pro Tour, something to strive for; the encouragement they could do something smart with their lives and go on to be, on some fundamental level, happy with themselves.

Think back to Mark Justice, the 'Stormin' Mormon' who stumbled into the Pro Tour spotlight just as his personal life was falling apart. As the pressure to perform got to him – and his marriage to a devout woman from within the Mormon faith fell apart – he slipped into a spiral of heavy drinking and drug use, which soon left him penniless, friendless and shut out by Wizards of the Coast. Still, he says, *Magic* saved him. At first, he clung on to the structure the Pro Tour provided. Then, even when he was way past playing cards, he sought out the still-glowing embers of self-esteem which had been ignited by the game. Thankfully, they would never go out.

He drifted for a while, not knowing how to rebuild his life. But, little by little, he cleaned up his act and came out the other side of his blackest days a stronger person. Justice realised it was time for him to do what he had always wanted to do: to get an education. Today, he is finishing his PhD, is happily married and has kids he hopes will one day discover *Magic* for themselves. Why? Because it filled him with belief when he needed it most. "*Magic* gave me confidence that I could do anything I want in my life," he says. "When I hit rock bottom in around 2000, with no money, having alienated every friend and every work contact I possibly could have and had no idea what I was going to do, I still knew that if I approached the rest of my life as I had done *Magic*, I could build it all back up again." While Justice's might be an extreme example, no-one mentioned in this book had anything but gratitude for the way the game had helped drag them into a wider world. From Peter Adkison, who discovered his business chops after a baptism of fire; to Jon Finkel, who went from bullying victim to world's best; from Marilyn, the Boeing janitor who became a millionaire; to Mark Rosewater, who went from frustrated screenwriter to funmaster-in-chief; via the inimitable Richard Garfield, who went from spacey maths student, to spacey millionaire. The Rob Hahns, Brian Weissmans, Olle Rades, LSVs... and many, many more like them all sense keenly just how much Garfield's creation has changed the last two decades of their lives. I am happy to join them, having been empowered to write this story by a community I am proud to belong to. After that, there is only one conclusion I can come to: *Magic: The Gathering* has changed the world, one grateful geek at a time. And you? You could be next.

ABOUT THE AUTHOR

Titus Chalk is a freelance writer based in Berlin, Germany. He has written and broadcast about sport, culture and games for outlets including *Deutsche Welle*, *Tagesspiegel* and *FourFourTwo*. He has been playing *Magic: The Gathering* since *Revised Edition* and even occasionally wins. Now, on the wrong side of 30, he is hatching plans to write fiction. Hatching little plans from little eggs beneath the skin.

ACKNOWLEDGEMENTS AND SOURCES

Thanks to Richard Garfield and Wizards of the Coast for a life-changing game, to Simon Hope for getting me hooked in the first place and to Kristina for getting me through the Berlin winters and into the library. Jon Hotten also lent me support and publishing knowledge – and let me nag him when I was tearing my hair out. Chris Barker and Thomas Lovegrove helped me over the finishing line. And then my agent James Wills showed me how far there was still to go. Thanks for helping me get there!

Thanks, too, to Jon Oliver and the team at Rebellion for taking a leap of faith in my story. I am very proud to be stable mates with Judge Dredd and Johnny Alpha.

I am also indebted to all of the fantastic people I spent time with and interviewed for this project. Without their help and belief, this book would never have been possible. Special thanks goes to Skaff Elias, whose knack for getting people to talk came along at just the right time, and to Brian Weissman for welcoming me as a friend into his home. Big up, too, to all the friends and family who gave me advice along the way – be it writing and publishing tips, design savvy or well-timed words of kindness. I owe you all many pints of beer.

While much of the content in this book came from my own interviews as well as a plethora of individual webpages, the following sources were invaluable:

BIBLIOGRAPHY

Print

De Vincentis Jr, Joseph; Jordan, Jeff; Moursund, Beth; Rosewater, Mark, *Magic: The Gathering Official Encyclopedia (Volume 1)*, London: Carlton Books, 1996.

Kushner, David, *Jonny Magic and the Card Shark Kids*, New York: Random House, 2005.

Various. *Totally Unauthorized Magic: The Gathering Advanced Players Guide*, Indianapolis: Brady Publishing, 1996.

Various. *The Duelist* (magazine), Renton: Wizards of the Coast 1994-99.

Online

classicdojo.org (particularly *Schools of Magic*)

channelfireball.com

crystalkeep.com

magiccardmarket.eu

oathsandfates.blogspot.com (Rick Marshall's personal blog on Wizards of the Coast's origins)

starcitygames.com

wizards.com/magic (especially columns by Mark Rosewater)

'I took a look – and was hooked.
Check it out. Fast-paced
fantasy-historical adventure.'

Michael Moorcock
on *Gideon's Angel*

The Guns of Ivrea
Clifford Beal

Acquel Galenus, former thief and now monk, uncovers a terrible secret under the Great Temple at Livorna, one that could shake the faith to its core. A secret that could get him killed. A secret that could enable an older, more sinister form of worship to be reborn.

Pirate princeling Nicolo Danamis, mercenary to the King and captain of the largest fleet in Valdur, has made one deal too many, and enemies are now closing in to destroy him.

Citala, fair-haired and grey-skinned, the daughter of the chieftain of the merfolk, finds herself implacably drawn to the affairs of men. She puts events in motion that will end her people's years of isolation but that could imperil their very existence.

All their fates will intertwine as they journey across the land, through duchies and free cities riven by political intrigue, religious fervour, and ancient hatreds. Alliances are being forged anew and after decades of wary peace, war is on the wind once again...

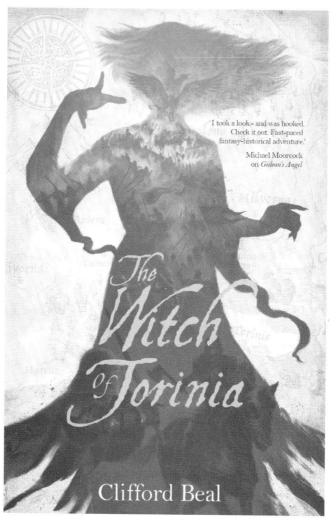

'I took a look – and was hooked. Check it out. Fast-paced fantasy-historical adventure.'

Michael Moorcock
on *Gideon's Angel*

The **Witch** *of* **Torinia**

Clifford Beal

Lady Lucinda della Rovera, the renegade canoness of St Dionei, secret sorceress of the "old gods", has cleverly split the One Faith into bitter factions and with the help of a pliant Duke of Torinia, launches a war to overthrow the king of Valdur and bring back the old ways. Brother Acquel Galenus, now Magister of the High Temple of Livorna, knows he must stop her, but doubts his own faith and ability. With powerful demons seeking to reenter the world through Lucinda, he must find allies, but how?

Julianus Strykar, now a coronel of the mercenary company of the Black Rose, finds himself thrust into the maelstrom of civil war but false pride leads him into a battle he may not be able to win -- or survive.

Captain Nicolo Danamis may have regained his fleet and command but the return of his long-lost father and lord, Valerian, has complicated his love affair with mer princess Citala. When his former lover -- the queen of Valdur -- demands his help, he and a suspicious Citala find themselves at the centre of palace intrigue as they try to avert an "alliance" with the predatory Silk Empire that will turn Valdur into a puppet kingdom. And then he learns that the crown prince may be his bastard son.

Friendships, loves, and the future of Valdur all hang by a thread.

 WWW.SOLARISBOOKS.COM

Follow us on Twitter! www.twitter.com/solarisbooks

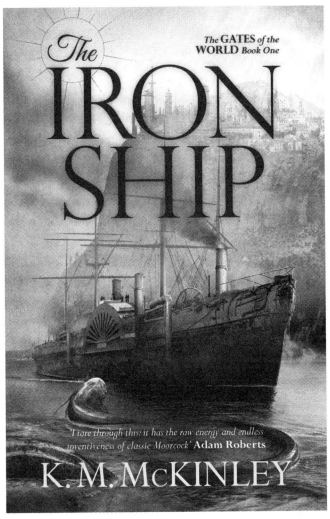

The **GATES** of the
WORLD Book One

The
IRON SHIP

'I tore through this; it has the raw energy and endless
inventiveness of classic Moorcock' **Adam Roberts**

K. M. McKINLEY

Merchant, industrialist and explorer Trassan Kressind has an audacious plan — combining the might of magic and iron in the heart of a great ship to navigate an uncrossed ocean, seeking the city of the extinct Morfaan to uncover the secrets of their lost sciences.

Ambition runs strongly in the Kressind family, and for each of Trassan's siblings fate beckons. Soldier Rel is banished to a vital frontier, bureaucrat Garten balances responsibility with family loyalty, sister Katriona is determined to carve herself a place in a world of men, outcast Guis struggles to contain the energies of his soul, while priest Aarin dabbles in forbidden sorcery.

The world is in turmoil as new money brings new power, and the old social order crumbles. And as mankind's arts grow stronger, a terror from the ancient past awakens...

This highly original fantasy depicts a unique world, where tired gods walk industrial streets and the tide's rise and fall is extreme enough to swamp continents. Magic collides with science to create a rich backdrop for intrigue and adventure in the opening book of this epic saga.

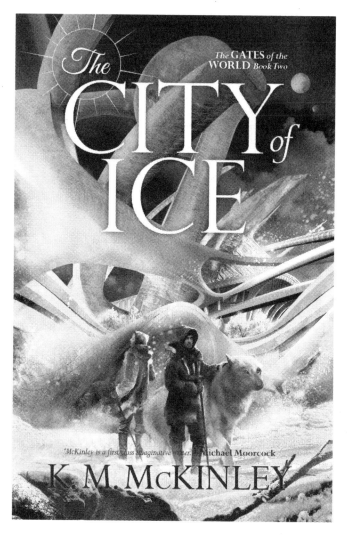

Deep in the polar south stands a city like no other, a city built aeons ago by a civilisation mighty and wise. Locked in a race with a rival engineer, Trassan Kressind's great iron ship crosses uncharted seas. The City of Ice promises the secrets of the ancients to whomever can reach it first. It may prove too little knowledge too late, for the closest approach of the Twin in 4000 years draws near, an event that has heralded terrible destruction in past ages.

As the Kressind siblings pursue their fortunes, the world stands upon the dawn of a new era, but may yet be consumed by a darkness from the past.

Industry and magic, gods axnd steam-power collide in the epic sequel to The Iron Ship.

'One of the most fascinating worlds I have read this year.'
— Sci-Fi and Fantasy Reviews on *The Iron Ship.*

 WWW.SOLARISBOOKS.COM

Follow us on Twitter! www.twitter.com/solarisbooks

'Steve Tem is a master: a genuine one.' — *This is Horror on Blood Kin.*

UBO

STEVE RASNIC TEM

Daniel is trapped in Ubo. He has no idea how long he has been imprisoned there by the roaches.

Every resident has a similar memory of the journey: a dream of dry, chitinous wings crossing the moon, the gigantic insects dropping swiftly over the houses; the creatures, like a deck of baroquely ornamented cards, fanning themselves from one hidden world into the next.

And now each day they force Daniel to play a different figure from humanity's violent history, from a frenzied Jack the Ripper to a stumbling and confused Stalin, to a self-proclaimed god executing survivors atop the ruins of the world. As skies burn and prisoners go mad, identities dissolve as the experiments evolve, and no one can foretell their mysterious end.

'Reminds you of what fiction is capable of being, of doing, of making, for the reader and the author.' — Neil Gaiman on *The Man on the Ceiling.*

 WWW.SOLARISBOOKS.COM

Follow us on Twitter! www.twitter.com/solarisbooks

When Captain Kel Cheris of the hexarchate is disgraced for her unconventional tactics, Kel Command gives her a chance to redeem herself, by retaking the Fortress of Scattered Needles from the heretics. Cheris's career isn't the only thing at stake: if the fortress falls, the hexarchate itself might be next.

Cheris's best hope is to ally with the undead tactician Shuos Jedao. The good news is that Jedao has never lost a battle, and he may be the only one who can figure out how to successfully besiege the fortress. The bad news is that Jedao went mad in his first life and massacred two armies, one of them his own.

As the siege wears on, Cheris must decide how far she can trust Jedao—because she might be his next victim.

'Ninefox Gambit is an effortlessly accomplished SF novel. Yoon Ha Lee has arrived in spectacular fashion.' – Alastair Reynolds

 WWW.SOLARISBOOKS.COM

Follow us on Twitter! www.twitter.com/solarisbooks

A fascinating collection of new and classic tales of the fearsome Djinn, from bestselling, award-winning and breakthrough international writers.

Imagine a world filled with fierce, fiery beings, hiding in our shadows, in our dreams, under our skins. Eavesdropping and exploring; savaging our bodies, saving our souls. They are monsters, saviours, victims, childhood friends. Some have called them genies: these are the Djinn. And they are everywhere. On street corners, behind the wheel of a taxi, in the chorus, between the pages of books. Every language has a word for them. Every culture knows their traditions. Every religion, every history has them hiding in their dark places.

There is no part of the world that does not know them. They are the Djinn. They are among us.

With stories from Neil Gaiman, Nnedi Okorafor, Amal El-Mohtar, Catherine Faris King, Claire North, E.J. Swift, Hermes (trans. Robin Moger), Jamal Majoub, James Smythe, J.Y. Yang, Kamila Shamsie, Kirsty Logan, K.J. Parker, Kuzhali Manickavel, Maria Dahvana Headley, Monica Byrne, Nada Adel Sobhi, Saad Hossein, Sami Shah, Sophia Al-Maria and Usman Malik.

JOE ABERCROMBIE // GEOFF RYMAN // LAVIE TIDHAR
PAOLO BACIGALUPI // ALIETTE DE BODARD // NAOMI NOVIK
DARYL GREGORY // CATHERYNNE M VALENTE // N.K. JEMISIN
GENEVIEVE VALENTINE // KEN LIU // ALYSSA WONG & MORE

EDITED BY **JONATHAN STRAHAN**

THE BEST SCIENCE FICTION & FANTASY OF THE YEAR

VOLUME ELEVEN

Jonathan Strahan, the award-winning and much lauded editor of many of genre's best known anthologies, is back with his tenth volume in this fascinating series, featuring the best science fiction and fantasy from 2015. With established names and new talent, this diverse and ground-breaking collection will take the reader to the outer reaches of space and the inner realms of humanity with stories of fantastical worlds and worlds that may still come to pass.

Featuring: **Joe Abercrombie, Geoff Ryman, Lavie Tidhar, Paolo Bacigalupi, Aliette de Bodard, Naomi Novik, Daryl Gregory, Catherynne M Valente, N.K. Jemisin, Genevieve Valentine, Ken Liu, Alyssa Wong** & more